Mastering Gephi Network Visualization

Produce advanced network graphs in Gephi and gain valuable insights into your network datasets

Ken Cherven

open source
community experience distilled

BIRMINGHAM - MUMBAI

Mastering Gephi Network Visualization

First published: January 2015

Production reference: 1220115

Published by Packt Publishing Ltd.
Livery Place
35 Livery Street
Birmingham B3 2PB, UK.

ISBN 978-1-78398-734-4

www.packtpub.com

Credits

Author
Ken Cherven

Reviewers
Ladan Doroud
Miro Marchi
David Edward Polley
Mollie Taylor
George G. Vega Yon

Commissioning Editor
Ashwin Nair

Acquisition Editor
Sam Wood

Content Development Editor
Amey Varangaonkar

Technical Editors
Shruti Rawool
Shali Sasidharan

Copy Editors
Rashmi Sawant
Stuti Srivastava
Neha Vyas

Project Coordinator
Leena Purkait

Proofreaders
Cathy Cumberlidge
Paul Hindle
Samantha Lyon

Indexer
Monica Ajmera Mehta

Graphics
Abhinash Sahu

Production Coordinator
Conidon Miranda

Cover Work
Conidon Miranda

About the Author

Ken Cherven is a Detroit-based data visualization and open source enthusiast, with 20 years of experience working with data and visualization tools. In addition to Gephi, he has worked with a variety of open source tools, including MySQL, SpagoBI, JasperServer, D3, Protovis, Omeka, QGIS, Leaflet, and Exhibit. He also has considerable experience using corporate software tools from Microsoft, Cognos, Tableau, and Oracle.

An automotive analyst and visualizer by day, he spends much of his personal time turning baseball data into web-based visualizations housed on his website, `http://visual-baseball.com`. He has previously authored *Network Graph Analysis and Visualization with Gephi, Packt Publishing,* as well as a self-published book, *MLB Pennant Races, 1901-1968: A Visual Analysis of Baseball's Pennant Races, Visual-Baseball Press*. His current areas of interest include visual dashboards, interactive networks, and anything involving geographic information.

Acknowledgments

I would like to thank the members of my family for their patience and understanding over the course of several months spent working on this book. This always starts with my wife, Karen, and extends to my children, Kellen, Kristopher, and Katie, as well as my always helpful mother-in-law, Carole Young.

This book would not have been possible without the considerable efforts of a group of thorough technical and content editors. I would like to sincerely thank Mollie Taylor, Ladan Doroud, Miro Marchi, Ted Polley, George Vega Yon, Marta Castellani, and Manasi Pandire for their considerable efforts to make this the best possible book. All of your input has been noted, and many improvements have been incorporated.

A special thanks also to Amey Varangaonkar at Packt Publishing for managing the entire process while also making recommendations that will result in a more enjoyable reading experience. Thanks also to others who helped in the early stages by providing useful feedback to get the book started. This list includes Joanne Fitzpatrick and Richard Gall at Packt Publishing, plus Gephi community members, Randy Novak, Mike Hughes, Matthieu Totet, Marco Valli, Gerry Wilson, and Carlos Benito Amat.

Finally, I would like to thank the creators and maintainers of Gephi for providing such a powerful tool that allows users to explore the fascinating world of network science. Thanks also to the growing community of enthusiasts who use Gephi to create some remarkable visualizations. My hope is that this book will make it easier for you to tap into the power of Gephi and, perhaps, even provide a few new approaches to leverage this powerful tool.

About the Reviewers

Ladan Doroud is a PhD candidate at the University of California, Davis. She received her master's degree in computer science from the same university in 2013. She is currently working on her PhD in computer science in Prof. Eisen's lab as a computational biologist and data scientist. Her research interests mainly lie in the area of large-scale network analysis, clustering and data mining with special focus on community detection, and function prediction of protein sequences in large-scale biological networks.

She has an extensive background in learner-centered education, including her collaboration with Udacity, Inc. in 2014 as a course manager on the data science track, as well as her collaboration with the California State Summer School for Mathematics and Science (COSMOS) in 2011. She can be reached at `ldoroud@ucdavis.edu`.

Miro Marchi is a PhD candidate at the University of Verona, Italy. He received his master's degree in cultural anthropology, ethnology, and ethnolinguistics from Ca' Foscari University of Venice in 2010.

He has authored *Self-Governance Lessons from Bali and Stephen Lansing, Cangiani M. (ed.), Alternative Approaches to Development, Cleup*, 2012, where he has reviewed the research of the interdisciplinary team coordinated by the anthropologist, Stephen J. Lansing, on farmers' cooperation network for rice cultivation in Bali.

His current research focuses on finding practical ways to foster the emergence of self-organization in social-economic networks. He is applying ethnographic methods coupled with community-based online network visualization, which is built with Drupal and D3 and available at `www.retebuonvivere.org/rete`, and he is interested in the use of complexity theory for sustainability and the commons. He can be reached at `miro.marchi@gmail.com`.

David Edward Polley is a social sciences librarian at Indiana University-Purdue University Indianapolis (IUPUI). Prior to joining IUPUI, he worked as a researcher at the Cyberinfrastructure for Network Science Center in the Indiana University School of Informatics and Computing, Bloomington. He is interested in the various ways people use data, generated in social science research. He is the coauthor of a book on data visualization with Dr. Katy Börner titled, *Visual Insights: A Practical Guide to Making Sense of Data.*

Mollie Taylor is the President of Proximity Viz LLC, located in Atlanta, Georgia, USA, which provides data visualization and mapping services to a wide range of clients. She holds degrees in economics and international affairs from the Georgia Institute of Technology. Her blog on programming for data analysis can be found at http://blog.mollietaylor.com/.

George G. Vega Yon is currently a PhD student at the California Institute of Technology. He holds a BA degree in business administration and an MA degree in economics and public policy from Adolfo Ibáñez School of Government (Chile).

He is the author of several R and Stata modules, including *ABCoptim: Implementation of Artificial Bee Colony (ABC) Optimization, rgexf: an R package to work with GEXF graph files,* and *Introducing PARALLEL: Stata module for parallel computing.* He has shown a deep interest in statistical computing and data visualization; furthermore, he is the founder of the Chilean R-Users Group (useR).

He is the cofounder of the entrepreneurship, NodosChile.org Social Network Analysis, one of the first companies in Chile to put the eye on applied SNA analysis. George's scholarly interests are focused on policy analysis, complexity and statistical computing—recognized by the community, as he has served as a reviewer of the *Journal of Computational Economics.*

www.PacktPub.com

Support files, eBooks, discount offers, and more

For support files and downloads related to your book, please visit www.PacktPub.com.

Did you know that Packt offers eBook versions of every book published, with PDF and ePub files available? You can upgrade to the eBook version at www.PacktPub.com and as a print book customer, you are entitled to a discount on the eBook copy. Get in touch with us at service@packtpub.com for more details.

At www.PacktPub.com, you can also read a collection of free technical articles, sign up for a range of free newsletters and receive exclusive discounts and offers on Packt books and eBooks.

https://www2.packtpub.com/books/subscription/packtlib

Do you need instant solutions to your IT questions? PacktLib is Packt's online digital book library. Here, you can search, access, and read Packt's entire library of books.

Why subscribe?

- Fully searchable across every book published by Packt
- Copy and paste, print, and bookmark content
- On demand and accessible via a web browser

Free access for Packt account holders

If you have an account with Packt at www.PacktPub.com, you can use this to access PacktLib today and view 9 entirely free books. Simply use your login credentials for immediate access.

Table of Contents

Preface

Gephi has rapidly become one of the most utilized tools for the exploration and analysis of network data, as users seek to understand the relationships between groups of people, institutions, events, and other connected phenomena. At the same time, Gephi can help us understand serious topics such as disease transmission, the diffusion of ideas and innovation, and changes over time to community structures. With the ability to import a wide variety of data formats both open and proprietary, Gephi is truly moving toward democratizing network information.

This book aims to assist both new and experienced users in fully leveraging the immense potential of Gephi, regardless of whether the end goal is exploration, analysis, visualization, or some combination of each. While not every nuance of Gephi is covered in this volume, the topics in the book should go a long way toward improving your capabilities for effectively using Gephi.

What this book covers

Chapter 1, *Fundamentals of Complex Networks and Gephi*, provides background into the world of complex networks and how we can use Gephi to explore and analyze network patterns.

Chapter 2, *A Network Graph Framework*, provides a process for creating and developing network visualizations using Gephi.

Chapter 3, *Selecting the Layout*, will introduce many available layout algorithms in Gephi, and help you to select the most appropriate types based on the characteristics of your network data.

Chapter 4, *Network Patterns*, examines several critical network patterns, including contagion, diffusion, and homophily. We then use Gephi to explore and understand these behaviors.

Chapter 5, Working with Filters, provides multiple examples for how and when to use the powerful filtering capabilities provided within Gephi.

Chapter 6, Graph Statistics, provides readers with background on some key statistical network measures, followed by examples for how to effectively apply these methods in Gephi.

Chapter 7, Segmenting and Partitioning a Graph, provides insight into the multiple approaches that can be used to effectively segment a network, based on categorical or behavioral attributes. The use of size and color to partition a graph will be thoroughly explored.

Chapter 8, Dynamic Networks, will introduce the concept of Dynamic Network Analysis (DNA) and how time-based networks can be explored and understood in Gephi.

Chapter 9, Taking Your Graph Beyond Gephi, gives an overview of available export options, followed by several examples for creating visualizations by combining Gephi with external tools.

Chapter 10, Putting It All Together, incorporates many of the methods covered earlier in the book to create both revised and brand new visualizations. We'll also introduce some new methods that will allow for further network customization.

Appendix, Data Sources and Other Web Resources, lists out all the important references that you can use to understand the book in much more detail.

What you need for this book

This book requires some degree of knowledge or curiosity about network graph analysis and how to use Gephi software and plugins. While a number of technical topics are discussed, the reader will not require a deep understanding of the mathematical complexities of graph statistics or layout algorithms.

To use this book effectively, the reader should have the following software installed, in order to follow along with the examples and use the referenced datasets:

- Gephi version 0.8.2 (0.8.1 should also work in most cases)
- Gephi plugins referenced in the book, and easily installed from within the application
- Java runtime version 1.6 or greater – 1.7 preferred
- Inkscape (or Adobe Illustrator) software for editing graphs outside of Gephi
- Microsoft Excel, OpenOffice Calc, Google Spreadsheet, or other spreadsheet software for editing and manipulating .csv files

Who this book is for

This book is designed for those who would like to use Gephi to view, explore, and analyze network data. It will also be valuable for those who wish to create network visualizations that can be deployed beyond Gephi, as static or web-based interactive versions. Both relatively inexperienced users as well as Gephi power users should find material that will make Gephi a more powerful tool for working with network data.

Conventions

In this book, you will find a number of text styles that distinguish between different kinds of information. Here are some examples of these styles and an explanation of their meaning.

Code words in text, database table names, folder names, filenames, file extensions, pathnames, dummy URLs, user input, and Twitter handles are shown as follows: "The .svg and .pdf options are also useful if your intent is to do further editing in Adobe Illustrator or Inkscape."

A block of code is set as follows:

```
<style type="text/css">
        body {
            margin: 0px;
        }
        #seadragon {
            width: 800px;
            height: 600px;
            background-color: Black;
        }
    </style>
```

New terms and **important words** are shown in bold. Words that you see on the screen, for example, in menus or dialog boxes, appear in the text like this: "Notice that at the top of the graph there are three tabs—the **SNA** page, **About analysis** tab, and **About us** page."

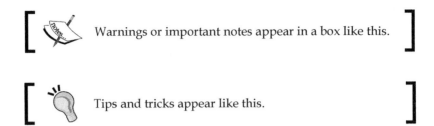

Warnings or important notes appear in a box like this.

Tips and tricks appear like this.

Reader feedback

Feedback from our readers is always welcome. Let us know what you think about this book—what you liked or disliked. Reader feedback is important for us as it helps us develop titles that you will really get the most out of.

To send us general feedback, simply e-mail feedback@packtpub.com, and mention the book's title in the subject of your message.

If there is a topic that you have expertise in and you are interested in either writing or contributing to a book, see our author guide at www.packtpub.com/authors.

Customer support

Now that you are the proud owner of a Packt book, we have a number of things to help you to get the most from your purchase.

Downloading the color images of this book

We also provide you with a PDF file that has color images of the screenshots/diagrams used in this book. The color images will help you better understand the changes in the output. You can download this file from: http://www.packtpub.com/sites/default/files/downloads/7344OS_ColorImages.pdf.

Errata

Although we have taken every care to ensure the accuracy of our content, mistakes do happen. If you find a mistake in one of our books—maybe a mistake in the text or the code—we would be grateful if you could report this to us. By doing so, you can save other readers from frustration and help us improve subsequent versions of this book. If you find any errata, please report them by visiting `http://www.packtpub.com/submit-errata`, selecting your book, clicking on the **Errata Submission Form** link, and entering the details of your errata. Once your errata are verified, your submission will be accepted and the errata will be uploaded to our website or added to any list of existing errata under the Errata section of that title.

To view the previously submitted errata, go to `https://www.packtpub.com/books/content/support` and enter the name of the book in the search field. The required information will appear under the **Errata** section.

Piracy

Piracy of copyrighted material on the Internet is an ongoing problem across all media. At Packt, we take the protection of our copyright and licenses very seriously. If you come across any illegal copies of our works in any form on the Internet, please provide us with the location address or website name immediately so that we can pursue a remedy.

Please contact us at `copyright@packtpub.com` with a link to the suspected pirated material.

We appreciate your help in protecting our authors and our ability to bring you valuable content.

Questions

If you have a problem with any aspect of this book, you can contact us at `questions@packtpub.com`, and we will do our best to address the problem.

1
Fundamentals of Complex Networks and Gephi

Welcome to the world of Gephi, the open source network graph and analysis tool. If you aren't already familiar with Gephi, this chapter will provide you a brief primer on both Gephi and the many ways in which it can be used to address real-world network analysis. For those who are already familiar with the software, this section will inspire you to take advantage of the many opportunities provided by this powerful tool.

Advances in computing power have helped to revolutionize the science of network graph analysis by putting complex datasets into the hands of thousands of users, and thus leading to the evolution of tools that help practitioners make sense out of previously unmanageably large datasets. Gephi is one of the tools at the forefront of this revolution, with a growing user community that produces some exceptional visualization. Gephi is far more than just a tool for producing attractive graphs; it is also a powerful instrument for exploratory data analysis that enables users to learn more about a given network.

This chapter will cover the following topics:

- First, we will examine a range of graph applications that represent some of the many ways we might choose to use Gephi in order to address real-world data
- The next section will provide an overview of the network graph vernacular, which will cover the primary topics of connectivity, network structure, and network behaviors

- Finally, we will begin to explore how we can use Gephi as the primary toolkit to move from the conceptual realm into a very hands-on, real-world application

Note that this chapter and the remainder of the book are focused solely on the Gephi desktop software, and not the Gephi toolkit. The toolkit provides Java library modules that can be plugged into new Java applications to deliver core Gephi functionality. More information on the toolkit can be found online at `http://gephi.github.io/toolkit/`.

Let's get started with some potential applications that will begin to illustrate the number of ways in which we can use Gephi to create compelling network analysis and visualization.

Graph applications

One doesn't have to look far to recognize the enormous growth of network graphs as a means to explore and explain networks. **Social Network Analysis (SNA)** has certainly been the most visible subset of network graph analysis, with thousands of cases where users have mapped Facebook, Twitter, and LinkedIn peer networks. While this has been, and continues to be, a viable use of the approach, there are many lesser known, but frequently more compelling, datasets with highly interesting networks that are available for our exploration. In the next few sections, we will walk through some of the primary categories where we can access data and use Gephi to construct highly informative graphs by employing definitions laid out in the book *Networks, Crowds, and Markets: Reasoning about a Highly Connected World*, by David Easley and Jon Kleinberg.

Collaboration graphs

Collaboration graphs represent one of the more frequently encountered categories in the world of network analysis. These graphs include networks where individual nodes are connected based on having some sort of collaborative relationship. The nodes might represent individuals or institutions; these graphs often depict collaborative research between universities and their staff within a specific discipline.

Who-talks-to-whom graphs

Another popular utilization of network analysis has been through the viewing of network graphs based on a variety of communication methods between the actors in a network, often within the confines of a single corporation, organization, or educational institution. These graphs can be constructed using e-mail or phone communications, and will often focus on the frequency of contact, thus exposing the true information flows and power structures within the organization.

Information linkages

Graphs that examine the flow of information across the Web are typical of this category of network analysis. These linkages can reference anything from connections between bloggers, pages on Wikipedia, or among scientific paper citation networks. This is a very popular type of graph, given the accessibility of information via the Web and its various applications.

Technological networks

This category often manifests itself through physical structures but, as David Easley and Jon Kleinberg note, there are underlying economic structures here as well, in the form of companies, regulatory bodies, and other organizations. In these sorts of networks, connections between nodes are likely to refer to a literal physical linkage, as in connections between routers or computers.

Natural-world networks

Another discipline that has received much attention through the use of networks is in the world of biology, where graphs are used to show relationships between predators and prey, neural networks within the brain, and a number of other science-based scenarios. Other network types are likely to emerge as well, and hybrids of these networks is also a possibility.

The idea here is to help stimulate thought processes about what sort of graphs you might be most interested in creating, and begin working toward their creation using Gephi. Specific examples of each of these network types are provided in the *Appendix, Data Sources and Other Web Resources*.

A network graph analysis primer

Network graphs are an element of what is termed as graph theory, defined by *Merriam-Webster* (http://www.merriam-webster.com/dictionary/graph%20 theory) as:

> "*Mathematical theory of networks. A graph consists of vertices (also called points or nodes) and edges (lines) connecting certain pairs of vertices*"

Stated simply, network graphs are collections of nodes (often called **vertices**) that are connected by edges (sometimes called **connections, links,** or **ties**) to form a graph. Nodes can be thought of as individual elements in a network that might represent persons, places, or objects that collectively define a network.

As you might have guessed, this definition could apply to an unlimited number of datasets, ranging from the obvious (Facebook or Twitter networks) to less explored examples, such as connections between staff, students, and facilities at a University; teammates in a baseball team; or musicians within a specific genre of music. In these cases, the nodes will represent the individual entities (people or structures), while the edges act as the connections that link them to one another. Each of your Twitter followers, for instance, represents individual nodes. They are then connected to you (a node) through a series of connections (edges). There are literally hundreds of thousands of opportunities to apply the principles of graph theory to interesting datasets spanning thousands of fields of interest.

So what can we learn from the principles of graph theory beyond creating a compelling visualization of a complex network? By the way, I will never downplay the visual output aspect of network graphs, as I am a strong believer in the power of aesthetics to enhance the story we are telling through our data. For example, refer to *Beautiful Visualization: Looking at Data through the Eyes of Experts*, edited by *Julie Steele* and *Noah Ilinsky, O'Reilly Media*. Still, there is much more to the basics of graph theory than a pretty picture. Let's examine a few of the most prominent principles in the next several sections.

Paths and connectivity

We can learn a great deal about how a network functions by looking at all of the connections within the graph and by understanding how they are structured. Perhaps the graph is loosely structured, with few connections between nodes, or it could be densely connected, or a combination of both with dense clusters interspersed with gaps or structural holes in the network. Why is this important? One example would be to understand the potential for the spread of an infectious disease (known as a **contagion** in network terms) across a large network. A network with many structural holes will not support the rapid spread of a disease, while a densely connected network can facilitate this spread. There are many such cases where network structure is critical to understanding the behavior of elements within the network. The following sections will touch on some of the key concepts employed to help us better comprehend the structure of a network, and how its member nodes interact with one another.

Paths

A **path** is quite simply defined as the set of connections required for one node to interact with another node. We can use paths to understand the shortest distance between nodes, or perhaps to determine the shortest route to reach a distinct cluster of nodes. The following figure illustrates an example of a path for Node **A** to reach Node E, using the *shortest path*, shown by the bold edges. The shortest path is also known as the **geodesic path**. Note that the path could also have passed through Node **D** on the way to Node **E**, but this is not the most efficient path, unless the direct connection from **C** to **E** is severed at some point.

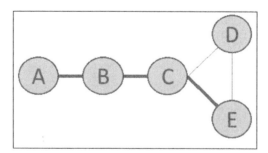

A network path

In some cases, a path might involve passing through a specific node more than once, but more often, this will not be true, especially if we are attempting to minimize the path distance. If our path does not repeat any nodes, it can be termed a **simple path**, as illustrated in the preceding figure.

Cycles

A **cycle** is an important variant of a non simple path, where there are a minimum of three edges and the first and last nodes are the same. All other nodes must be distinct; the cycle cannot traverse any of these nodes more than once. Cycles are critical to understand shortest paths through the network. Here is a simple cycle diagram—let's suppose we start at Node **A**:

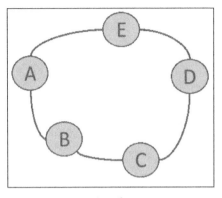

A cycle

This cycle is easy to follow, as we would simply move from **A** to **B**, **C**, **D**, **E**, and return to **A** in order to complete the cycle. We could also move in the reverse order, moving in a clockwise direction starting at Node **E**. This would become a little more complex, when there were additional nodes that do not flow around the perimeter as we have shown in the following figure. For example, a cycle could not move through the newly added Node **F**, since it would need to pass through Node **C** a second time to complete the entire path:

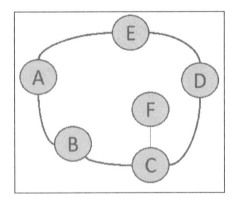

A cycle with extra node F

Connectivity

Connectivity is defined as the degree of connectedness of a graph, and can be measured using several formulas. At its essence, connectivity is a measurement of the robustness of a graph, as defined by the relative number of connections within a network. Networks with low connectivity are inherently fragile, as the removal of a small number of edges serves to weaken the network, and can actually disconnect some members from the components of the graph.

A few of the more common forms of connectivity measures are the **beta**, **alpha**, and **gamma** indexes. The beta index is a simple measure that looks at the number of edges divided by the number of nodes in a graph. Very simple networks will have a score of less than one, while more complex, densely connected graphs will exceed a value of one, and might go much higher in many instances. This is a very simple equation: $\frac{e}{v}$, where **e** equals the number of edges, and **v** represents the number of nodes.

An alpha index evaluates the number of cycles in a graph relative to the possible number of cycles. At one extreme, a simple tree network would have an alpha value of zero, as there is no way to cycle through the network without repeating nodes. A perfectly connected network would have a score of one, but this is both rare and impractical, as this would indicate an inefficient network.

Finally, a gamma index measures the number of actual or observed links relative to the number of possible links, which gives us a value between zero and one. Scores closer to one indicate a more densely connected graph, although it is unusual to find a network that approaches that level. The gamma index is particularly useful to assess temporal (time-based) changes in a network. There are two equations, one for a planar graph with no crossing edges, and a second for non-planar graphs.

More details on connectivity and its various measures will be provided to you in *Chapter 4*, *Network Patterns*.

Network structure

We have thus far focused on the concepts of paths, cycles, and connectivity, all of which help us to understand the interactions within the graph and even provide us with some statistical measures of the composition of the network. Yet these approaches fall short to convey all the information about the overall structure of the graph, such as how influential individual nodes or clusters are within the network. Fortunately, there are many ways in which we can statistically measure the structure of a network. If our graph is limited to a small number of nodes and edges, it is not difficult to see connectivity patterns, node groupings, and the overall topology of the graph, and we might not be terribly concerned with the statistical output.

However, when the network grows to more than a few dozen nodes, simple visual assessment will not provide us with all of the information within the graph, so we need to rely on more sophisticated formulas that provide us with detailed insights into the data and its structure.

The following sections will provide some details on many of the primary measures that tell us more about our graph. Further details are provided in *Chapter 6, Graph Statistics*. There are also many additional sources that provide further details on these, as well as more advanced network concepts, statistics, and theory. If you have not already consulted some of these resources, I would encourage you to do so. A listing of many available sources is provided in the *Bibliography* section of *Appendix, Data Sources and Other Web Resources*.

Centrality

One of the key constructs within network graph analysis is the idea of centrality, where we make an attempt to understand the relative influence of individual nodes within the network. As one might anticipate, there are several ways we can measure centrality, with each method providing a different definition, and often, very different results. Let's assume in each of the following cases that we are examining a subset of a network, rather than its entirety. Each centrality measure will be measured across an entire network, but we will use the following measures for illustrative purposes. The general principles do not differ.

There are four primary centrality measures to explore, which we will look at in no particular order. The first measure of centrality is **closeness centrality**, a measure of the proximity of a selected node to all other nodes within the graph. A node with strong closeness centrality would typically have very short paths to all other nodes within the network. Note that the result will be a lower average number, as we are talking about how many steps it takes to reach all other nodes. Here is a simple example:

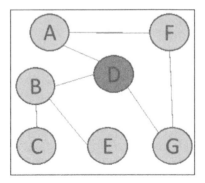

Closeness centrality

Note that Node **D**, despite having direct connections to just three of the six remaining nodes, has a maximum distance of two to reach any other point in the graph, while all other nodes have paths that might require three or even four steps. The central location of **D** makes traversing the graph very simple. Generally speaking, we would expect this type of node to lie at or near the physical center of a graph, although this is not always the case. In any event, this category of node is very prominent within the graph, and is also likely to have strong **degree centrality**, which we will discuss in a moment.

Another key measure is **betweenness centrality**, which often returns a very different result than the other centrality measures. In this case, we will find nodes that are highly influential in connecting otherwise remote regions of a graph, even though these nodes might have low influence as measured by other centrality measures. These nodes form a **bridge** between parts of the graph and thus play a key role in reducing path distances when traversing the graph. An example of this might be a jazz musician of relatively limited stature who managed to perform with both Duke Ellington in the 1940s and Wynton Marsalis in the 1990s, thus forming a bridge between musicians of different eras.

Here is a simple illustration of betweenness centrality, again using the Node **D**:

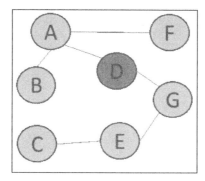

Betweenness centrality

In this case, **D** has just two first degree connections yet it plays a pivotal role in the network structure by being the bridge between the **BAF** and **CEG** clusters, which otherwise would be unable to connect.

Another critical centrality measure is **eigenvector centrality**, where the influence of a particular node is defined by the connectedness of its closest neighbors. This can be thought of as the *who you know* type of centrality, wherein an individual node might not be thought of as important on its own, but its relationship to other highly connected nodes indicates a high level of influence. In our modern society, you might view this type of node as being a confidant of a popular celebrity, athlete, actress, and so on (perhaps a gatekeeper for some highly influential neighbors).

Let's examine a basic illustration of eigenvector centrality at work:

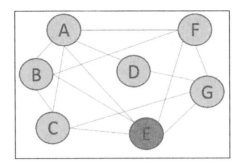

Eigenvector centrality

In this instance, **D** has only two first degree connections, but is surrounded by a host of very well connected nodes. Node **D** would thus score highly on the eigenvector centrality measure due to the relative importance of its first and second degree neighbors.

Finally, we consider the **degree centrality** measure mentioned earlier, which examines the number (or proportion) of other nodes linked to a specific node, either through inbound, outbound, or undirected connections. This type of node might act as a sort of hub for information flow — it might not be the source of direct information, but plays a critical role in dispersing this information to others.

The following example illustrates a node with a high degree centrality (once again using Node D):

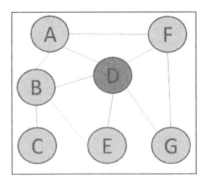

Degree centrality

In this case, **D** has direct connections to five of the six remaining nodes, while no other node has more than three such edges, making **D** a hub within the network. Based on this structure, information is likely to flow though **D**, particularly as nodes communicate across the network (say from **B** to **G**).

To summarize, centrality is an essential measure for how information flows within a network, and should be assessed using a combination of the above measures to achieve a complete understanding of the network. We will go into greater detail on this critical topic in *Chapter 4*, *Network Patterns*, where a number of more detailed visual examples will be presented, so that we can begin to apply these concepts to real-world graphs.

Components

Graphs can be termed as **connected**, where all nodes are joined through a fully linked network, and **disconnected**, in which there are separate groups of nodes with no relationship between the groups. It is in this latter instance where components take root with multiple groups of nodes standing alone with no linkages to other portions of the graph. Let's look at a hypothetical group of friends' network, first in a connected state, and then in a disconnected state with two components.

First, in the connected state, (as shown in the following figure) all member nodes can reach one another, with a maximum path distance of four Nodes (from **G** to both **C** and **E**). This is a rather loose set of connections yet it remains fully connected:

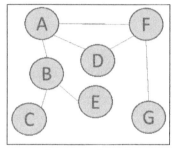

A connected graph

Next, let us suppose that Node **F** has done something to alienate both nodes **A** and **D**, forcing them to break off their connection to **F**. Now not only is **F** cut off from the remainder of the network, but so is **G**, who was previously connected through **F**. We now have two distinct components to the graph, as shown here:

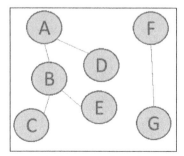

A disconnected graph

Many friends' networks exhibit this type of behavior, albeit on a larger scale than we have shown here. One of the more notable examples in the literature comes from *Berman, Moody*, and *Stovel* published in 2004 (http://www.soc.duke.edu/~jmoody77/chains.pdf) and shows the romantic connections in a selected high school, with a graph composed of nearly 20 distinct components.

Let's take a brief look at a specific type of component—the **giant component**.

Giant components and clustering

A giant component (http://en.wikipedia.org/wiki/Giant_component) might be thought of as the largest cluster in a network assuming it follows a specific mathematical formulation. For simplicity, we might refer to this as **large** components or **largest connected** components. These might also qualify as giant components, but will not require the same level of qualification. In our prior example where we saw a split in our friends' network, nodes **A** through **E** all remained connected within one cluster, while nodes **F** and **G** formed their own smaller cluster. In this case, the first cluster becomes the large component, by virtue of its larger size relative to the two node cluster represented by **F** and **G**. Now let's consider a case where we have more than two distinct clusters.

Take a look at the following network:

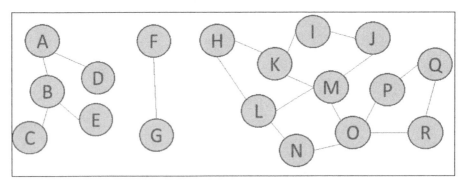

A large component composed of nodes H-R

We started with the same two clusters from our disconnected network example, but added nodes **H** through **R**, which have formed a new cluster that is clearly the dominant grouping in the graph. This is now the giant component, as it encompasses 11 nodes, compared to the other clusters with five and two, respectively. In *Chapter 4, Network Patterns*, we will take a look at how giant components form using various connectivity thresholds and assumptions.

Even when graphs are connected within a single component and we no longer have multiple components, clustering still plays a critical role in helping us to understand relationships, information flow, the spread of disease, and other relevant topics. We can assess the degree of clustering through statistics such as the **clustering coefficient**, applied at both global and local (that is, neighborhood) levels. Many clustering applications will be covered in greater detail in *Chapter 4, Network Patterns*, and the statistical measures will be covered in *Chapter 6, Graph Statistics*.

Homophily

Homophily is one of the key concepts that we need to understand when we examine network graphs, and is critical in helping us to assess networks with significant clustering. The term refers to what is often characterized as "birds of a feather stick together", wherein individuals tend to congregate with other like-minded individuals to form tightly knit clusters. Homophily might be driven by gender, race, age, occupation, education level, social status, or some other salient characteristic possessed by individuals within the network. These attributes might act individually, but will often interact with one another to define subgroups within a graph. Here are a few simple examples of groups we might find within a network graph:

- Women with a postgraduate degree
- Electricians belonging to the same union
- Executives serving on overlapping boards of directors

I think you get the idea, and could no doubt come up with many other relevant combinations. Once our graph is created, we can test for homophily and begin to examine its causes by exploring the tightly knit clusters that characterize its presence. In *Chapter 4, Network Patterns*, we will learn more about the critical role of homophily as it relates to the spread of information and innovation, while some of the statistical measures covered in *Chapter 6, Graph Statistics* will help us understand the presence of homophily in a network.

Density

Graph density is a measure of how tightly interconnected a network is calculated by examining the proportion of edges relative to the possible number of connections. A network with a high degree of homophily will tend to have a low density (due to the lack of connections beyond the local clusters), while networks that show a high degree of interaction across the network will have higher density levels. This will depend to some degree on whether we are viewing the entire network or a more localized sample. Two networks with identical numbers of nodes might have very different density levels; even the same network measured at different time intervals is likely to have differing density measures as links are formed or broken over time. A more detailed exploration of this measurement will be included in *Chapter 6, Graph Statistics*.

Network behaviors

We have just completed a brief overview on network structure and how it helps us to explain the patterns we see within an already existing network. Now it is time to touch on some of the behaviors that can take place within those structures and how they might develop or fail to develop according to features of the graph.

There are two terms used almost interchangeably to explain the evolution of a process within a network—**contagion** and **diffusion**. We will provide a basic overview in this section and then explore this concept in much greater detail in *Chapter 4, Network Patterns* and *Chapter 8, Dynamic Networks*.

Contagion and diffusion

The concept of contagion is typically associated with the spread of disease, but it can be used to describe a variety of phenomena in the marketing and social spaces. At its essence, contagion refers to the ability of something—a disease, an idea, or a book—to spread rapidly based on its network structure. Given the typical verbal association of contagion and the spread of disease, I will use that term in cases where we examine the progression of a disease. In all other contexts, the book will default to the use of diffusion, as that seems to be the predominant term when we look at how ideas propagate through a network.

To understand the potential of diffusion, we need to comprehend both, the structure of the network and the influence of various actors (nodes) within the network. If our subject (idea, book, information, and so on) flows through highly influential nodes within the network, we would then anticipate a rapid spread throughout the graph. To the contrary, if an idea is launched from a distant, poorly connected node, it is highly likely that there will be a very low level of diffusion, and only a small portion of the network will be exposed to the idea.

The following figure shows a hypothetical diffusion of a new product through a small network, using the simple assumption that each node requires 33 percent of its neighbors to adopt the product before it tries the product. Note that whenever this criterion is not met, the diffusion will cease in that part of the network. This figure shows the first four rounds of diffusion, beginning with the purchase of the new product by Node **A**:

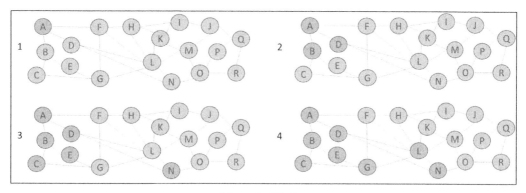

Network diffusion

In addition to the influence factor just mentioned, the basic structure of a network will help to determine the rapidity with which information spreads. Networks with lots of localized clusters tend to limit or even terminate the flow of information, while densely connected networks with few gaps promote the transmission of information. As noted earlier, we will explore these concepts in greater detail in *Chapter 4*, *Network Patterns* and *Chapter 8*, *Dynamic Networks*, with visual examples that illustrate information flows through the existing networks.

Network growth

Much of what we have considered until this point has been by looking at an existing set of networks without regard for additional growth or expansion of the network. In reality, we know that networks do grow, often very quickly and unpredictably. There exist a number of models in the literature that attempt to predict network growth using a variety of assumptions. These include the Erdos-Renyi random growth model as well as the Barabási–Albert model of preferential attachment, plus a host of variations on these themes.

Barabási offers a concise definition of a random network model (`http://barabasilab.neu.edu/networksciencebook/downlPDF.html#`):

> *"A random network consists of N labeled nodes where each node pair is connected with the same probability p."*

> – *Barabási, L. (2012), Network Science*

Given this definition, we can quickly determine that random graphs could take on a variety of structures, especially as we increase or decrease the p value. If p is high, say 0.8, then our graph will tend toward a dense structure, while a p value of 0.2 would lead to a very sparse graph with few connections between nodes. Random networks have been criticized for being unrealistic in modeling network growth (refer to *Social and Economic Networks* (2010), P. 78, *Matthew Jackson*, which can be retrieved from `http://books.google.com`), yet they continue to serve as a useful starting point in understanding how networks evolve.

Preferential attachment, on the other hand, has been shown to correlate much more closely, if imperfectly, to real-world situations, such as the structure of connections on the Web. Barabási notes the basic premise behind preferential attachment. The following is retrieved from `http://barabasilab.neu.edu/networksciencebook/downlPDF.html#`:

> *"Preferential attachment is a probabilistic rule: a new node is free to connect to any node in the network, whether it is a hub or has a single link… if a new node has a choice between a degree-two and a degree-four node, it is twice as likely that it connects to the degree-four node."*

> – *Barabási, L. (2012), Network Science*

In the preferential attachment model, new nodes are more likely to connect to nodes that have higher degrees, a pattern often referred to as *the rich get richer*. Thus, our network winds up with a number of hubs with many connections, surrounded by a greater number of nodes with fewer edges. Many real-life examples have shown this sort of behavior, from mathematical processes to citation networks and on to the Web.

We will defer further discussion on this subject until *Chapter 4, Network Patterns* and especially in *Chapter 8, Dynamic Networks*, where we will discuss the potential ways a network might grow, how quickly it will evolve, and what it might look like at some future point in time. Gephi provides the capability to perform this type of analysis, which can lead to powerful illustrations for how a network has changed over time.

Overviewing Gephi

Before moving into a discussion of the components of the Gephi interface, it will be helpful to provide you with a more holistic view for you to understand Gephi. Many of you might already be quite familiar with the general philosophy behind Gephi and how it is laid out. If so, feel free to skip ahead. For everyone else, let's step back for a moment and take a view at the big picture. You might think of this as viewing the entire building before visiting each of the individual rooms.

If we carry our building analogy a step further, Gephi has three primary sections, surrounded by a host of smaller rooms. The three main sections are as follows:

- **The data laboratory**: This houses all of our original data, plus additional calculated values created when we apply statistical or partitioning methods.

- **The overview window**: Most of the actions here will take place as we test layouts, set filters, and perform many more operations on our network.

- **The preview window**: This is where graph window output is refined, typically starting with the original graph and then using an array of tools to add aesthetic appeal. This is also where we can choose to export the graph to a new output format, such as a PDF or SVG file.

Beyond these three main sections lie a host of tabs, or smaller rooms, that allow us to perform many functions that will primarily be carried out inside the graph window. You might wish to rearrange these tabs to suit your work style, but I find the default setup quite intuitive and easy to work in.

So now that we've taken a very simple look at how Gephi is laid out, let's examine each of the primary and secondary windows in slightly greater detail.

Primary windows

The three main operating windows discussed earlier are covered in the following sections. While there will be some details provided within each of these sections, this book will not provide a comprehensive guide to the functionality of each and every option. Additional information is available via the Gephi documentation and forums, as well as through my introductory book on Gephi—*Network Analysis and Visualization with Gephi*, *Packt Publishing*.

Let's begin with the data laboratory, which will be the repository for our graph data.

Data laboratory

All data that feeds our network graphs will reside in the data laboratory. The laboratory is built around the concepts of nodes and edges, which we covered extensively earlier in this chapter. While the data laboratory might have a spreadsheet-like appearance, do not confuse it with the likes of Excel, Calc, or Google Spreadsheet. Certain aspects of data manipulation can be done here, but it is best to have your base data largely prepared prior to importing it into Gephi. For instance, I find it much easier to utilize a spreadsheet tool when there is a need to create distinct values within a categorical field. Likewise, any field values that are based on a specific sorting scheme might be best created outside of Gephi.

This is not to say that data held within the laboratory is fully static. For example, all statistical and clustering calculations will automatically append new values to each node when a process is run. You can also add columns, copy data from one column into another, and so on. Still, making individual node or edge-level changes here can become tedious (and very time consuming), especially if your dataset consists of hundreds or thousands of values.

There are several ways we can add data to the laboratory, from the very basic to more complex (albeit, more powerful). Here are a few ways:

- Manual entry
- CSV import
- Excel import
- MySQL import
- Graph file imports

Let's briefly discuss each of these options. I will not attempt to go into each and every use case, as that alone could fill an entire book. Instead, we'll look at some generic examples, and I recommend you the Gephi forums for cases that are beyond the scope of this book. Example processes for each of these processes will be provided in the *Appendix, Data Sources and Other Web Resources*.

Manual entry

If you are working with a very small dataset, or are very skilled at data entry, there is a manual option to create a Gephi dataset. This approach can be useful for those who wish to experiment; this is discouraged for all, but the smallest networks. Importing data from a .csv format is so easy that it makes little sense to choose the manual option beyond the simplest of scenarios.

CSV import

One of the simplest ways to move data into Gephi is through the use of comma separated values (.csv) files. Users can start saving and exporting data in Excel, Calc, Google Spreadsheet, or any application that allows the files to be saved and exported in the .csv format. To make the data transfer even simpler, only an edge file is actually needed by Gephi, as it will create a node file automatically. However, if you wish to add more detail to describe your nodes, I recommend that you create separate node and edge worksheets.

Excel import

Excel users have the ability to easily load data into Gephi using the `Excel/csv converter to network` plugin from the Gephi Marketplace. This plugin uses a more flexible approach as compared to the data laboratory import spreadsheet process. More information on this approach can be found at the Gephi Marketplace at `https://marketplace.gephi.org/`.

MySQL import

Gephi users that have data housed in the open source MySQL database are also able to directly import data by creating specific tables for nodes and edges, and then pointing Gephi to the database using connection parameters.

Graph file import

Gephi also enables the use of multiple graph file formats, making it very easy for the users of other software (UCINET, Pajek, GUESS, and so on) to import existing files into Gephi.

As a final note, we also have the ability to merge files in Gephi using either the data laboratory or simply through opening a second (or greater) file.

Graph window

All visual output is initially viewed using the graph window, with Gephi providing a somewhat crude initial view of your network. The initial view is very simple given that we have not selected any sort of layout at this stage; this is an issue that will soon be rectified. It is highly likely that the majority of your time will be spent working within the graph window, observing the patterns within your network. All applications of filtering, partitioning, sizing, coloring, and any layout adjustments will be seen here first, so it is wise to become very familiar with this space, if you haven't already done so.

You will observe that the graph window is adjacent to multiple toolbars, each with an array of functions. The functionality behind each of these options is generally intuitive, and should be explored for further understanding. This book will not spend considerable time with each of these functions. For a primer on these, my introductory book on Gephi provides greater detail, or, alternatively, takes some time to play with each option and represents what happens to your graph.

Preview window

The Gephi preview window allows the user to adjust a variety of graph attributes that have been created in the original graph window. Here, we can customize node labels by adjusting font size, font color, outlines, specifying whether to use boxes for the labels, and electing whether to display the labels at all. These decisions can be made based on the density and complexity of our graph; dense graphs might benefit from labeling only the critical nodes. Using Inkscape or Adobe Illustrator to create labels after exporting the graph is another option that allows the greater customization.

Node appearance is also addressed by providing border width, border color, and opacity options. As with the node labels, you can elect to use external tools to provide a greater degree of customization, where you have the ability to color individual nodes and edges rather than applying a one size fits all approach. Remember that you can always toggle to the overview window to do many of these customizations in Gephi, and then simply refresh the preview window.

Additional options are provided for adjusting the appearance of graph edges. Edge thickness, color, opacity, radius, and curved edges are all available options. Likewise, edge arrows (for directed graphs) and edge labels are customizable.

The preview window is also where some of Gephi's built-in export options reside, specifically, in the SVG, PDF, and PNG formats. Let's briefly consider each of these options, and why you might select one over another:

- **PNG**: This represents the simplest choice. It creates an image of your network, making it easy to share it online or elsewhere, provided you have no desire to further enhance the graph. This option is ideal for sharing a quick snapshot of your work on the Web or via e-mail, but is obviously limited from an editing standpoint.

- **SVG**: The SVG export creates a scalable vector graphic that can be edited in other programs such as Inkscape, although the large file size of this format might be most suitable for graphs without a high degree of complexity.

- **PDF**: The PDF export offers some of the advantages of SVG minus the large footprint. This format is also editable in Inkscape and Illustrator, and will ultimately allow you to customize every aspect of your graph, as well as to add titles or other notations describing the graph.

Secondary windows – tabs

As we noted earlier, Gephi provides an array of secondary tabs that surround the main workspace, permitting the user to execute actions on the graph without the need to toggle between multiple windows. With this approach, the impact of filters, partitions, color and size adjustments, and much more can be seen instantly, making it easy for the user to take an iterative approach to manage and analyze the graph.

The next several sections will provide an overview of how to use each of these tabs, without going into greater detail at this point. Some of these options, such as filtering and statistics, will be covered in much greater detail later in the book, while further information on other functions can always be found on the Gephi wiki or in the user forums.

The filtering tab

The filtering tab is where we will eventually examine our graph output using a range of criteria, so that we gain a better understanding of our network. Many times, our network will be very large, dense, and thus difficult to navigate in its entirety. In these cases, filters provide us with the necessary tools to begin probing the graph systematically, searching for specific attributes or graph features. Note that Gephi gives us the ability to create individual or compound filters, where multiple conditions are nested.

The application of filters in Gephi is not always easy, so we will devote an entire chapter (*Chapter 5, Working with Filters*) of the book to them, as they can and should become a very powerful component of our Gephi skillset.

The statistics tab

Not all graphs are created with the end goal of analysis or measurement, but for those who wish to understand network interactions and patterns, the statistics tab can provide a wealth of information. Gephi provides an array of statistical graph measures that can be employed to better understand the structure of a network, and ultimately can be used to compare networks to one another.

Chief among these statistics are a variety of centrality measures to be applied at the node level, including betweenness centrality, eigenvector centrality, closeness centrality, and eccentricity. Other measures include graph diameter, clustering coefficients, edge betweenness, and average degree measures. Many of these are included with the base Gephi installation, while others are available through selected plugins. *Chapter 6, Graph Statistics*, will be devoted to discuss these statistics using individual graph examples to drive a greater understanding on how to measure the network, and what the numbers mean.

The layouts tab

The selection of an appropriate layout can make the difference between creating an impenetrable graph that fails to communicate a story versus an easily accessible visualization that not only communicates, but also has aesthetic appeal. In perusing the network graph literature, one is bound to come across the term **hairball**, a description for a very dense network with many connections that is all but undecipherable using standard graph algorithms.

By using Gephi, we have the ability to test many layout algorithms before settling on a final choice. This provides us with an opportunity to not only avoid the hairball issue, but also to find a layout that is most complimentary to the underlying network. Many of the layout algorithms provide options that allow the user to determine the ideal spacing within a graph by tinkering with attraction, repulsion, gravity, and other available settings.

We can also determine whether to employ a force-directed graph that displays a network based on the aforementioned attraction and repulsion settings, or to select a predetermined layout that arranges the network in a circle or set of concentric circles ordered by some sort of categorical ranking. In other words, Gephi makes it possible to explore network data using a wide variety of layouts, making it possible for us, the users, to select the best possible option for our graph.

We will explore many of these layout options in greater detail in *Chapter 4, Network Patterns*, by comparing and contrasting outputs using a variety of methods.

Essential plugins

Plugins used in Gephi do not abide by the primary and secondary workspaces model that we just covered. Instead, they logically wind up where they are designed to be used; layout plugins are placed in the layout tab, formatting plugins can be found at the perimeter of the graph window, and so on.

The basic idea with Gephi plugins, as with plugins for other software, is to add features that are not readily available in the core software. In some cases, this will be in the form of functions that help users to better format their graphs, while in other cases the plugins represent full fledged layout algorithms or graph generators that provide users with additional choices for graph creation and analysis.

There are a number of Gephi plugins which we will use later in this text, so it might be the best to download and install them early on so that you can follow along with some of the examples. While the Gephi Marketplace plays host to some excellent plugins that extend the core Gephi functionality, the number is very manageable. If you wish, download and install them all as the installation process is very simple, and the space requirement is minimal.

Here are some of the most essential plugins I refer to, and often use within the course of this book, along with a brief description of their category and functionality. If you need more detailed information, please navigate to the Gephi Marketplace site to learn more. Many of these plugins will be used within the book, so it might be a good idea to download them all up front so that you will have a fully capable Gephi installation to work with as you follow examples in the book.

I'm going to walk you through these plugins by category, providing brief descriptions of each. We will go into greater detail as each plugin is used within subsequent chapters.

Clustering – Chinese Whispers

Gephi provides several options for partitioning and/or clustering graph data, including this useful plugin. The goal of this clustering approach is to partition your network data into individual clusters, which can then be used to color or size the graph nodes, creating a more intuitive and easily interpreted visualization. While it is possible to color nodes in Gephi manually or through partitioning, the Chinese Whispers clustering provides another option that is based on an analysis of network patterns.

Data laboratory

The data laboratory is where all the data manipulation takes place. While the base installation provides several helpful functions, others can be added using plugins.

Data laboratory helper

For users frustrated with the limited ability to edit data in Gephi, this plugin provides the ability to recast the column type (from string to numeric, for example) as well as to create new columns based on existing values.

Exports

The ability to export data and graphs from Gephi to other formats is highly useful, as it makes Gephi a very flexible tool for further interaction with or deployment of network data. We'll provide a brief overview of a few plugins that can be used to display network graphs beyond Gephi.

Sigma.js Exporter

One of the best ways to make your network graph even more powerful is to deploy it on the Web and make it interactive using `Sigma.js`, with the zooming, grouping, and filtering capabilities. This is an easy to use tool that provides a template approach to publish interactive graphs, making it especially easy to replicate a series of graphs using a consistent approach. Once the graph has been exported to Sigma, additional customization is possible using the CSS, JavaScript, and HTML methods. We will learn more about `Sigma.js` and explore actual examples in *Chapter 9, Taking Your Graph Beyond Gephi*.

Seadragon Web Export

Another option for deploying a graph to the Web is through **Seadragon**, which permits graph users to zoom in and out of your graph, which can be especially useful in the case of large or very dense networks. While this option does not provide the full range of capabilities found with `Sigma.js`, it does provide a quick solution to make your graph accessible through the Web.

Graph Streaming

One of the most powerful aspects of network analysis is its ability to see how a network evolves over time, rather than viewing a static graph. There are a couple of ways we might approach this, the `Graph Streaming` plugin providing perhaps the most powerful approach. All that is required to use this tool is a JSON dataset with time elements.

ExportToEarth

Users with geography-based datasets are able to use Gephi to create their initial graph before exporting the network in the `.kmz` format used by Google Earth and other GIS programs. All that is required to leverage this tool is some geocoded information in your data file, such as latitude and longitude data.

Generator – the Complex Generators plugin

A wide range of fundamental network graph types can be generated using this tool, including Erdos-Renyi (random graphs), Barabási-Albert (preferential attachment), and Watts-Strogatz (small world) graphs. These generators help to provide a quick visual understanding of several classic network growth theories, and can ultimately help us to comprehend network behavior while viewing existing graphs.

Here are three simple examples created in Gephi using the Random Graph, Barabási-Albert scale-free model, and the Watts-Strogatz small world model Alpha generators, all using a 20 node specification.

First, let's take a look at the random graph example, which is as follows:

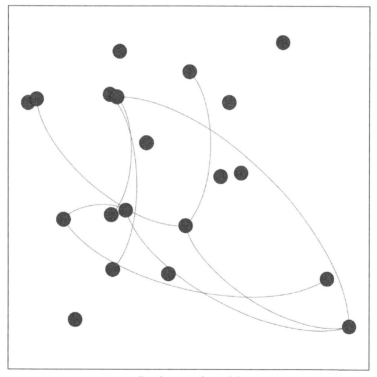

Random graph model

Next, a scale-free model is as follows:

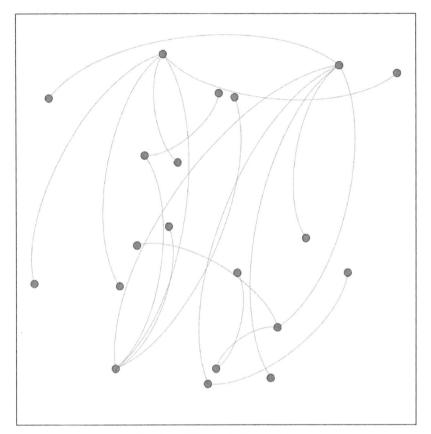

Barabási-Albert scale-free model

Lastly, a small world graph is as shown here:

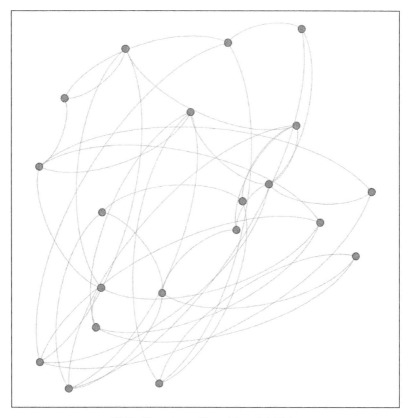

Watts-Strogatz small world model Alpha

Note the dramatic differences in network structures between the three models, all based on underlying assumptions of network growth. As mentioned earlier, the generators are very useful to understand and visualize network structures using different assumptions, which can then provide insight when we create graphs from our real-world datasets.

Layout

One of the most powerful ways to extend Gephi is through the use of a wide array of layout algorithms available through plugins. These layouts, when paired with the multiple layout options already available in base Gephi, will provide you with a wealth of choices to map your networks. Some of these choices will be useful for very specific use cases, while others are much more generally used for a variety of networks. Let's take a quick look at a handful of highly useful layout algorithms, and the situations where we might find them most appropriate.

The Multipartite layout

A **multipartite graph** is a network with multiple nodes (vertices) that belong to different groups, where all edges are between members of different partitions, and no edges can be found between members of the same partition. One can think of this in terms of members of a category (a sports team, for instance) that are connected to the top level of the category, but not to one another. If the team and team members represent the only two partitions, we have a **bipartite graph**; but we could also have many cases with more than two partitions. This becomes especially useful in cases where we have a temporal network, where players are associated with Team A initially, but are later traded to Team B or Team C.

The primary purpose of the multipartite layout in Gephi is to minimize edge crossings, thus making it easier to view and interpret the graph.

The Hiveplot layout

A Hiveplot is a graph layout that attempts to overcome the so-called **hairball effect** produced by large, highly connected networks. The hiveplot addresses this by placing nodes along multiple radial axes based on network structure. This approach is particularly appealing in cases where there are three or more definable levels, as it will position nodes in an effort to avoid some of the unintended or misleading effects that might appear while using other algorithms. We'll examine this approach further in *Chapter 4, Network Patterns*.

The Concentric layout

Networks are often most easily viewed using familiar visual forms such as circles. Concentric layouts allow us to take advantage of this, particularly while working with small to medium datasets. Nodes are arranged in a series of concentric circles based on the distance from our central node. Thus, nodes with direct connections are arranged in the first circle followed by nodes that are at a distance of two nodes away from the center, and so on. By arranging nodes in this concentric fashion, viewers are able to more easily navigate small network structures and see the closeness of relationships to a single node, and to each other.

The OpenOrd layout

The OpenOrd plugin helps to generate network graphs very rapidly, and is best suited to very large networks due to a loss of precision in the interest of greater speed. This approach is based on the classic, but much slower, Fruchterman-Reingold algorithm provided with Gephi. In cases where you are dealing with hundreds of thousands of rows of data, this algorithm enables a rapid look at the network structure.

The Circular layout

The circular layout plugin actually provides three distinct layout types—the circular layout, dual circle layout, and radial axis layout. A variety of options allow users to order nodes by degree, ID, attribute sort, or randomly. This can be especially useful to arrange a network based on predefined characteristics, as opposed to calculated relationships within the network.

The Layered layout

The layered layout is a useful layout for cases where we wish to visualize a small world phenomenon using numerical values to assign the layer, or orbit, that each node resides in. Stronger relationships to a key node will occupy inner orbits, with more distant connections occupying the perimeter of the graph. This approach is similar to the one used by the concentric layout.

The ARF layout

The **Attractive and Repulsive forces** (**ARF**) layout provides a useful layout tool that affords considerable flexibility through attraction and repulsion settings. ARF outputs tend toward a more circular appearance than many of the other spring-based algorithms such as the Fruchterman-Reingold and the Force Atlas models.

Additional plugins

A number of additional plugins are provided for Gephi, with new ones being added on a regular basis. Here are a couple tools that provide even more utility as you create and analyze your network graphs.

Link Communities – metrics

Link Communities is a clustering approach that assesses links in undirected and unweighted networks and then classifies nodes into communities based on their similarity. Nodes can be placed into multiple communities, making this approach differ from other clustering approaches. Once the metric has been computed, users can then select a layout algorithm of their choice to display the network.

Give color to nodes – tools

One of the most effective methods to convey network information is through the use of color. Gephi provides the ability to color individual nodes within the graph window, but this useful plugin lets you provide colors within your dataset that can be used to color the entire graph, versus making ad hoc changes using the Gephi toolbars.

Summary

As you might have gathered from this introductory chapter, there are an almost infinite number of graphs that can be created by pairing network data with a wide variety of algorithms provided either in base Gephi or through one of the many available plugins. Whether your end goal is simply to create a compelling visual image that communicates a specific story or you intend to perform some thorough network analysis using filters, graph statistics, and other tools, Gephi provides a robust framework for your explorations.

Before moving on, you might wish to learn more about the specific plugins—most of them provide some level of detail about their purpose and methodology. There are additional plugins not covered here which you might also find highly useful to create your own graphs.

In the next chapter, we'll walk through a process that will help you to scope your graph needs, and then provide an overview on how to create or access a dataset and import it into Gephi. Finally, we'll provide a brief overview on how to manage your data in the Gephi data laboratory, before moving on to creating and testing some actual graphs in *Chapter 3, Selecting the Layout*.

2
A Network Graph Framework

As one embarks on the task of creating a network graph, it quickly becomes apparent that neither is there a shortage of topics to visualize, nor is there a lack of data detailing many potential sets of network relationships. The more difficult task is to determine what we choose to visualize and how to move from a simple idea to a finished graph. In this chapter, you will be exposed to a proposed framework that details how this author goes through the entire process from the initial idea to a final published graph. The chapter will then take you through an actual example, where we can begin creating a network graph together.

In the following sections, I will discuss my personal approach to create a finished graph using the following:

- Identifying an idea or topic to pursue
- Determining the final output
- Identifying the data source(s) needed to populate the graph
- Formatting the data for Gephi according to the required naming conventions
- Importing data into Gephi to begin working on the graph
- Viewing the initial network created by Gephi to help understand the network structure
- Selecting a layout that will be appropriate for the network
- Analyzing the graph using a variety of Gephi filters and statistics
- Modifying the graph with color, size, and other features provided within Gephi
- Exporting the graph to external formats for additional customization or deployment (optional)

After completing the process, we'll create and export our own graph. By the end of the chapter, you should be comfortable with a general process to prepare and create network graphs using either the steps presented in this chapter, or through using a flow of your own creation.

A proposed process flow

This process might seem like a lot of steps, but it is meant merely to provide a framework to move an idea from your imagination to a final published graph. In fact, you might find a better approach or might already be using a different workflow that suits your particular style or specific needs. By all means, if it works for you, keep using it. On the other hand, if you are new to this discipline and need some direction, then follow this process to get started. I have found that especially in cases where there are multiple graphs to be created around a common theme or dataset, this process can make graph creation more efficient to move from start to finish. So let's get started, and we can ultimately get to the best part—actually creating and publishing some graphs.

Identifying an idea or topic

The world around us is literally filled with examples of networks, ranging from our own social media connections through very complex webs of information, such as the connections between millions of websites. What story do you want to tell the world, and how would you propose going about it? Think of your graph as you would if you were writing a paper or preparing a speech. Do you want to inform, persuade, educate, or entertain? While it is possible to create a graph that serves multiple functions, it will still be useful to narrow our focus to one of these possibilities, as it will help us reduce the level of complexity to a slightly more manageable scope.

Now, we need to find a more specific idea or topic that we feel comfortable working with, as that will make the process of creating graphs easier. While it is certainly possible to take a previously unfamiliar topic and create an exceptional graph, it is typically far simpler to start with a familiar subject. Think of your hobbies, professional interests, personal networks, or educational background. Are there potential network topics in one of these areas where you already have a high degree of knowledge? Allow me to digress for a moment and describe how I would proceed using the upcoming topics in which I have either professional or personal experience.

My personal list of potential topics is as follows:

- **Wine**: I have been in the business for several years—mostly as an interested consumer—and I also have a respectable collection of books on many aspects of the wine business

- **Baseball**: I have spent many years performing statistical and visual analysis, attending games, and collecting a considerable library on the subject

- **Jazz**: I have been listening to recorded music, attending concerts, and reading jazz histories for 25 years

There are perhaps others, but if I start with these three topics that I feel very comfortable with, they are likely to make the process of ideation, data gathering, graph creation, and so on much easier, as opposed to attempting to work with a less familiar topic. In addition, while I cannot be considered one of the true experts in any of these areas, I do have enough background to lend credibility to my work and be able to address potential questions that might be encountered during the creation process.

Here are a couple examples of graphs that I created using this approach:

Topic	Graph	Location
Miles Davis studio album network	Bi-partite graph with 351 nodes and 581 edges	`http://visual-baseball.com/gephi/jazz/miles_davis/`
Detroit Tigers player network	Complete network with 1566 nodes and 47905 edges	`http://visual-baseball.com/gephi/teams/tigers_network/`

Enough about me and my interests! What is it that you would feel comfortable pursuing? Do you avidly follow political issues, a particular sport, or a specific aspect of history? One of the beauties of networks is that they can be found in almost every endeavor if one looks for them. So, start considering your own interests, make a list if needed, and then begin to narrow down the possibilities to the one idea that sparks your interest at the moment. It is important to keep the list manageable initially. There will always be time to return to your backup choices; the goal at this point is to get started with an idea. Don't worry about viability just yet—you might find out that the data you need is not available, although this is becoming less and less of an issue due to the remarkable array of data sources made available through the Web.

Determining the final output

After developing your topic, the next logical question concerns the final format: who will view the graph and how? This will help you make decisions along the way about how to use layouts, color, sizes, and so on. For example, if this is simply a project intended for personal use, then design considerations will most likely take a different direction versus a project to be displayed on the Web or exported to a PDF format for high-resolution printing.

Consider some of these questions and how it will have an impact on your graph:

- Will my project be interactive or static? If the answer is interactive, then you have the luxury of allowing users to navigate and discover the network, so the network can be quite dense while still telling a good story. If, however, the output is static, then special formatting such as size, color, and text might be needed to help guide users through the story.

- Where will the final network output reside? If you wish to post to a blog, Facebook, or Twitter, then a simple PNG output will suffice, although you might need to give users a larger version to click through to, depending on the complexity of the graph.

- Will the graph need further enhancement beyond what can be done in Gephi? Is there a need for textboxes, callouts, legends, or other adornments using an editing tool such as Illustrator or Inkscape? If this is likely to be the case, then exporting to an SVG or PDF format is a logical choice. My personal choice is to use a PDF format that can be fully disassembled in Inkscape for detailed editing and then easily reassembled for the final output.

- If the graph is intended to be navigated via the Web, then Gephi offers multiple options, including Seadragon, Sigma.js, and the Loxa Web Site exporter. If you have geographic data, then the Google Earth export is yet another option.

There are a few other options besides those listed in the preceding bullet list. The main point is to begin thinking about your end goal to display and share the network. In many cases, your network will translate well to several of these methods, giving you a bit more freedom and the ability to produce multiple versions for different audiences. In other cases, such as a network with tens of thousands of nodes, you might find that a static image yields dismal results, so you might need to orient your project toward an interactive version early on. There are no hard and fast rules that dictate the final decision; instead, the best solution will come through trial and error coupled with visual assessment.

Identifying the data sources

Courtesy of the Web, we live in a magnificent era of data availability and transportability, with ever faster processing and connection speeds. This has had an enormous impact on the ability of both theorists and practitioners to create complex graphs that were unimaginable just a generation ago. There are tens of thousands of sites that provide rich datasets, and many of them are free of charge. All that's required is a local device, a web connection, a bit of tenacity, and some innate curiosity.

To help you get started, I have listed a variety of available (and free) data sources in *Appendix, Data Sources and Other Web Resources*, but the list is far from exhaustive. Take some time to scan the Web for data sources in your interest areas—you will almost certainly find some sources to download and begin preparing for Gephi.

While there is an incredible number of datasets available, not all will be suitable for network analysis and graphing. You will need to find resources that provide some sort of relationship data or at least data that can be converted into relationships. Think of datasets that can be structured this way or that can be adapted to show the connections within a network. Relatively few data sources will be fully prepared for this purpose, but with a little tweaking and an understanding of the objective, many can quickly be converted into powerful resources for network graphing. If you would like to begin with some prepared data, the Gephi wiki is a good place to start, or you could visit **Stanford Large Network Dataset Collection**, which is found at `http://snap.stanford.edu/data/`.

Formatting the data for Gephi

To work with data in Gephi, it must be in the form of nodes and edges. Otherwise, there will be no possibility to create a network graph. In theory, you could have nodes only, but this defeats the point of creating and analyzing a network. Gephi provides the ability to convert an edge-only source into nodes, saving you a potential step. However, this approach has some limitations from a node perspective, particularly if you are working with supplemental fields that hold incidental node information to be used for partitioning, ranking, filtering, or any other possible use.

Fortunately, it isn't difficult to prepare data for use with Gephi as long as the basic Gephi naming conventions are followed. At a minimum, the following fields are required by the nodes and edges sheets in Gephi:

Attribute	Required	Optional
Nodes	Nodes, ID, and label	Other fields that provide information about individual nodes
Edges	Source, target, and type, ID	Label, weight, and other descriptive information

Note that in cases where data is entered directly into Gephi, some fields will be automatically populated based on the initial entry. However, this will not be the typical data entry process, so our focus will be on structuring the data for import into Gephi. The simplest way to do this is by employing these naming conventions in your data source file, making for a seamless process on the Gephi side.

Importing data into Gephi

Gephi provides multiple options to import data from other sources, including spreadsheets, databases (MySQL), GraphML files, Pajek NET files, GEXF data, RDF files, and several additional formats. The Gephi website provides further details on how to create many of these data files as well as some examples showing the required structure for each type. Start with `https://gephi.github.io/users/supported-graph-formats/`

Probably the easiest way to get data ready for Gephi is to create a pair of simple `.csv` files, using one file for nodes and another for edges. As I mentioned in *Chapter 1, Fundamentals of Complex Networks and Gephi*, Gephi will create a nodes table if you first import an edge file, but this approach will limit your options, so it's a good idea to create both the node and edge files using a spreadsheet tool. In cases where you have no node data beyond the basics (ID or label), this might be fine. However, if your dataset has additional node information, start your import with the node file to preserve all of your data. This will enable the creation of ad hoc fields that are relevant to your nodes.

Likewise, MySQL can be used to create both node and edge tables that can be pulled into Gephi by providing database connection parameters. This approach has the advantage of porting data directly from an existing source if you happen to be a MySQL user. Other options exist, although they require some extra effort using an appropriate database wrapper.

If you choose to work with existing datasets, there are many examples on the Web that are already in one of the available graph formats, such as CSV, GEXF, GML, GraphML, and others. Gephi will be indifferent to your data format once the import is complete and will allow you to export your network data to many of these same formats. Just remember to create the required fields—the source, target, and type for edges and the node and label fields for the node file. For a CSV file, you can do your work in any spreadsheet platform, such as Excel or OpenOffice Calc.

Viewing the initial graph layout

Once the data has been successfully imported by Gephi, an initial graph will appear in the graph window. This will be a barebones random graph to be certain, but it does provide us with a starting point to assess some basic features inherent in the data. Some of the questions we can address at this point include:

- Does the graph have enough nodes to make a simple visual analysis difficult or impossible?

- Are the nodes loosely or densely connected?

- Is the network fully connected via a single giant component, or are there a number of disconnected nodes?

- Is there some sort of observable network structure, or do things appear to be random? Do we see a small world effect and/or considerable clustering?

Some of these points will become easier to detect after employing some sort of layout algorithm, but we still might get a glimpse prior to that stage. Gephi allows you to zoom in using a mouse wheel or tracking pad, which can help us answer some basic questions about the network. If the graph is too large or complex, it might be difficult to answer some of these questions without resorting to some more advanced techniques, which will be discussed in subsequent chapters. For now, let's address each of these points from a theoretical perspective. Later in this chapter, we'll use actual network data that will further illustrate these ideas.

Now on to the question of nodes, more specifically, what we mean when we say that a network has a lot of nodes. For instance, a network might have a few dozen nodes, or it might have tens of thousands (or even more). So, when we pose the question about assessing the number of nodes, it is somewhat relative as well as subjective. Certainly, a network with 20 nodes will always be thought of as small, and a network of 10,000 nodes will be thought of as large, but what about those points in between? Is 200 nodes a lot? What about 500? From a practical perspective, if your screen display feels crowded, with very little spacing between any nodes, then you might consider that network to have a lot of nodes, and thus, a high degree of complexity. Again, the size of your display, the intent of your graph, and the final format (paper/screen or static/interactive) all play roles in determining the visual density of your graph. If it feels too crowded to you, the creator, then users will almost invariably find the graph difficult to navigate.

What of the connectedness of the network, then? When we speak of connected nodes, we refer to the edges between two nodes, either undirected or directed. In some cases, the number of connections relative to nodes is rather low, which is an indication of a sparse or loosely connected network. In other instances, the graph will have many nodes with high degrees, leading to a considerable number of edges populating the graph. The former instance is related to the concept of random graphs, while the latter is more aligned with real-world graphs exhibiting the small-world phenomenon.

What about disconnected versus fully connected networks? Some networks will have multiple small clusters that are distinct from a single large component connecting many of the nodes. In some cases, there might not even be a large component but rather a series of small clusters. In either case, these are termed disconnected networks, as discussed briefly in *Chapter 1, Fundamentals of Complex Networks and Gephi*. There are many examples in literature that show this type of network, with one of the more notable recent examples showing the romantic relationships at a single high school, titled *Chains of Affection* (`http://www.soc.duke.edu/~jmoody77/chains.pdf`). In other cases, including many examples from the social network analysis field, networks are fully connected, with all nodes having the ability to traverse the graph and link directly or indirectly to every node in the network.

Finally, and in a slightly more subjective vein, we'll talk about the subject of network structure. In some cases, it is quite simple to view a network and see patterns defined by association, homophily, or some other network behavior. Many of these graphs will have multiple clusters that connect to one another through a single node that acts as a conduit between otherwise unconnected groups. However, in many cases, determining whether a graph is random or has a more defined structure is not so easily done; therefore, we rely on tools such as Gephi to aid in discovering the underlying structure. In certain cases, we will see visual evidence of networks where the power law distribution is at work, resulting in a small number of high degree hubs surrounded by a large number of less influential members. These structures can be confirmed by examining the degree distribution of a network. One very simple approach is to size nodes according to degree; another is to simply browse the node table using the data laboratory.

Now that we have walked through a brief primer on what to look for when viewing a network, the next step is to find the best way to display the graph to take advantage of the underlying network structure. This is also a somewhat subjective decision, although we can apply a degree of rigor to the process by testing many of the varied layout options provided in Gephi.

Selecting a layout

One of the most critical steps to create a network graph is to make sure that we select a layout that helps us tell the story most effectively. Technically speaking, any layout will perform the basic function of showing you the network; at the same time, some will be far more effective than others, and it is not an exact science to determine which layout will yield the best results. For one dataset, a **Force Atlas** algorithm might be ideal, while for another network, a different approach will create far better results.

 The technical results (centrality measures, network diameter, and so on) will be the same regardless of the selected layout. It is only the visual result that will differ, so we must rely on our visual assessment of the graph to determine which layout is most powerful.

As it is unlikely that you will be totally satisfied with your initial attempt at creating a perfect graph, I recommend an iterative approach, which is otherwise known as trial and error. Gephi makes this process quite painless, although certain algorithms will take a bit of time to run depending on the complexity of the network. Unless you are working with a familiar data structure you have previously graphed to your satisfaction, it is a good practice to try a minimum of three or four algorithms before selecting a favored approach.

Network complexity and structure are other factors that will help determine your final layout selection. If your dataset is small, and the goal is to show the known relationships between entities (perhaps members of specific groups), then your choices will be quite different than for a network where the goal is to explore and discover the interactions between nodes. For the former, some of the circular layouts might prove ideal, as they will allow ordering using a specific criterion. However, this would not be suitable in the second case; here is where algorithms based on spring mechanisms such as repulsion and attraction are probably far more useful in drawing the network.

In the end, it will be your visual inspection of the graph that rules the day. So, given that the final layout selection will be highly dependent on this visual inspection, what is it that should be inspected? The next section will walk you through some of the more critical criteria to be examined when judging the effectiveness of a graph.

Analyzing the graph

Regardless of which layout is selected, recognize that the graph might not be in a finished state and will most likely require multiple modifications. In fact, it would be surprising if this weren't the case, as even the most appropriate layout algorithm cannot possibly define everything we wish to see in the finished graph. With that in mind, let's discuss some of the nuances we are looking for when we analyze the graph, starting with this list:

- Is the graph cluttered? Many graphs, even when they have a rich underlying dataset, are hampered by the so-called *hairball* effect, which renders them visually unintelligible to most viewers. This can be seen as a virtually impenetrable concentration of nodes and edges that are typically concentrated near the center of the graph. One of the critical steps to produce a finished graph is to prevent this effect using a wise algorithm choice coupled with some custom settings. This will often involve adjusting the default settings for attraction, repulsion, and gravity depending on the choices provided by the individual algorithm. Ironically, many well-known network graphs suffer from an excess of clutter, although this can be offset to a degree through user interaction, such as panning and zooming.

- Do distinct features of the dataset stand out? For instance, if the network has a number of large hubs, are we able to see that in the graph? Gephi provides opportunities to make these hubs stand out from the clutter using size and color options in addition to the previously mentioned settings that help space out the network properly.

- Are important connections in the network visible? If the relationships between particular nodes are critical to the story, viewers should be able to easily determine that from the graph. Gephi enables edges to be sized to reflect the strength of a connection, making it more easily seen by the end user. Edges are the guilty party in many of the aforementioned hairballs, so it is essential to minimize those that are not critical to the story. This can be done through effective weighting, the use of opacity, and subtle edge coloring.

- Are there key groups, segments, or partitions that should stand out in the network? If so, there are several approaches to make these stand out, including colors, labeling, and special formatting. Gephi provides both native and plugin-based features to address this using partitions or clusters to identify the groups within the dataset.

There are additional considerations, but paying attention to the ones just shared will go a long way toward making your graphs more attractive and powerful. So, now that we've discussed a few of the important factors in making a graph more effective, we'll look at what can be done within Gephi to achieve these outcomes.

Modifying the graph

Graph modification is the final step prior to exporting or publishing your network, and it can be done both manually and programmatically. On the manual side, there are an endless number of small tweaks that can be made within Gephi using a variety of toolbar and plugin components. Here are a few options that can be performed manually in Gephi:

- The **Painter** function: This function on the toolbar can be used for color-specific nodes, making them stand out or recede from the remainder of the network. This is a quick method that you can use when there are a small number of nodes you wish to edit; if you wish to color a large number of nodes, there are other options (we'll touch on them shortly).

- The **Sizer** function: This function will enable the resizing of individual nodes in much the same fashion as how the Painter icon enables recoloring. This is particularly effective if nodes in the network are not already sized based on the degree and you simply want to call out important members within the graph.

- The **Brush** function: This function makes it easy to see diffusion patterns relative to a selected node, allowing you to highlight neighbors (first degree), neighbors of neighbors (second degree), predecessors, and successors. This is an effective way to understand behavior within the network while highlighting network behaviors for viewers through the use of specific colors.

- The **Node Pencil** and **Edge Pencil** tools: These tools enable users to create new nodes or edges, respectively, without the need to manually add these features in the data laboratory.

There are other tools within Gephi and its plugins that will also facilitate the manual manipulation of your graph—take time to explore each of these features to see how to best leverage them for your network. All changes made using these tools persist between the **Overview** and **Preview** tabs and into the final output regardless of format.

There is one step remaining in our process, assuming you wish to share your work with others through the Web or some other outlet. Now that all the graph modifications are complete, it is time to export your work from Gephi to a more universal output format such as PNG, SVG, or PDF, or publish it to the Web using one of several available tools.

Exporting the graph

So, you've arrived at the point where your graph is ready to be shared. The next question, if you haven't already considered it, is what do you intend to do with your work. If the goal is to share it through social media or on a blog, then you might well be content to export your work as an image using the .png format made available by Gephi. However, if you intend to make it interactive or plan to do some additional modification using Illustrator or Inkscape, then other options need to be considered.

Let's walk through a number of available export options, and the use cases associated with each one, using the following table. Note that this list isn't exhaustive and isn't intended to provide great detail for each approach. The Gephi website and discussion forums provide additional insight into these and other export methods.

Format/tool	Potential uses	Strengths	Weaknesses
.png	Sharing via e-mail, blog post, Facebook, Twitter, and Flickr	Quick, compact, web friendly	No interaction, not editable, and thus, limited value for complex networks
.svg	Post-Gephi editing, embedding in a web page	Scalability, small file size for large networks, editable, panning, zooming, and higher quality image	Not as familiar for many viewers
.pdf	Sharable in PDF format, additional edits in Illustrator or Inkscape	A widely available format for users and possibility for further editing	Limited interactivity
Seadragon	Interactive network for users to navigate	Zooming, panning capabilities, and easy creation	Limited functionality and no additional customization
Sigma.js	Interactive network for users to navigate	Searching, filtering, zooming, panning, and customization using template approach	Web browser only. Won't work locally with Chrome or IE generally. Can use the rgexf package in R to work around this limitation

Format/tool	Potential uses	Strengths	Weaknesses
Loxa Web exporter	Interactive network for users to navigate	Searching, filtering, zooming, panning, and exporting `.gexf` settings	Web browser only. Will not work locally with Chrome or IE
Graph file	Suitable for use with a variety of other network analysis tools, including Pajek, Tulip, GraphML, and others. Can also be exported to a `.kmz` file when geocoding is part of the dataset for further use in Google Maps and Google Earth	Allows use in other tools for portability and further exploration	Not a visual network export in the sense of the other options listed here

Creating an example graph

Now that we've been through the process, it's time to have a little fun by following the preceding steps from start to finish using actual network data. Think of this as a bit of a case study where we put the theoretical process to work with a real dataset. The goal here is to get you acquainted with many of the capabilities within Gephi and to see how they might be used when you create your own graphs first hand.

So let's follow the process outlined earlier, walking through each step. Only this time, we're going to come up with an idea, retrieve the data for it, and create a network graph.

Identifying the topic

Choosing a topic for a network graph is not an easy task, given the hundreds of thousands of possibilities available to us, courtesy the Web and its numerous datasets. Even when a topic area is narrowed down to a specific genre (say, infrastructure networks), there are often multiple potential networks that could be created. Let's pursue the infrastructure network idea for this illustration and then find a suitable dataset that we can work with to create a compelling graphic.

This is a very broad topic, as infrastructure is manifested in many different settings and places and can have multiple meanings. For our purposes, it is merely referring to a set of physical places (nodes) that connect to form a network. This could be a series of connected routers that physically enable the Internet, a set of physical plants and connections forming a power grid, and so on.

Finding the data source

There are many places where infrastructure network data can be found, but for the sake of simplicity, we'll work with an example available on the Gephi website. This dataset examines a Power Grid, specifically referred to by *Watts* and *Strogatz* as "An undirected, unweighted network representing the topology of the Western States Power Grid of the United States". The file can be found on multiple locations across the Web, including `https://gephi.org/datasets/power.gml.zip`.

Once this file is unzipped, you'll note that it is in the `.gml` **Graph Modeling Language (GML)** format, which is another form of the XML-style graph formats that are frequently used for the creation of networks using one of many tools that support this format.

Formatting the data for Gephi

In the current situation, the data is already neatly formatted for us in the `.gml` format, making the import step extremely simple. Prior to completing the import, let's examine the file in a text editor to get a better idea of the structure of `.gml`, as it is often encountered when searching for network datasets.

Here's a glance at the beginning of the file:

```
Creator "Mark Newman on Thu Aug 31 13:33:32 2006"
graph
[
  directed 0
  node
  [
    id 0
  ]
  node
  [
    id 1
  ]
  node
  [
    id 2
  ]
  node
  [
    id 3
  ]
  node
  [
    id 4
```

For those of you acquainted with XML or JSON, this will have a familiar look to it, with the highest level representing the graph, followed by the attribute level, which then incorporates each individual node. Likewise, when we move further into the file, we see how the nodes are connected to one another using edge attributes:

```
edge
  [
    source 8
    target 6
  ]
  edge
  [
    source 8
    target 7
  ]
  edge
  [
    source 9
    target 8
  ]
  edge
  [
    source 10
    target 9
```

Note how each edge contains two previously created nodes and simultaneously provides the source and target attributes required by Gephi. Based on the node and edge values, we can also detect this as a barebones dataset without labels, weights, color fields, or any other sort of identifier values. Therefore, we'll need to add any of these values once we've brought the data into Gephi. That's alright for this example, but there's a good chance that you'll want future datasets to be richer prior to importing them into Gephi, as opposed to making manual edits using the Gephi data laboratory.

Importing the data

Now that we've had a preview of the data, it's time to launch the import process. Depending on the data type, there are different approaches to import the data. We won't spend a lot of time on this, as there is plenty of information available on the Gephi site and in the discussion forums. Here are some quick tips to import your data file based on the formats:

- For MySQL data, simply navigate to **File | Import Database | Edge List**, and set up the database driver and location information.

- For multiple CSV files (one for nodes and another for edges), navigate to **Data Laboratory | Import Spreadsheet** and follow the prompts for both node and edge tables.

- The Excel and CSV files can also be imported using the `Excel/CSV Converter` plugin. Once that has been installed, navigate to **File | Import Spigot** and follow the prompts.

- If you are working from graph file formats, including output from other network graph software, simply navigate to **File | Open** and locate your source file. This is where you can import anything, such as `.gml`, GraphML, Pajek `.net` files, Tulip `.tlp` files, and several additional formats. A graph information window will follow, allowing you to identify the column attributes that are being imported.

For our example, we'll use the last option, which will create a Gephi graph directly from the `.gml` file. So, let's proceed with that step and then move on to view the actual graph.

Viewing the initial network

Network data loaded into Gephi will not look very interesting at first glance. If our dataset runs into the hundreds or thousands of nodes, the initial view will appear very crowded and certainly won't shed a great deal of insight into the structure of the network. You need not worry about this—Gephi provides a multitude of options to rectify this very quickly.

Let's take a first look at the network after importing the data:

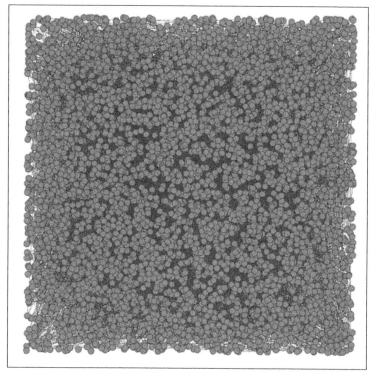

The initial network view

This looks much like what we might have anticipated, given the nearly 5,000 nodes and more than 6,500 edges in the network (as shown in Gephi's **Context** tab, which is often located in the upper-right corner of the workspace). The initial shape doesn't provide a clue to the network structure either, as Gephi simply created an incredibly congested square. This square layout, without an apparent form or function will, however, provide a great opportunity to utilize many of the capabilities within Gephi.

Selecting an appropriate layout

Let's take an opportunity here to see how this network looks using several different layout algorithms. We'll take a deeper look at layouts in *Chapter 3*, *Selecting the Layout*, but viewing some of the layouts now will help us see some quick examples of how they work with this data. Rather than moving directly to an effective layout, it might be more useful to survey a handful of approaches with our dataset.

Gephi makes it exceptionally simple to test multiple layout algorithms, which can be observed doing their work in real time. Over the next few pages, we'll see the results generated by a few different algorithms in an effort to make some sense out of the network. Feel free to replicate the results using your own version of Gephi, and by all means, don't feel constrained by the layouts selected here; try a few others on your own, play with some of the settings, and learn more about your network through different approaches.

If you installed the recommended plugins from *Chapter 1*, *Fundamentals of Complex Networks and Gephi*, your version of Gephi will have each of the following layout options available already. If not, you can install them now or simply follow along with the text and get the plugins at a future date. The following layouts will be shown in an order:

- Force Atlas (the faster Force Atlas 2 will be explored in *Chapter 3*, *Selecting the Layout*)
- Fruchterman-Reingold
- Radial Axis
- Yifan Hu
- ARF

At the end of this exercise, we will select a single layout that seems to provide the best initial results and then begin modifying the graph to make it tell a more effective story. So, let's begin with our survey of layout algorithms.

The Force Atlas layout

The Force Atlas layout is a classic force-based algorithm that draws linked nodes closer while pushing unrelated nodes farther apart. For this illustration, we'll retain the default settings, although we have the ability to tweak attraction, repulsion, and gravity criteria, among others. *Chapter 3*, *Selecting the Layout*, will take a deeper look at how to work with many of these settings to optimize a graph, but for now, let's run with the default. Also, be aware that many force-based algorithms will run indefinitely if allowed to, but in many cases, you will notice very little incremental improvement beyond a few minutes of runtime depending on the size of the network.

Let's take a look at the network after 10 minutes of runtime on my own laptop. Note that your time might vary considerably depending on the processing power of your machine; more processors are better, as network algorithms are very demanding! Take a look at the following:

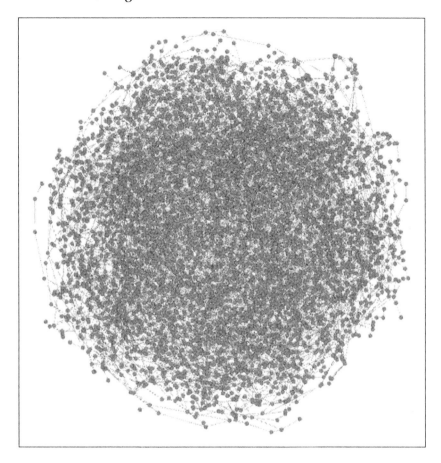

The Force Atlas layout

There's certainly improvement compared to where we started, yet there is still a very high level of density in the center of the graph. On a positive note, the edge of the graph is showing connected nodes that have been pushed out from the center. However, our results might have been improved by increasing the default repulsion setting in order to spread the graph out or by reducing the gravity criteria, which would move nodes away from the center of the graph.

The Fruchterman-Reingold layout

Next is the Fruchterman-Reingold layout, which is another force-based approach that has slightly different settings available. While we are still working with the defaults, it is possible to adjust settings for this algorithm—although not to the same degree as with the Force Atlas model. The primary adjustments we can make here involve the graph size area and the gravity. Thus, a dense network can be forced to spread out by manipulating the graph area rather than adjusting repulsion or attraction settings. Here's the result using the same 10 minutes allotted to the Force Atlas method:

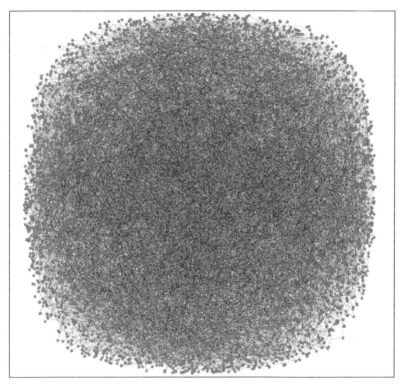

The Fruchterman-Reingold layout

A first appraisal suggests that the Fruchterman-Reingold layout was not very effective with this dataset, as it failed to spread out the network as effectively as the Force Atlas layout managed. Instead, we are left with the dreaded hairball effect, potentially overcome by some clever interactivity and modifications to color or node size, but overall, this method was not particularly effective for this network.

The Radial Axis layout

One of the beauties of working with Gephi lies in the sheer number of layout algorithms as well as the variety of options. In cases where traditional force-based methods are not as effective as we would like, Gephi provides the ability to turn to other approaches, including the Radial Axis layout. This algorithm positions nodes along radial axes using a predetermined number of radians. This method is not force-based, giving it a significant speed advantage. Instead, users specify how they wish to group nodes, how the nodes should be laid out, and several additional selections. Here is the same network seen through the Radial Axis approach:

The Radial Axis layout

 Note how the use of forced axes spreads the nodes out, enabling far greater visibility of the edges running between each pair of nodes. This might or might not be the best algorithm for this network, but it clearly demonstrates another option as we seek to portray the network in the most flattering light.

The Yifan Hu layout

Yifan Hu is another force-based algorithm but one that is designed to run more quickly than many of the other force-based algorithms while still providing a reasonably accurate result. Yifan Hu also has the advantage of shutting itself down after optimizing the network. The following result was achieved in just over 2 minutes of runtime:

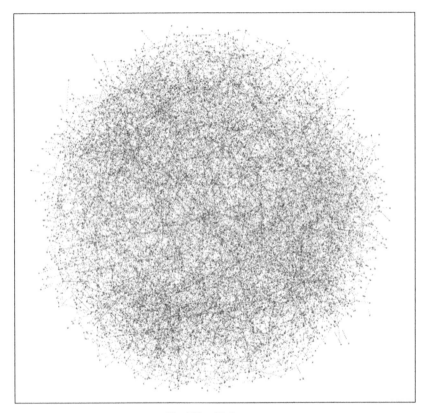

The Yifan Hu layout

Now we seem to be making more progress, as our network has spread out considerably, allowing some separation of nodes and edges and becoming considerably more understandable than some of our prior efforts. This is still certainly nowhere near a finished work, but it has done a better job of illustrating the network structure.

ARF

Finally, we'll turn to the **Attractive and Repulsive Forces (ARF)** ARF algorithm. This, as you might have guessed, is another force-based algorithm, which allows users to adjust settings to better optimize the network display. In this case, as with the other layouts, the default settings will be applied.

As these layouts have helped demonstrate, a network of this nature is not easily drawn due its complex structure. In contrast, many social networks, web networks, and citation networks will have far greater levels of clustering, more hubs, and additional attributes that often make them far easier to graph. In our infrastructure example, where there are nearly as many nodes as edges, it becomes far more difficult to spread the network out, as there are few, if any, hubs that dominate the graph, and clustering is effectively nonexistent:

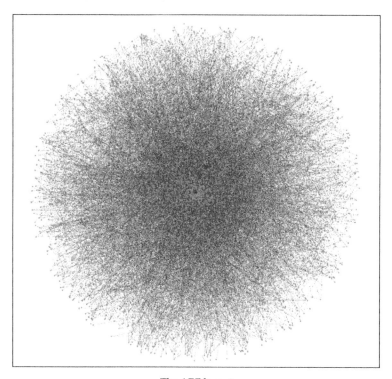

The ARF layout

Running the ARF algorithm for 10 minutes spreads the graph out at the edges but leaves a dense cluster in the center of the graph, which makes it very difficult to detect connections between nodes. Setting the repulsion value higher might have improved the output, but the default settings have left us with a bit of a hairball in the center of the network.

After assessing each of the five layouts, it looks as though Yifan Hu has provided the clearest picture of the network, so we will use it for the remainder of this chapter. The Radial Axis layout also cleaned up the network but feels less intuitive with the current network, where we would hope to see all connections across the power grid as opposed to groupings of connections based on selected attributes, which is the approach taken by the Radial Axis layout. This is not a negative commentary on the other methods; in fact, in another situation with a different dataset, our choice might be completely different.

Analyzing the graph

Now that we have settled upon a layout, let's take some time to perform a cursory analysis of the network to see what patterns can be identified and begin understanding relationships within the network. In *Chapter 4*, *Network Patterns*, and *Chapter 6*, *Graph Statistics*, we'll venture much further into analyzing some graphs from both visual and technical perspectives, but let's get a head start on the process.

Here's the Yifan Hu layout we saw previously:

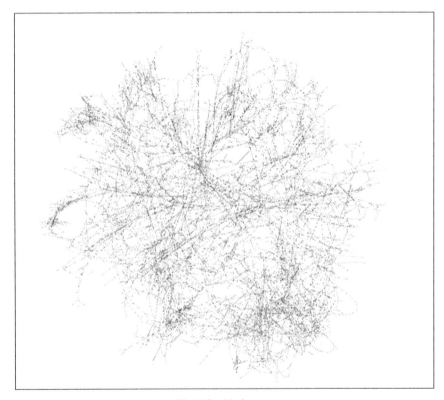

The Yifan Hu layout

Let your eyes scan the graph for a few moments to understand more about the network. Ready? Here are a few things you might have noticed:

- The graph is still somewhat difficult to navigate
- A number of nodes have been forced away from the center and appear to have single edges in many cases
- There are no obvious hubs (high degree nodes) to be seen
- Several linear connections appear, with several nodes connected in sequence— although this is only evident when zooming into the graph

Now let's use some automated approaches provided by Gephi to learn a bit more about this network. To begin this process, go to the **Statistics** tab in your Gephi workspace. *Chapter 6, Graph Statistics*, will provide additional details about a number of critical statistical functions, but for now, we'll get acquainted with a few of the common ones. Let's start with the **Network Diameter** option, as this provides three distinct measures that serve as important windows into every network's structure. Be sure to select the **UnDirected** option before you run your statistics.

The output screen gives you a few telling statistics, followed by some distribution graphs. This graph has a diameter of 46, which simply means that it would take 46 steps to traverse the graph between its two most distant points. This is a far cry from the notion of a small world graph, which is often known through the **six degrees of separation** term. Clearly, power grid networks are very different from social networks in structure. We also note an average path length just under 19; the typical node in this grid is about 19 steps away from any other point in the graph.

Scrolling down to the third graph (we'll bypass the first two for now; there's more in *Chapter 6, Graph Statistics*), we can see a very informative distribution on the eccentricity measure, which is shown by a bell-shaped curve. Eccentricity refers to the distance of a single point in the graph to its most distant point. Note that the minimum value here is 23, with very few nodes represented. These nodes can be thought of as being the most central within the structure of the network, as they require fewer steps to traverse the entire network. The mode value here is 33, with nearly 600 nodes requiring 33 steps to connect to the most distant point. Finally, the maximum value is 46, which is equivalent to the diameter of the network. These are the least central nodes in the structure and are very likely to be represented on the perimeter of most layouts.

Let's visit another simple statistic: **Average Degree** (we'll cover many more in *Chapter 6*, *Graph Statistics*). This measure will help any visual impressions we might already have about hubs and perhaps clustering by informing us about the typical number of neighbors per node. In this case, the answer is displayed via another distribution chart, where we can see that the overwhelming majority of nodes have either one, two, or three degrees, with an average of nearly 2.7. Again, we can contrast this with the familiar social network examples, where average degrees will often be in excess of 100.

For a final statistic, let's examine the clustering coefficients for this graph, which will give us a very clear indication of the graph density. The traditional clustering coefficient measured at the network level turns out to have a value of just 0.08, which means just eight percent of all possible graph triangles are complete. This indicates a graph that is not very dense. The average clustering coefficient, with more emphasis on local cliques, measures slightly higher at 0.107. In both cases, we confirm that the network is low density.

Now let's move on to the **Filters** tab, where some further network insight can be developed using a range of tools. Filtering is especially helpful when working with a dense graph, such as our power grid example; therefore, let's examine a couple of the most useful functions here with *Chapter 5*, *Working with Filters*, which is devoted to a deeper exploration of these capabilities. For these examples, go to the **Topology** folder within the **Filters** tab.

Assume that we want to focus on only the most highly connected nodes in the network, given that these points might serve as some sort of hub (albeit small ones in this network) with a high degree of importance. If we select the **Degree Range** option and drag it to the **Queries** portion of the tab, we see that nodes might have degrees ranging from a minimum of **1** to a maximum of **19**. Using the slider bar and then clicking on the **Filter** button, we can then restrict the display to show only nodes with degrees of five and above, 10 and above, or whichever setting is selected. This can help dramatically reduce clutter in the graph and allow us to focus on the most important details while potentially identifying additional patterns in the network.

Next, we'll navigate to **Attributes | Range** and select the **Eccentricity** option. Recall our from earlier discovery that eccentricity values ranged between 23 and 46, with the most frequent value at 33. Let's suppose we wish to see only nodes with an eccentricity level below 30, representative of the nodes with the shortest paths across the network. Following the same process of dragging the **Eccentricity** attribute to the **Queries** space and then setting the maximum value to 30, we now see a graph with a greatly reduced number of nodes on display. If even more precision is needed, the maximum value can be set to 25, or any value of your choice, using either the slider bar or by manually entering a value.

Now that we have seen some of the basic functionalities with statistics and filters, it is time to move on to the process of modifying the graph for user consumption. The goal is to take actions to make the graph more navigable for users. Let's examine some of these actions in the next section.

Modifying the graph

No network graph is ever perfect, no matter how much time one spends tweaking it, but every graph can be substantially improved from the original output, whether you are using Gephi or any other graph analysis tool. Even a well-selected algorithm using carefully prepared data is unlikely to provide the exact output we seek. This is why the final modifications, either manually applied or executed using some broad criteria (clusters, partitions, and so on), invariably add more power to the finished graph. Whether the modifications address aesthetic, technical, or navigational aspects of the network, these final tweaks will lead to a better output than that provided by total dependence on the data and the layout algorithm.

Recall our earlier selection of the Yifan Hu output for the power grid network display. While the network had improved considerably from its original version, there are still some simple actions that will make the network far more useful for viewers. Let's begin with the simple steps to adjust the size of nodes based on their level of influence.

The first step is to find the **Ranking** tab, which is found on the left-hand side of the workspace in the default Gephi settings. The **Size/Weight** icon (second from the left-hand side) will enable adjustments of either the nodes or edges based on the tab that is selected. In this case, select the **Nodes** tab, click on the **Size/Weight** icon, and select **Degree** from the listbox. As there are so many nodes in this network with low degree levels, it helps if we increase the size settings. Let's try a range of 20 to 100 and see how it looks:

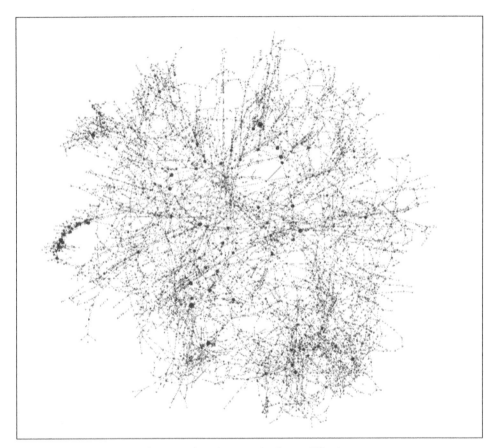

The network with size and color modifications

Notice how much more easily we can spot patterns in the network simply by employing these two changes. Now it is easy to see a cluster of high degree nodes to the extreme left of the graph (perhaps all interconnected) as well as a number of other high degree nodes that might serve as some sort of localized hub. These two findings alone can help in learning more about the network in an efficient manner, as opposed to a completely random approach.

We will make one more small change, and then we'll move on to learn more about exporting the graph. In this case, we'll focus on the cluster of nodes just identified in the prior step and apply one more modification to make them stand out. Recall that we just colored all nodes based on their respective degree levels. Now, for this selected group, we can apply a different color to draw attention to this part of the graph (this is most easily done by zooming in to that section of the graph) using the **Painter** tool on the main toolbar. Select a distinct color, and then click on each node while the **Painter** icon is highlighted to see something like this:

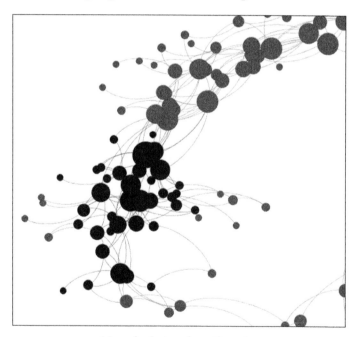

Manual coloring of specific nodes

Now, this portion of the graph has been more clearly identified for eventual users of the graph without the need to do postediting in Illustrator or Inkscape.

We'll explore the topic of modifications further in *Chapter 3*, *Selecting the Layout* and again in *Chapter 7*, *Segmenting and Partitioning a Graph*, but I hope this little exercise has helped show you the power of making some simple cosmetic changes to the graph.

Exporting the graph

Now we need to think back to the start of this process, when we were considering what our visualization was intended to do and how it would ultimately be used. For now, let's assume we don't want an interactive graph but simply a static network in two versions: one for quick display and another that can be modified for future use. *Chapter 9, Taking Your Graph Beyond Gephi*, will explore the interactive options in considerable detail as well as delve a bit further into the default static types.

There are two quick ways in which we can export a static version of the network graph. The first is to navigate to **File | Export | SVG/PDF/PNG file**, which will load a dialog window with some basic options available dependent on the export type selected. An alternative way to arrive at the same place is to use the **SVG/PDF/PNG** button available at the bottom of the **Preview** window.

The PNG option will create a simple graph image suitable for sharing through e-mail or social media. Both the PDF and SVG selections will allow for further editing using Inkscape or Adobe Illustrator and will also provide higher image quality. We'll explore these options further in *Chapter 9, Taking Your Graph Beyond Gephi*.

Summary

In this chapter, we discussed and learned how to think through the process of creating a graph, starting with the initial idea and then following a process through to a completed project. This has given us the opportunity to begin understanding how Gephi works with network data, how to visually assess the network, and how to select an appropriate layout based on the visual output of several approaches.

Once the layout type was settled on, we then discussed some approaches to analyze the network, both visually and programmatically, using some simple graph statistics and filters. We then explored the utility of making some simple modifications to the graph, providing viewers with a much clearer view of the network. Finally, we learned about using some simple export options that take the network beyond the Gephi application and into general use formats such as `.png` and `.pdf`.

With a basic understanding of networks and how to work with them in Gephi, it is now time to move on to more highly detailed sections of the book, starting with the next chapter, which will explore the growing number of interesting layout options available for Gephi. We'll walk through the pros and cons of many layout algorithms and determine which options can work best depending on specific network attributes.

3
Selecting the Layout

The nature of your dataset, coupled with the goals you defined earlier, will go a long way to help you select a layout algorithm. It is important to note that while the patterns and statistics within your data will remain unchanged by your layout selection, the impression your graph makes can be remarkably different depending on your selected algorithm. As you become more experienced in creating graphs, your ability to filter these choices will likely be enhanced, and you will instantly reject some approaches as inappropriate for your data. However, there will still be multiple options to choose from, particularly when many of the exceptional layout plugins are used. Your final choice might become evident only after a significant period of experimentation and visual assessment.

In this chapter, we will look at several critical steps that will help and guide you toward a final choice that fits both your data and the intent of your graphical output. Remember, there are no absolute right or wrong answers here; some portion of your final selection will be determined subjectively, using your own visual judgment. So let's begin walking through the steps that will help you make an informed choice about using actual data in order to move from the theoretical to the practical realm.

Overviewing the layout types

This section will neither attempt to answer all questions about each layout, nor will it dive into the technical aspects of how each algorithm works. For those answers, the Gephi website has resources to be explored at your leisure. Instead, we will provide a synopsis of many of the layout options available with Gephi, along with the strengths and weaknesses of each algorithm and some tips on when and where a specific layout is appropriate.

I recommend you consider your options from a holistic point of view. The end goal is to create a network graph that is not only comprehensible, but also tells a compelling story. If the layout looks impressive while achieving these goals, even better! However, any perusal of the literature and online world will quickly reveal that many graphs look impressive while failing to communicate the underlying stories within the network, and many are so dense that they are effectively unreadable. Do not fall prey to creating something impressive for its own sake — always remember that you are communicating with the graph viewer, and make every attempt to communicate clearly.

Now that we have these priorities straight, we can move on to the examination of many of the Gephi layout offerings, which reflect a number of the primary methods used in the network graph world. There are some popular graph types that are not directly covered by Gephi — arc layouts. However, Gephi does provide multiple examples within genres, such as force-based and circular layouts, that provide network analysts with a rich toolkit for creating powerful graphs.

There are several primary types of layouts used in Gephi, with a few of these containing multiple variations within the broader theme, as just noted earlier. The following sections will examine the general types, how they work, and when they might be the best method to use in your network analysis. Our discussion will focus on the practical application of these layouts, rather than any deep technical understanding. Additional technical specifications can be found in the document available at `http://sebastien.pro/gephi-esnam.pdf`.

Let's start our overview with probably the most frequently encountered network graph approach, the force-based (or force-directed) layouts, for which Gephi provides multiple alternatives.

Force-based layouts

The force-based (or force-directed) algorithms constitute one of the most popular layout categories, often using some combination of methods based on **attraction**, **repulsion**, and **gravity**. Here are the brief definitions for each of the three terms:

- **Attraction**: This refers to the process of drawing nodes closer together based on their similarity or relatedness. Direct connections will draw nodes together, as will indirect connections through common neighbors. Many algorithms allow you to adjust the attraction settings to pull nodes closer together based on their similarity. Many force-based layouts use the concept of springs that can be used to pull nodes closer together or force them apart. Higher attraction settings will typically pull nodes closer together by minimizing the value of the springs.

- **Repulsion**: This is a process that forces unrelated or distantly related nodes further apart from one another, which helps to space a graph and makes it easier to see relationships within the network. As with attraction, many layouts provide the ability to adjust this setting to force nodes away from one another. Higher repulsion levels will use the aforementioned springs to force nodes apart.

- **Gravity**: These settings allow users to define how nodes are drawn relative to the center of the graph. Lower gravity levels will disperse nodes toward the perimeter of the graph, with higher settings pulling points into the center.

Even when these settings are not explicitly available, the general idea is similar; with individual nodes *springing* closer or farther from one another based on their shared (or unshared) characteristics. Some of these layouts enable additional enhancements using spacing or size parameters to help make a graph more navigable.

The following force-based layouts are available either in base Gephi or through an installed plugin. For each layout, we'll use the same small network dataset and the default layout settings, so you can see the difference in how the various algorithms portray an identical network. The summaries provided are not focused on the technical aspects of each algorithm (many resources are available via the Web and published papers), but are rather focused on how they display a graph based on your network data. We will look at these from a user-centric view — what will the graph appearance look like, and will it help me to create a powerful story using my selected dataset?

The ARF layout

The ARF layout is one of the many force-based methods offered in Gephi, and operates in a similar fashion to others in this genre, while providing its own distinct settings. Here is a quick overview of several available options, and how they function:

- **Neighbor attraction force**: This is used to pull neighboring nodes closer together, or conversely, further apart. The default setting is 3.0 and can be adjusted downward to spread neighbors apart, or can be set higher in an effort to pull connected nodes into a tighter space. This option can be used in tandem with the general attraction force to set differing behaviors based on relatedness within the network, a feature not available to a number of force-directed algorithms.

- **General attraction force**: This is applied to all nodes in a network, without regard for their neighbor status. This can be used to spread the network out or draw it closer together, independent of how the neighboring nodes relate to one another. The default setting is 0.2, which will tend to create a small graph with all nodes close together. Changing this setting to 0.1 will have a dramatic impact on the scale of the graph, and the spacing nodes considerably move further apart from one another.

- **Repulsive force**: This option is another means to spread the network apart. In this option higher settings will force the nodes away from one another, especially in cases where they are not closely related. Again, this setting can be used together with the pair of attraction options to optimize the spacing in your network and to be consistent with the story you are aiming to tell.

- **Precision**: To make your graph as accurate as possible, adjust this setting to a higher level. High levels of precision will result in a longer running time and harder work for the layout algorithm, as it will try to maximize accuracy, and at some point, of maximum necessary precision there will be minimal benefit derived. As with the other options, it is wise to experiment with this level; you might find that the default setting is sufficient for your network.

Force Atlas

Force Atlas is a classic force-directed approach that uses the principles of repulsion, attraction, and gravity to provide a high degree of accuracy for small to fairly large datasets. On the downside, this accuracy comes at the cost of speed, with Force Atlas being one of the slowest layout methods in Gephi. Fortunately, Gephi makes it possible for us to stop a layout before completion if you sense the results are not what you intended.

There are many settings available for this algorithm, but we'll focus on the primary ones that will help to draw your network. For additional information on the methodology, refer to the Gephi forums. Here are the brief overviews of several options that can help you create an effective network graph.

Repulsion strength is a measure to determine how strongly each node rejects other nodes, similar to what we just discussed in the ARF layout settings. Higher levels force stronger rejection levels and tend to create a graph that has greater spacing between nodes, all else equal. As with other force-directed layouts, this option can be used together with the opposing attraction effect, which is discussed next.

Higher levels of **attraction strength** will draw connected nodes together, leading to a network that is potentially more clustered, depending of course, on the underlying dataset. If your goal is to create a network graph that is dependent on isolated groups within the network, then a high attraction setting coupled with a high repulsion setting can help us to achieve this result.

Gravity settings play an important role to achieve the look you desire from your network. Higher settings will draw nodes toward the center of the graph, preventing extreme dispersion at the perimeter, while lower settings can help the network to spread in cases where extreme crowding exists at the center of the network.

Another useful feature, especially when nodes are sized according to their importance (based on centrality or degree levels), is the **Adjust by Sizes** checkbox, a simple toggle that tells the algorithm to avoid overlapping of nodes, or conversely, not to be concerned with the node size. This is highly useful when we have a network with large hubs that could easily land atop smaller nodes, despite our best efforts to spread the graph. This could be done manually of course, but this option makes for less work on this front.

Finally, the **Speed** function works in much the same manner as the **Precision** setting in the ARF options. Higher speed sacrifices accuracy, so it will be up to you to determine the proper trade-off, which will be highly dependent on the nature and complexity of your network.

Force Atlas 2

Force Atlas 2 is a faster, updated version of Force Atlas that replaces the attraction and repulsion settings with a single scaling setting, which allows users to set a repulsion level that spreads the graph out for better readability. Once again, there are many available options, but our discussion here will focus on those most likely to be used for designing your layout. For a complete overview of this methodology, refer to `http://www.medialab.sciences-po.fr/publications/Jacomy_Heymann_Venturini-Force_Atlas2.pdf`.

We'll begin with the **Threads number** setting, which lets you take advantage of multicore processing when it's available, giving you more dedicated processing power to run the layout. The default setting is 2, but can obviously be raised based on the capabilities of your local machine.

Another unique option is to position hubs away from the graph center using the **Dissuade Hubs** checkbox. When the checked box is set to yes, the algorithm will tend to push hubs away from the center of the network, providing a rather different perspective than the traditional layouts. The result can be of a very different view of your network, again this is highly dependent on its data structure.

The Prevent Overlap setting can be used to keep larger nodes from obscuring our view of other components in the network, again through a simple checkbox selection.

Another interesting option is to use the **Edge Weight Influence** setting to control the appearance of your network. A setting of 1.0 equates to a normal influence, while 0 tells the algorithm not to refer to the edge weights at all in the layout computation. Levels above one will become increasingly dependent on the edge weights, resulting in strongly connected nodes being pulled closer together than would otherwise be the case.

We mentioned in the introduction to this method that explicit repulsion levels are specified using the **Scaling** function. As with all repulsion settings, higher levels will create a sparser graph with greater spacing between nodes.

As with the most force-directed layouts, Force Atlas 2 contains a **Gravity** option, which gives users the ability to pull nodes toward the center of the graph (through higher settings) or push them away from the center when better visibility in the middle of the network is required. The settings selected will once again depend heavily on the density and structure of your dataset. As usual, the recommendation is to experiment until you achieve a satisfactory result.

Force Atlas 3D

The Force Atlas 3D layout is identical to Force Atlas 2, with the additional option of setting the graph to 3D via a simple checkbox selection. If you have a benefit to display your graph in three dimensions, then use this layout; but beware that 3D graphs can lead to certain nodes being obscured from view. The differences between the two versions are often quite minimal, mostly related to how the nodes are visually depicted.

The Fruchterman-Reingold algorithm

Another force-directed alternative is the Fruchterman-Reingold method, considered as one of the standard approaches, but is also saddled by lengthy runtimes. The implementation of this layout in Gephi provides a few simple options, which we'll review here.

Instead of repulsion and attraction settings, Fruchterman-Reingold uses a single **Area** function, which acts as a surrogate for both, by spreading the network farther apart or by drawing it closer together. Providing a single function in place of two or even three distinct choices places more dependence on the algorithm and less on the end user, so this is a bit of a limitation if you choose this approach.

Once again, we encounter a **Gravity** function, which works in the same manner as the previously discussed version in other layouts, where higher values pull the network in toward the center of the graph.

The one remaining selection is **Speed**, which can be used to hasten the convergence of the network at the cost of higher levels of accuracy.

The OpenOrd algorithm

OpenOrd is an algorithm expressly intended for very large networks that operate at a very high rate of speed while providing a medium degree of accuracy. This is often a nice trade-off for large networks, but is often not desirable for smaller graphs where the loss of accuracy can be substantial compared to other layout approaches.

Many preferences can be set using OpenOrd, with several trying to optimize the time allocation of the algorithm across five distinct stages. We will not go into great detail on how each of these stages work, instead you can refer to the literature for this methodology at `http://www.researchgate.net/publication/253087985_OpenOrd_an_open-source_toolbox_for_large_graph_layout/file/3deec5205279e8c66a.pdf`.

In order, the five stages are **Liquid**, **Expansion**, **Cooldown**, **Crunch**, and **Simmer**. Each can be allocated a percentage of the total process, totaling to 100 percent in all. This full process controls the levels of attraction and repulsion while also determining node locations within the network, by varying parameters in an attempt to optimize results. The default settings are based on extensive research done by the authors of the algorithm, but you can choose to vary the settings to see if there is a tangible impact on your network layout.

The remaining settings include a concept called **Edge Cut** (or Edge Cutting in the paper), which gives users the ability to dictate how long the edges are handled. A value of 0 corresponds to the Fruchterman-Reingold approach, and can potentially result in clusters abutting or overlapping one another. Setting higher values allows the layout to increase white space between clusters and to become more visually appealing.

Num Threads and **Num Iterations** both affect how the layout is processed, first by allowing greater processing power, and then to employ additional optimization to occur through a higher number of iterations. Going beyond the default iteration levels is only recommended (or even useful) for very large networks.

The Yifan Hu algorithm

The original Yifan Hu produces faster results compared to other force-directed methods by focusing on attraction and repulsion at the neighborhood (rather than the entire network) level, thus placing a far lower computational burden on the local machine. It also has the advantage of stopping itself by using adaptive cooling, so that it can generally run much more quickly than methods such as Force Atlas.

Among the multiple options for Yifan Hu is its ability to set **Optimal Distance** levels, with higher values pushing nodes farther apart, without explicitly setting a repulsion level. This is a more generic way to set the lengths of the springs used to space the network.

For repulsion and attraction preferences, Yifan Hu employs a combined ratio titled **Relative Strength**, which measures the relationship between repulsion and attraction levels. The default setting for this is 0.2; increasing this number puts a relatively higher weight on repulsion, and will spread nodes apart. Changing the setting to a value of 0.1 will invariably draw nodes closer together, as attraction is given much greater weight than repulsion.

The Yifan Hu Proportional layout

All options for the Yifan Hu Proportional layout are identical to the original Yifan Hu, with the only difference being a different displacement scheme. One of the benefits of this model versus other force-based approaches is that this model has a better optimization of distances between nodes, with outer nodes and central nodes spaced appropriately. Some of the traditional force-based algorithms are biased in this respect, with outer nodes being placed closely relative to central nodes, even when the graph distances should be equivalent.

The Yifan Hu multilevel approach

This approach provides another option for very large graphs that speeds up the processing, which results in a slightly coarser graph. A couple of new settings are critical for this layout, which will be further discussed in detail. One of the great benefits of the Yifan Hu models is their rapid computational speed, achieved by working with nodes at a neighborhood level, rather than across the entire network, for each iteration. From an end user standpoint, this results in an exceptionally fast graph creation paired with relatively high accuracy.

The **Minimum level size** and **Minimum coarsening rate** options are both intended to set the number and structure of levels in the model, resulting in optimized layouts. Minimum level enables the users to specify a threshold level for nodes per level. The higher this value is set, the fewer levels will be created by the algorithm.

Minimum coarsening dictates the relative differences between levels; a value close to 1 will create more levels, as it implies smaller steps from one level to the next. Conversely, to have fewer levels in your layout, set this value closer to 0 (the default is 0.75), which will force a higher level of coarsening to occur. This could result in a somewhat less accurate graph, although the difference might scarcely be noticeable, again depending on the structure of your network. Experimentation is in order if you wish to understand the impact of these settings.

More technical information on this approach can be found at `http://yifanhu.net/PUB/graph_draw_small.pdf`.

Tree layouts

Tree layouts are frequently seen in the network literature, although not to the same level as force-based networks. Certainly, this is reflected by the limited number of available layouts in Gephi, with many options for force-based graphs and a scarcity of algorithms for displaying trees. While tree layouts are useful in portraying selected network structures, it is reasonable to question how often this is the case. Organizational structures are traditionally portrayed in this fashion, but anyone who has spent time working in a large organization knows that this is not an accurate representation of who talks to whom or even for how things actually get accomplished.

Nonetheless, there is a place in network analysis for this type of graph, especially if the algorithm provides the flexibility to modify the tree structure into something that more accurately reflects the underlying data, rather than an artificial construct. In Gephi, the **DAG layout** can be used to create this type of network graph, as we will discuss in the following section.

DAG layout

DAG is an acronym for **Directed Acyclic Graphs**, and is designed to handle datasets that are nonlooping; the resulting network will resemble (to a certain extent) an organizational chart, with a top to bottom flow. This will likely not resemble a true tree structure, unless the data forces that behavior. It will, however, provide a top to bottom view that can help to show the relationships in the network. In certain instances, this will help illustrate the network structure more effectively than we might get from a force-directed approach, as edge crossings and node placements should be optimized in a vertical plane.

Just four settings are available in the Gephi DAG implementation, which we'll cover in brief. The **X Distance** option is used to create either a narrow (by decreasing the value) or wide horizontal axis, and is highly dependent on the size and structure of the network. The default setting of results is set to 100 results in a relatively narrow horizontal view, which might be optimal in some instances; be sure to test your network at different levels.

Similarly, the **Y Distance** function is used to set vertical (y axis) spacing, and will again be heavily dependent on the size and depth of your network.

Speed is used here to vary the animation speed of the graph, and can be set to a value between 0 and 1. Finally, we have **Random Optimizations per Pass**, which can be raised from the default level in an effort to find the best solution.

To learn more about the general method, refer to `https://www.cs.umd.edu/class/sum2005/cmsc451/topology.pdf`.

Circular layouts

Circular layouts provide an intuitive structure for networks with a limited number of nodes, although there are variations that allow slightly more complex structures. Nonetheless, these are generally not suitable for graphs with hundreds or thousands of nodes, due to the inefficient use of space whenever circular structures are employed. On the other hand, for relatively small networks with a high degree of connectedness, a circular layout provides a familiar, intuitive framework for viewers of a particular graph.

Gephi provides several circular options, with three easy to use methods discussed in the following sections. We'll briefly discuss each of these layouts and then show how they display the *Les Miserables* network found on the Gephi website.

The Circular layout

The Circular layout can be used effectively to display a network with a limited number of nodes, especially when there is an intuitive sorting pattern in the data, using either degree values or alphanumeric labels, for example. The diameter of a circle can be set manually to create very compact displays as well as larger ones that can accommodate dozens of nodes. Once we get into the hundreds of nodes, other layouts tend to make more sense from a user's perspective.

The individual options provided in Gephi include several options, beginning with **Node Layout Direction**, which simply tells the algorithm to arrange your nodes in either a clockwise or counter clockwise manner. This might not be meaningful in some cases, but if your graph is sorted by labels or even by degrees, then a clockwise display will likely feel more intuitive to the end users.

Prevent Node Overlap is available in a number of Gephi layouts, and can be essential in cases where your network nodes are in close proximity, or have significant size variations, with large nodes prone to obscuring smaller nodes.

The Fixed Diameter and **Diameter size** options are used in tandem to predetermine the size of a graph. In order to have a custom diameter display, the **Fixed Diameter** checkbox must be checked. Also understand that in cases where you have elected to prevent node overlapping, the graph will rescale itself to accommodate this request, thus overriding the specific diameter size.

To sort your graph using some meaningful criteria (alphanumeric label, node size, and so on), specify the selection using the **Order Nodes by** criteria. This will enable you to tailor the graph using one of the many possible choices based on the data in your nodes file.

There are also a couple of transitions criteria we won't cover here, but feel free to investigate these as well. Their main purpose is simply how to go about drawing the graph.

The Concentric layout

The Concentric layout allows users to select a root node to build the network around, with the remaining nodes surrounding the target at multiple distances, based on the degree distance from the selected node. This is an effective approach in cases where there is a specific network element to be highlighted. As with many of the circular layouts, this is best suited for relatively small networks, although several circles can be used to display up to several hundred nodes without difficulty.

Here's an overview of the key settings that will help you optimize a graph using this layout—quite simple in this case. **Distance** sets the value between consecutive circle, allowing cases where there is a need to show multiple rings within a limited space. Knowing the graph diameter is critical for this layout. If your selected node is within three degrees of the most distant member of the network, the distance setting can be high, as it will not significantly increase the size of the graph. If, however, the maximum distance is six or seven degrees away, then distance settings might need to be minimized in order to create a full display within a reasonable screen size.

The **Node** option requires a target node to be set at the center of the graph. If you fail to enter a value, Gephi will select one for you, and most likely it will not be the node you wish to analyze (the odds are not very favorable!). Find the Node ID in the **Data Laboratory** tab, or by displaying the node information in the **Preview** window.

The **Speed** and **Coverage** settings each affect how the layout is constructed and should not have a material impact on the final graph.

The Dual Circle layout

The Dual Circle layout bridges the gap between the Circular and Concentric layouts we reviewed in the last two sections, allowing the users to specify the number of upper order nodes to place either inside or outside the main circle. This can be an effective layout when there are a specific number of nodes to be focused on as part of the story, as we can visually isolate them from the others. For example, if our story wants to focus on the three most connected characters in *Les Miserables*, we could sort them by degree and place only these nodes in the center of the larger circle.

Several settings are made available to optimize this layout, with some related to selections in the Circle layout. There are, however, some options unique to this layout that play an essential role in creating a finished network. These are the ones we'll focus on in the following sections.

The **Upper Order Nodes Outside** checkbox gives users the alternative of placing the selected group of nodes outside the primary circle, rather than the default inner setting. Thus, our three selected nodes reside toward the outer edge of the network. In most cases, this is not the typical display, which might be why the default setting is unchecked, leaving the selected nodes in the inner circle.

We have already discussed the use of upper nodes; now we can take a step back and see how to specify the number to place in this status, using the **Upper Order Count** function. There is no real rule for how high this value can be set, although an error message will appear if it happens to exceed the total number of nodes. What should this value be, you may ask? The answer, as usual, is that it depends on the specific network. This might mean a value of one, in a case where the focus is on a single member of the network. Or it could be equivalent to the number of nodes in a specific cluster—perhaps the members of a single crime family or some other defining criteria. Think about the goal of your analysis, and then find the appropriate value to enter here.

Radial layouts

Gephi provides a couple of radial layouts that can be used to display networks in a similar fashion to the circular networks discussed earlier. Radial layouts present some interesting advantages than other approaches, although they will not always be appropriate. However, if your data has some natural partitions or clusters, a radial layout can often display these groups quite effectively, by giving users the ability to specify certain graph settings.

The radial layouts resemble circular ones, in the sense that radians extend out from the center of the graph, although in this case, rather than forming a connected circle, the radians extend out in a series of lines defined by the user. For instance, if there are eight distinct clusters in a network, it might be instructive to view each one along its own axis. A circle is not capable of this, nor is a force-directed method. This is an advantage offered by a radial approach.

Another advantage lies in the ability of radial axis layouts to minimize edge crossings by ensuring the positioning of nodes along their respective axes. This can have the desirable effect of ordering the network such that we don't wind up with a high degree of clutter in the center of the network. Let's examine two offerings available in Gephi—the **Hiveplot** and **Radial Axis** layouts.

The Hiveplot layout

The Hiveplot layout is considered highly accurate as well as very fast and provides a way to improve networks that might otherwise suffer from considerable clutter at the center of the graph—the so-called hairball effect. User settings differ a bit from most other layout algorithms, so let's walk through them to gain a clear understanding of how to use them.

The first option is the **Refresh** button, which simply resets the available fields for other selections. In some cases, these fields will not load automatically; click on the **Refresh** button to address this. Next, the algorithm provides you a choice (using the **Nominal** axis assignment property) between assigning a nominal axis (by selecting the radio button) such as **ID** or **Label**, versus another field in the dataset (perhaps a cluster or partition). To see a network based on a grouping variable, make sure the radio button is not selected.

The **Axis Assignment Property** option provides the fields that can be used for drawing the graph—typically ID and Label for the nominal, than whatever other fields can be used to aggregate the network when the nominal option is not selected. This is followed by the **On-Axis Ordering Property** option, which effects how the network is displayed after the axis assignments have been made. Think of this as a two-step process:

1. Define how to draw the axes.
2. Decide how they should be sorted or arranged.

Finally, there are a series of axis settings to define. I recommend that you adjust the axis settings a few times to understand how they affect the display of your graph.

A paper providing the full details of the Hiveplot layout is available at `http://www.hiveplot.net/talks/hive-plot.pdf`.

The Radial Axis layout

The Radial Axis layout differs considerably in execution from the just discussed Hiveplot, yet it delivers a vaguely similar output in some cases. However, in many ways, this layout is far more closely related to the various circular layouts, and will in fact deliver the network in a circular form in some cases.

There are many settings that can be leveraged using this algorithm, some already familiar and others unique to this method. We'll begin with the familiar **Scaling Width**, which simply adjusts the size of the entire network. Adjusting the default setting from 1.2 to 2.0 (or other larger value) will enlarge the graph, while smaller values do just the opposite.

The next couple of items — **Resize Nodes** and **Node Size** — each address node sizing, the first dependent on the value set in the second. These options allow us to resize all nodes to a common value, which can be useful in some cases, but might undo some of your prior work if each node is independently sized based on the data values. So be careful not to create more work for yourself, although it is relatively easy to rectify this using the **Ranking** tab.

Five items are provided in the next section and all are geared to generate node placement on the graph. The first two of these should be somewhat familiar: **Group Nodes by** and **Node Layout Direction**. As a refresher, the first of these lets you determine the grouping criteria for your network (by degree, ID, cluster, and so on), while the second is simply a clockwise versus counter clockwise selection. On the slightly less familiar side, but still quite intuitive, is the **Order Nodes in Spar/Axis by** option, which follows the same logic as the recently learned Hiveplot technique for on-axis ordering.

The remaining selections in this section are **Ascending Order of Spar/Axis** and **Draw Spar/Axis as Spiral**. In the first case, we decide whether to sort along each axis in ascending or descending order, using the attribute just selected to order the axis. The spiral option is used in an effort to increase the readability of edges between nodes along the same axis, which can often be a bit challenging in a highly connected network.

Geographic layouts

In cases where your network data has a geographic component, such as latitude and longitude (or at least country), Gephi provides several choices to leverage this information in order to create a geo-based network. These networks can take advantage of the users' innate ability to view and interpret spatial data by overlaying networks on a geographic foundation. We'll take a look at two such layouts; others are available as well from the Gephi marketplace at `https://marketplace.gephi.org/plugin_categories/plugin-layout/`.

The Geo layout

The Geo Layout offers several parameters that can be adjusted to fit your geo-based network file. The first and foremost parameter to use this layout is the presence of latitude and longitude data in your network. The field names are not critical, as you will have the ability to point each of these options to the matching values in your node file.

Like many other algorithms, the Geo layout offers a simple **Scale** value for sizing the graph. More important for this algorithm is the **Projection** function, which offers eight distinct map projections to display your data. It is not in the scope of this book to discuss map projections, but here is an external resource for that purpose `http://www.csiss.org/map-projections/`.

The Maps of Countries layout

With the Maps of Countries layout, users have the ability to show all countries of the world or alternatively, specific ones by region and subregion. The idea behind this tool is to synchronize geo-based network data from your own network with the mapping capability delivered by the layout. Several options are available to do this, including the following ones discussed here.

The Country, **Region**, and **Subregion** options provide the functionality one would anticipate — the ability to draw maps of the world, region, subregion, and country levels. There is also the **Projection** functionality found in the Geo layout (with the same eight projections), with **Scale** and **Center** functions.

Latitude and longitude data can also be accommodated via the Geo layout offering, although the fields must use precise field names (`lat`, `lng`) in order to work.

Additional layouts

Gephi offers some additional layouts that don't fit neatly into a specific category, or else they are the only representative of their category, so they are included in this section. Each of these layouts offers at least some specific capabilities that are not present in our previously covered layouts.

The Isometric layout

The Isometric layout gives Gephi users the ability to add a third dimension (z) to their datasets, making it possible to display a network beyond a simple x, y space. Users simply need to have a node field containing the character (z) that indicates the presence of this additional dimension. The advantage of this algorithm lies in its ability to effectively stack data points in a vertical fashion, indicating rank levels or something similar.

Several menu items can be set, including **Z-Maximum Level**, which tells the algorithm the total number of levels available in the network, based on the underlying data. Each level will correspond with a unique node cluster; a maximum level of five will lead to a graph with five levels, and so on. Next in line is **Z-Distance**, which sets the distance between each layer for display purposes. Higher values will lead to greater vertical spacing, but this will need to be weighed against the number of levels for best results.

Scale is once again included and functions as it does elsewhere, while **Horizontal Z-Axis** lets users flip the graph on its side for a lateral display. Finally, **Reverse 0-Level Origin** inverts the ordering of the levels, placing Level 0 at the top (or far right), with the highest z values at the graph origin.

The Multipartite layout

The Multipartite layout arranges the data in a series of distinct levels with nodes that connect between (but not within) levels. Think for example, of professors in a large university, with each professor linked only to their own department, but not to other professors. This would constitute a **bipartite graph** which can be used to show the relationship between professors and departments, but not to one another.

The objective of the Gephi Multipartite layout is to minimize edge crossings by optimizing the node arrangement. There are just two available settings to work with in the Gephi Multipartite layout: **Speed**, which controls how rapidly the algorithm executes, and **Layer Attr.** (short form for attribute) where users select the data field that will parse the graph along multipartite lines. For example, in a dataset with ten departments, the result would be a graph with all the professors pointing to one of the ten opposing nodes.

The Layered layout

The Layered layout is another simple algorithm that splits the graph using some sort of partitioning or clustering provided by one of the original (or calculated) data fields. Just three selections for a Layered layout are provided for users: **Attribute**, **Layer Distance**, and **Adjust**.

The **Attribute** parameter is where we determine how to segment the graph; if, for example, we have a dataset with eight clusters, the algorithm will create a network with eight distinct layers. **Layer Distance** is simply a device to create distance between layers, and will be largely contingent on the number of layers in the network. Finally, the **Adjust** mechanism provides a toggle where users decide whether to utilize size as an additional criterion.

Network Splitter 3D

The Network Splitter layout uses settings similar to what we just reviewed for the Isometric layout, incorporating a z axis variable to parse the network into multiple levels. Four settings are available, shown as follows:

Z-Maximum Level uses a data field to set the number of levels for splitting the graph along a vertical axis. This number could range from 0 (no split will occur) to 10 or more, although practical viewing considerations might limit this number. The **Z-Distance Factor** spaces each layer using the specific value entered by the user. You can increase or decrease this value to adjust the network to best fit the viewing area.

Z-Scale sets the number of pixels to use for the vertical scale; a value of 100 provides a vertical axis of 100 pixels. Again, this should be sized to optimize the viewing space of your graph. Too small of a value will fail to take advantage of the strengths of the algorithm.

Additional layout tools

Gephi also provides some simple tools that don't qualify as layouts, but do assist in creating optimal network graphs. These options provide you with the ability to adjust spacing, rotate the graph, and customize label settings. These functions are included here, as they are found in the same location as full layout algorithms. Unlike various alternatives available within specific layout settings, each of the following are layout agnostic:

The **Clockwise Rotate** tool lets you rotate the graph by specifying the number of degrees of rotation using the **Angle** specification. This is useful for repositioning your graph to a desirable viewing perspective, perhaps based on a specific node or cluster to be featured. **Counter Clockwise Rotate**, as you might expect, turns the graph in the opposite direction.

Graph displays can be resized using the **Contraction** function and its **Scale factor** setting. Contrary to the name of the function, displays can be both reduced or enlarged, simply by specifying a decimal value (say 0.8 or 1.3). **Expansion** works in the same fashion.

Noverlap enables better spacing within a network, using the **Ratio** and **Margin** settings, while **Label Adjust** also contributes to an improved layout by positioning all labels so that they can be easily read without overlapping.

Assessing your graphing needs

Now that you have seen the broad array of available layout options and a bit of their respective capabilities, it is time to step back and reconsider what story you want to tell through the data. As you have just seen, there are many directions you can take within Gephi, and there is no absolute standard for right or wrong in your layout selection. However, there are some simple guidelines that can be followed to help narrow the choices.

If you are experienced with Gephi or another network analysis tool, you might wish to dive directly into the next section and begin assessing each layout type using your very own dataset; I will not attempt to convince you otherwise. This is a great way to quickly learn the basics of every layout offering and can be a great experience. On the other hand, if you wish to take a more focused approach, I will offer you a brief checklist of considerations that might help to narrow your pool of layout candidates, allowing you to spend more time with those likely to provide the best results. Think of this as akin to shopping for clothes — you could try on every type of clothing on the rack, or you can quickly narrow your choices based on certain criteria — body type, complementary colors, preferred styles, and so on. So let's have a look at some of the basic points to consider while shopping for an appropriate layout:

- What is the goal of your analysis? Are you attempting to show complementarity within the network, as in the relationships between nodes or sets of nodes, or is the goal to display divisions within the data? Does geography play a critical role in the network? Perhaps you are seeking to sort or rank networks based on some attribute within the data. Each of these factors can play a determining role in which layout algorithm is best for your specific network.

- Is the dataset small, medium, or large? Admittedly, this is a subjective criteria, but we can put some general bounds around these definitions. In my mind, if the number of nodes is measured in tens or dozens, then this is likely a small dataset that can be easily displayed in a conventional space — the Gephi workspace window or a simple letter-sized paper for a printed version. If, however, the nodes run into the hundreds, we are now moving away from a very simple network and potentially reducing the number of practical layout options. When the number of nodes in a network moves into the thousands and beyond, we have what can practically be considered a large network, at least for display considerations. With datasets of this scope, additional display considerations come into play, such as judicious use of filters, layers, and interactivity.

- How densely connected is the network? In our previous example using the power grid data, we had a fairly large dataset numbering in the thousands, but one that was not highly connected, at least as compared to social networks. In that case, we might have an easier time selecting and applying an effective layout, while the highly connected nature of social networks presents an additional challenge.

- Does the network exhibit certain measurable behaviors such as clustering and homophily? In some cases, we might not know this until the network has been visually and programmatically analyzed, but in others we might already know that the data is likely to cluster based on certain attributes that influence the network structure, including geographic proximity, alumni networks, professional associations, and a host of other possibilities. Knowing some of these in advance might help guide us either toward or away from specific layout types.

- Will the network be displayed on a single level, or will it be bipartite or multipartite? In this case, as covered briefly in *Chapter 1, Fundamentals of Complex Networks and Gephi*, some networks might be hierarchical, with individuals (for example) linking only to an organization, and not to other individuals in the network. There are many instances where we will wish to present hierarchical networks in this fashion. This could be used to display corporate structures, academic hierarchies, player to team relationships, and so on, and requires some different considerations than networks without this structure.

- Does the data have a temporal element? In simple terms, will the story be told more effectively by viewing network changes over time? This can be very effective in showing diffusion/contagion patterns, random growth, and simple shifts in behavior within a network, for example—were Thomas and James friends at T1, but no longer so at T3 (where T equals time)? If our data has a specific time element, this leads to identify layouts that will best display these changes and tell an effective story.

- Will the network be interactive on the user end, or will it be static? This can ultimately lead to a different layout selection when users have the ability to navigate a network via the Web.

You might have additional considerations, including the speed of the layout algorithm, but the preceding list should help you to narrow the list of practical layouts, allowing you to test the remaining candidates.

Actual example – the Miles Davis network

Let's walk through a process following the preceding guidelines, and applying them to a project previously created by me. This will help us migrate from the theoretical constructs above to a practical application of many of these principles. The project I'll use as our example traces the studio albums recorded by the legendary jazz trumpeter, Miles Davis—48 in all. Here are the details for this project, following the above progression.

Analysis goal

The goal of the analysis was to inform viewers, who might or might not be jazz fans, about the remarkable, far reaching recording legacy of Miles Davis. Since the career of Davis moved through many stages, he crossed paths with and employed an incredible number of artists across a diverse range of instruments that ranged far beyond the normal jazz instrumentation. Therefore, part of the goal of the analysis was to expose viewers to this great diversity, and give them the ability to see changes and patterns within the scope of his career.

Dataset parameters

The dataset in this case is not insignificant—while 48 albums would represent a small network if left on its own, we know from the data that there are typically at least four musicians per recording, and often far more, numbering into the 20s in some cases. Many of the musicians are represented on multiple recordings, but there is still a multiplicative impact on the size of the network, which turns out to have about 350 nodes. While this certainly doesn't rival the enormous datasets often seen in social networks, it is large enough that we need to be thoughtful about the layout and how users will interact with the project.

Here is a look at some of the underlying data for the nodes:

Nodes	Id	Label	Group	Nodes	Size	Released	Color
● Alto Flute - Dave Liebman	Alto Flute - Dave Liebman		Alto Flute		1		#d2d2d2
● Electric Violin - Michal Urbaniak	Electric Violin - Michal Urbaniak		Electric Violin		1		#a52a2a
● Shaker - Juma Santos	Shaker - Juma Santos		Shaker		1		#f6f6df
● Handcuffs - James Prindiville	Handcuffs - James Prindiville		Handcuffs		1		#ececec
● Synthesizer Bass - Robert Irving III	Synthesizer Bass - Robert Irving III		Synthesizer Bass		1		#626258
● African Percussion - James Mtume Foreman	African Percussion - James Mtume Foreman		African Percussion		1		#f5f5dc
● Cello - Paul Buckmaster	Cello - Paul Buckmaster		Cello		1		#731d1d
● Synclavier - George Duke	Synclavier - George Duke		Synclavier		1		#cfcfcf
● Triangle - Billy Cobham	Triangle - Billy Cobham		Triangle		1		#c4c4bo
● Conductor - Gil Evans	Conductor - Gil Evans		Conductor		4		#101010
● Baritone Sax - Gerry Mulligan	Baritone Sax - Gerry Mulligan		Baritone Sax		1		#998100
● Whistling - Hermeto Pascoal	Whistling - Hermeto Pascoal		Whistling		1		#e5acb6
● Berimbau - Airto Moreira	Berimbau - Airto Moreira		Berimbau		1		#7a7a6e

Miles Davis nodes

Notice that the nodes are a combination of an individual musician and a specific instrument, since so many of these musicians play a second (or even third) instrument. The data is then grouped by instrument, which allows you to partition and custom color the data.

Now, the following figure illustrates a partial view of the edge's data:

Source	Target	Type	Id
Trumpet - Miles Davis	Album - Blue Period	Undirected	221653
Trumpet - Miles Davis	Album - Dig	Undirected	221654
Trumpet - Miles Davis	Album - Blue Haze	Undirected	221655
Trumpet - Miles Davis	Album - Walkin'	Undirected	221656
Trumpet - Miles Davis	Album - Miles Davis and Horns	Undirected	221657
Trumpet - Miles Davis	Album - The Musings of Miles	Undirected	221658
Trumpet - Miles Davis	Album - Blue Moods	Undirected	221659
Trumpet - Miles Davis	Album - Quintet/Sextet	Undirected	221660
Trumpet - Miles Davis	Album - Miles: The New Miles Davis Quintet	Undirected	221661
Trumpet - Miles Davis	Album - Collectors' Items	Undirected	221662
Trumpet - Miles Davis	Album - Bags' Groove	Undirected	221663

Miles Davis data edges

In the preceding screenshot, we see only album level connections, with Miles Davis as the source and each album as the target, although the edges are left undirected. If we move further into the edge's data, we can see how the network is structured a bit more clearly:

Source_base	Target_base	Source_detail	Target_detail
Miles Davis	Blue Period	Trumpet	Album
Miles Davis	Dig	Trumpet	Album
Miles Davis	Blue Haze	Trumpet	Album
Miles Davis	Walkin'	Trumpet	Album
Miles Davis	Miles Davis and Horns	Trumpet	Album
Miles Davis	The Musings of Miles	Trumpet	Album
Miles Davis	Blue Moods	Trumpet	Album
Miles Davis	Quintet/Sextet	Trumpet	Album
Miles Davis	Miles: The New Miles D...	Trumpet	Album
Miles Davis	Collectors' Items	Trumpet	Album
Miles Davis	Bags' Groove	Trumpet	Album

Miles Davis data edge details

This data shows some of the musician level connections to specific recordings, as well as the instrument played on that album. This completes the basic structure of the network, as each musician will have an edge connecting them to any and all albums they played on. So this gives us a basic understanding of how the data will be represented in the network—Miles at the core, all albums at a second level, followed by every contributing musician at a tertiary level.

Network density

We have all seen many highly connected networks with edges crossing between nodes or groups within a graph that become virtually impenetrable for the viewer. Fortunately, this was not a major concern with this network, given its relatively modest size, but it could still play a role in the final layout selection. As always, the goal is to provide clarity and understanding, regardless of the relative size of the network, so minimizing visual clutter is always a priority.

Network behaviors

Examining the network behaviors can be an interesting exercise, as it often leads us to findings that were not necessarily anticipated. In the case of this project, we know from viewing the data that *Miles* played with certain musicians on a frequent basis, but would then often play with an entirely new group during his next phase, before switching yet again to a completely unrelated group of musicians. In other words, there were multiple aggregations of musicians who only occasionally intersected with one another. This is very nearly a proxy for homophily, with distinct clusters connected to each other through a single node (*Miles Davis* in this case) or perhaps a small subset of network members who act as bridges between various clusters.

Based on this knowledge, we would anticipate a highly clustered network with a significant level of connectedness within a given cluster, and a limited set of connections between clusters. The next decision to make was how best to display this network.

Network display

We just saw the underlying data structure, which had a bipartite nature to it, with each musician connecting to one or more albums, rather than to other musicians. Given this type of network, we want to select a layout that eases our ability to see not only the connections between Miles Davis and each recording, but also from each album to all of the participating musicians. This will require a layout that provides enough empty space to make for clear viewing, but also one that manages to combine this with a minimal number of edge crossings. Remember that many of these musicians played on multiple recordings, so they must be positioned in proximity to several albums at the same time, without adding to a cluttered look.

After testing several layouts, some of which simply didn't work effectively with the above two needs, I settled on the ARF algorithm for its visual clarity to display this particular network. The ability to see patterns within the network, even prior to adding interactivity, is a plus; if the network passes that test, it should be very effective once users interact with the information.

Temporal elements

Another interesting aspect of the network that could have been utilized was the timeline for the recordings. With more than four decades of recordings, this could have provided a wealth of information about changes over time in the musicians' network and instrumentation on each album. This element was not highlighted, but it does make its presence felt in the final network, with albums from one period with a consistent cast of musicians occupying one sector of the graph, while other types of albums with many infrequently used musicians land in another area.

Interactivity

The final decision was whether to make the network interactive, giving users the ability to learn more through self-navigation of the graph. This was considered important from the very start, so that the viewers could see not only the body of work represented by the 48 recordings, but also the evolution of which musicians were involved, as well as shining a light on the wide array of instruments used as Miles' career evolved.

After each of these considerations was evaluated, and through a period of testing the network using multiple layouts, I settled on the ARF force-directed layout coupled with the `Sigma.js` plugin for interactivity. Here's a look at the final output, which includes options using the `Sigma.js` plugin:

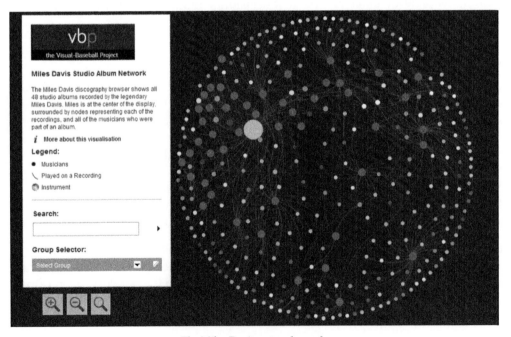

The Miles Davis network graph

The link to the project can be found at `http://visual-baseball.com/gephi/jazz/miles_davis/`.

I hope this example helps to generate some ideas or at least opens up the possibilities for what Gephi is capable of creating, and that the process illustrated earlier helps to provide at least a foundation for your own work. The data files used for this project are also available at the link in the *Web Resources* section of the book, so you can create your own version—and perhaps improve on the original!

Layout strengths and weaknesses

We've walked through an overview of many layouts in this chapter and provided a number of external links for those who wish to learn the full technical details of a specific algorithm. What we have not done to this point is compare these approaches to give you a bit of guidance in how and when to use various layouts, and what their relative strengths and weaknesses are. The following table will attempt to remedy this, giving you a fairly high level overview across a few broad categories. Remember, there are few absolutes in this space, and there are no substitutes for trial and error and visual evaluation, but it is hoped that the following will provide some guidance as you evaluate various layouts:

Algorithm name	Type	Strengths	Weaknesses	When to use
ARF	Force-directed			
Circular layout	Circular	This is simple, easy to interpret, and easy to set parameters	This is limited to small networks for easy viewing; it has potential for excessive edge crossing	This layout can be used in cases where you have a particular order in mind for the data—by clusters, size, and so on
Concentric layout	Circular	This is good for focusing on a single node within a network	This is not ideal for large diameter networks as graph size increases geometrically	This is useful for featuring a single node at the center and displaying their neighbors in descending order from direct to distant

Algorithm name	Type	Strengths	Weaknesses	When to use
DAG layout	Tree	Ordering hierarchical data	This is impractical for very large networks	This can be used in cases where you wish to see levels of data in a top to bottom order
Dual Circle layout	Circular	This has the ability to focus on a group of nodes within the larger network	This layout results in very large networks that might create viewing issues	This layout can be used in instances where a second circle is desirable to focus on a limited group of nodes
Force Atlas	Force-directed	This includes many options and has a high level of accuracy	This can be very slow and is not suited to large networks	This layout is useful for network analysis and discovery, and for measuring network behavior
Force Atlas 2	Force-directed	This is faster than original Force Atlas and handles very large networks	This suffers slightly on overall accuracy	This is used as a good tool for network analysis and discovery, and for detecting behavioral patterns
Fruchterman-Reingold	Force-directed	This is accurate, and tends to be easy for viewers	This is very slow and not suited for large networks	This is good for a generalized view of small-to medium-sized networks
Geo layout	Geographic	This uses lat/lon data for geo-based networks	This is limited to geographic data, and must have lat/lon attributes	This can be used with any geo-based data

Algorithm name	Type	Strengths	Weaknesses	When to use
Hiveplot layout	Radial	This provides a good solution for network hairballs by spreading connections along radial axes	Can be difficult to see interactions within groups along each axis	This is ideal for viewing cross-group interactions in small-to medium-sized networks
Isometric layout	Layered	Adds third (z) dimension to help spread crowded networks	More difficult to determine relative positioning of nodes within the larger network	Useful for cases where the network has natural groupings or layers
Layered layout	Layered	This is an easy way to view a network with distinct layering patterns based on clusters or groupings	This has very few options for setting layer behavior and layout	Useful for simple graph creation where layers are a key part of the story
Maps of Countries	Geographic	This provides a background of countries and regions for use with other networks; this also works with lat/lon overlays	This requires country-level data to be useful	This is used in cases where national affiliations are part of the story — perhaps author networks or research collaborations
Multipartite layout	Multipartite	Minimizes edge crossings, best suited to multitier network structures	This has few options to customize the graph	This is best used when the network data shows linkages between individuals and organizations or other level of aggregation

Algorithm name	Type	Strengths	Weaknesses	When to use
Network Splitter 3D	Layered	This adds a third (z) dimension to help in viewing crowded networks with natural layers	This separates layers, making it more difficult to perceive the whole network	This is ideal for splitting crowded networks along a specific criteria, such as clusters or groups
OpenOrd	Force-directed	This is very fast, and can handle large networks	This is not highly accurate on smaller networks	This is used for a rapid understanding of large network structure
Radial Axis layout	Radial/ Circular	This is flexible, and is a good layout for clustered datasets	This can be challenging with large networks, and is not ideal for viewing intragroup connections	This is ideal for viewing connections across groups
Yifan Hu	Force-directed	This is fast compared to other force-directed algorithms	This lacks separate repulsion and attraction variables	This has an easy to understand approach for rapidly viewing small to medium networks
Yifan Hu Proportional	Force-directed	This handles relatively large networks; and has fast graph creation	This has moderate quality versus other force-based layouts	This has an easy to understand approach for rapidly viewing small-to-medium networks
Yifan Hu Multilevel	Force-directed	This handles very large graphs, fast	Quality is sacrificed as a trade-off for processing speed	Very fast method for viewing large networks

Testing layouts

In my experience, selecting a perfect layout on the first attempt is highly unlikely; even if the best possible algorithm is chosen, it is almost a certainty that the graph display can be improved through adjusting the base settings, not to mention all of the downstream cosmetic enhancements. Knowing this makes it essential to sample multiple layouts for your network data, which can be a very efficient process for all but the largest networks.

In the next few sections, we will walk through the process of testing a few layouts using the same dataset, and will go into greater detail compared to our exercise in *Chapter 2, A Network Graph Framework*, by modifying settings within each algorithm to demonstrate the resulting impact on the network graph. We'll work with the *Les Miserables* dataset found in the Gephi samples (available when you open Gephi), as it provides an interesting network to work with, while still being small enough to easily interpret.

Our focus during this process will be limited to the actions that we can control primarily from the layout algorithms, in the hope that there will be sufficient differences that favor certain layouts over others. In later chapters, there will be a focus on additional modification that can be made once the base layout has been selected.

For this exercise, we will visit algorithms from several of the main categories discussed earlier—force-based, circular, and radial, and walk through a simple testing process. The goal is to not overwhelm you with image after image of each layout type, but rather to select a few layouts and then work within the layout to adjust settings and improve the graph appearance. This will be a nonjudgmental process as well, which will allow you to choose the layout that works best per your individual perception.

Testing the ARF layout

While there are many options for the force-directed layouts, the ARF algorithm provides a fast, simple, and easy to interpret layout that will aid in understanding the fundamentals of the force-based layouts. If you wish to follow along, use the *Les Miserables* dataset from the Gephi samples to get started. This is an undirected network that shows the interaction between characters in the famed novel.

Here's a look at what we see after opening the network in Gephi:

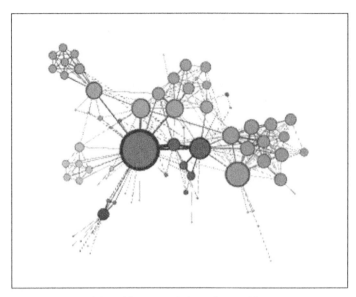

Les Miserables network from the .gexf format

Not bad as networks go—this one has obviously been worked on to some degree, with sized and colored nodes, weighted edges, and some sort of clustering tied into the colors. Still, we will work with our layout algorithms to see what improvements can be made.

Now, select the ARF layout if you choose to follow along (as you can recall, this must be installed as a plugin). Here are the default settings we'll use for the first iteration:

- **Neighbor attraction force** = 3.0
- **General attraction force** = 2.0
- **Repulsive force** = 8.0
- **Precision** = 2.0
- **Maximum force** = 7.0

Here is the result, after letting ARF run for about a minute:

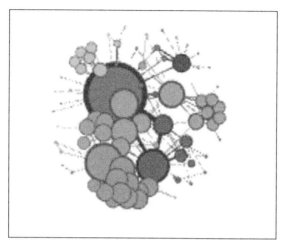

Les Miserables in ARF

Notice that the network has actually drawn closer together compared to the original, making it more difficult to interpret. To remedy this, we'll adjust the repulsive force higher—say from `8.0` to `20.0`, in an effort to spread the graph out by putting greater distance between unrelated nodes:

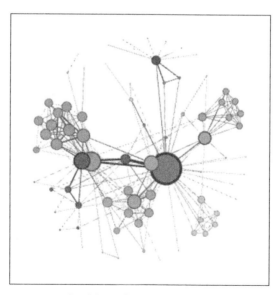

Les Miserables in ARF (Step 1)

That's much better, although it still hasn't really surpassed the original, given that we have a few overlapping nodes that require attention. Let's give it one more try, this time adjusting the general attraction from 0.2 to 0.1. Reducing this value will minimize the likelihood that nodes are drawn together, thus preventing the overlapping (we hope!):

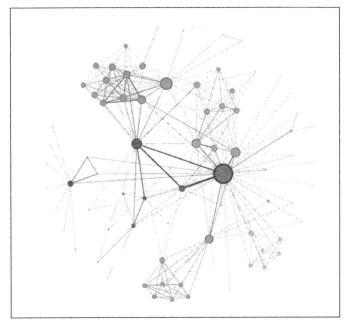

Les Miserables in ARF (Step 2)

This is definitely an improvement over our first two attempts. The clustered nodes group together better than before, there are no overlaps, and peripheral characters have been pushed further toward the perimeter of the network, thus minimizing edge crossings and making for a cleaner layout. This final version feels like a good foundation we could take to subsequent stages in Gephi, assuming that we prefer the result versus the upcoming layouts we're about to view.

The Concentric layout

Our next effort will focus on the Concentric layout, available again as a Gephi plugin. The Les Miserables data provides an interesting use case for a concentric graph, given the dominance of a single character, Jean Valjean. If you are unfamiliar with the story, Valjean is the central character, and is thus represented by the largest node in the network, based on the number of connections to other characters. As you can recall from earlier, a single node is featured at the center of a concentric network, with other nodes spaced based on the number of degrees they are away from the selected node (for example, direct connections are represented in the innermost circle).

In theory, this would make a concentric layout an attractive option for telling this story, assuming that Valjean is at the center of our story. Let's have a look at whether this is as effective as it sounds. The default settings are as follows:

- **Distance** = 100
- **Node** = 0
- **Speed** = 10.0
- **Coverage** = 0.6

One change we do need to make is to set the node to Valjean's ID, which happens to be 11. Otherwise, the algorithm will do the selection for us, forcing an extra iteration to get things right. The initial result looks like this:

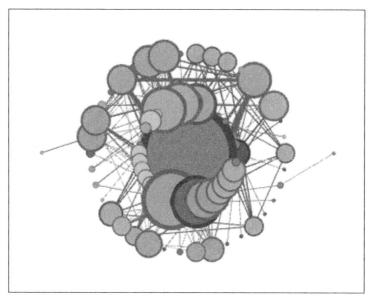

Les Miserables Concentric layout

These settings result in a very crowded graph that won't be effective in telling any sort of story. Perhaps if the nodes were not previously sized, this might work better, but we would then lose the impact conveyed by the multiple sizes. So let's increase the distance settings from 100 to 500 to spread the rings out from one another. Note that this is easily done given the small diameter of the network.

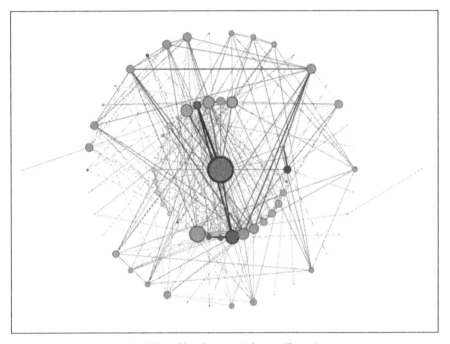

Les Miserables Concentric layout (Step 1)

Much improved! Now we can clearly see the structure of the network, and the fact that virtually all nodes are within two steps of the central character, with only a couple of instances three degrees out from the center. On the downside, the concentric approach isn't as effective in grouping the clusters compared to the ARF method, but at least it now presents a viable option for further use.

Testing the Radial Axis layout

A Radial Axis layout resembles circular layouts to a considerable degree, but presents another option to consider that is different in one critical sense. The difference lies in the manner in which nodes are arranged and displayed using a series of axes rather than one or more circles. This would appear to be a reasonable approach for our current dataset, especially given the existing clusters in the network. Let's have a look at where this approach leads us, once again starting with default settings as follows:

- **Scaling Width** = `1.2`
- **Group Nodes by** = `Degree`

We'll leave the remainder of the settings untouched for now, although there are several more selections that could be used to tweak the layout. Here's the initial network graph:

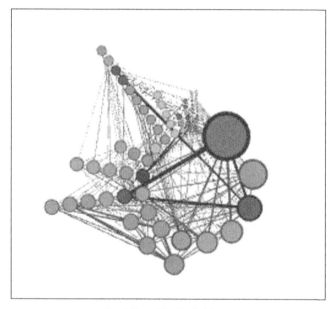

Les Miserables Radial Axis

As with the other layout selections, the default settings have created a crowded graph, albeit somewhat more readable than our previous examples. Still, there are a couple of simple choices we can make to improve the layout quickly. Our first step, as with the other layouts, will be to spread the graph out for easier interpretation. Let's raise the **Scaling Width** option from 1.2 to 2.5 and see whether that level is sufficient for our purposes.

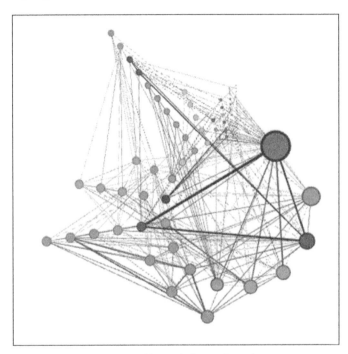

Les Miserables Radial Axis (Step 1)

This is certainly an improvement, although a slightly higher setting might be even better, especially if we need to draw attention to some of the smaller nodes. For now, let's stick with this setting while making an important adjustment to the **Group Nodes by** option. Rather than using the default setting of **Degrees**, we're going to change this to group based on the clustered nodes, here shown as **Modularity Class (Attribute)**. Let's check out the results of this change:

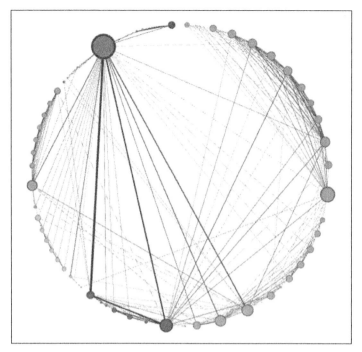

Les Miserables Radial Axis (Step 2)

Interesting—our Radial Axis layout has formed a circle, confirming our earlier statement about the similarities between circular and radial layouts. Also note how clean and easily followed the network is, with the various clusters ordered by size around the perimeter, and the Valjean node easily seen at the upper-left corner of the graph. This layout also highlights the strongest connections in the network, seen here through weighted edges between Valjean and some other prominent characters in the story.

While this layout worked quite well in this instance, note that it would probably be far less effective if we had 500 nodes rather than a mere 76 in this network. This is where your trained eye needs to make some decisions about how much is too much within a specific layout context, guided by how the network will ultimately be deployed.

Layout selection criteria

Now that you've had the opportunity to see the impact of different layouts and settings on the same network data, it's time to determine what the best option is before proceeding with your graph. This is not always an easy task, and can certainly be influenced by subjective factors such as differing layout preferences among individuals, different layout needs (for example, print versus interactive), and personal decisions on what story to tell with the network graph. After all, the same data can often lend itself to many narratives, depending on the perspective of the individual analyst.

Even with the above caveats in mind, there are certain criterias that are at least somewhat objective, and can thus help in making the graph selection process a bit easier. Here are a few measures we might start with to select an appropriate layout:

- Does the network graph communicate any sort of story when you examine how it appears in a specific layout? After all, if even the creator of the graph has a difficulty in perceiving the meaning from the network, then users who are unfamiliar with the data are likely to have an even more difficult go at interpreting the story. If you have spent considerable time in tweaking and adjusting the layout, and it still fails to reveal further meaning from the data, then you should find a layout that is more effective for your network.

- If you do see evident patterns within the data that lend themselves to a story, but find they are being crowded out by comparatively meaningless clutter (a common issue with dense graphs), there is still hope for using that particular layout. If you haven't already attempted some of the available spacing options, by all means begin working with these. Set your attraction settings lower and/or your repulsion settings higher to help spread the graph in a meaningful fashion. Many layouts allow you to adjust the gravity setting, which will pull nodes toward the center or, alternatively, push them out towards the perimeter of the graph.

- If the network has the dreaded hairball appearance, with large numbers of nodes and edges creating a dense, difficult to read graph, then it is likely that your layout is either a poor choice for the selected data, or that it has yet to be optimized. There are opportunities to segment dense networks using a layered or partitioned approach or through the use of intelligent filtering to focus attention on the relevant relationships within the graph. In instances with very large datasets, it is often difficult to completely avoid the hairball effect regardless of the chosen layout, but there are still ways to work around it, using the suggested approaches.

- Will the final layout be interactive or static? If the network will be navigable for end users, then a higher degree of complexity is possible, although this should not be used as an excuse for failing to optimize the layout. Regardless of the final output, the goal should be to create the best (and often simplest) graph that tells the story. An interactive format will typically allow you to explore a larger graph, but it should adhere to the same basic principles we use to produce a graph for the printed page.

Keep these guidelines in mind when you are assessing the viability of a layout, and trust your own judgment as well. This is certainly an area where experience is a valuable asset. By following this process, or something similar to it, you will build a level of confidence while viewing future network graphs, and will be able to make better, faster decisions for future network layouts.

Graph aesthetics

Part of what makes certain graphs memorable goes far beyond the data or the layout algorithm used by the analyst. What takes these graphs to the next level is often some relatively simple tweaking of graph attributes using styling options within Gephi. The intelligent use of spacing, sizing, coloring, and labeling can elevate a graph from being merely informative to being both, informative and aesthetically pleasing, and indeed eye-catching. We should not set out to create the graph simply as a work of art, compromising the relationships in the network, but we can and should make the graph visually attractive, in order to successfully convey the meaning of the data. Use aesthetics to enhance, not obscure, the meaning of the data.

In this spirit, we can learn from the information visualization approaches of *Edward Tufte* and *Stephen Few*, albeit with some appropriate caveats that apply specifically to network graphs. Some readers will consider their approaches to be rather Spartan, and indeed that might be the case when taken at face value. However, it is the basic principle, suggested by *Tufte* and *Few*, as well as *Cleveland*, *Bertin*, and other data visualization experts, that we are concerned with, and how best to integrate their ideas into the world of network graph design.

Subsequent chapters focusing on filtering (*Chapter 5, Working with Filters*) and partitioning (*Chapter 7, Segmenting and Partitioning a Graph*) will take this to another level, but in the meantime there are some simple steps that can be taken to enhance the appearance of our graph. In the following sections, we'll walk through a makeover process where a plain, uninspiring graph is elevated step by step to a much higher level, simply by using some basic Gephi functions.

Working example of graph aesthetics

For this example, we'll begin with an unadorned dataset, and then make step-by-step modifications using only the tools in the Gephi **Preview** toolbars. The idea is to demonstrate how easily we can make a graph more attractive, even without utilizing more sophisticated clustering, ranking, and filtering tools. Think of this as graph aesthetics 101, where we will learn to take advantage of base Gephi functionality. Some of you might find this information very basic, and might want to skip ahead to the next chapter, but if you are not in this group, then join me in this basic example.

We're going to use the *Les Miserables* dataset again, but this time it won't be in the neat form we've previously used, but rather in a simple, unformatted version, available from the Gephi website. This can be found in the Gephi wiki under datasets in a .gml format. After opening the file in Gephi, the result is a very plain, somewhat undecipherable network:

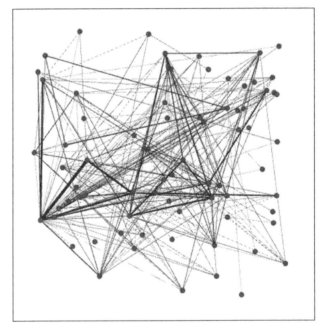

Les Miserables .gml

Perform the following steps:

1. Our first step will be to choose a layout; at this point, nearly any choice should improve the graph. We'll work with the ARF algorithm, which creates this result:

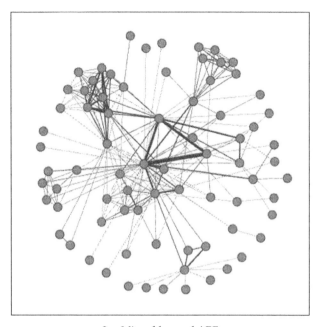

Les Miserables .gml ARF

2. For the second step, let's size and color a selected node; in this instance, we'll choose node 55, the character *Marius* (full name *Marius Pontmercy*). We'll assume that our story revolves around this important character, so all efforts will be made to highlight his network position and connections. These simple steps can be done by using the **Sizer** tool followed by the **Painter** tool, both located on the toolbar to the left of the **Preview** window:

Styling elements in Gephi toolbar

Now we at least have an element that stands out from the remainder of the network:

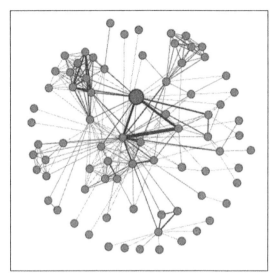

Les Miserables .gml ARF (Step 1)

3.   Marius now stands out from the remainder of the network, by virtue of his size and color, which helps to identify him from the more generic nodes that comprise the remainder of the network. Let's learn a bit more about Marius and his connections by using the **Brush** function, which enhances our graph even further:

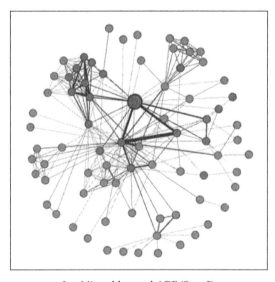

Les Miserables .gml ARF (Step 2)

4. All the closest neighbors of Marius are now highlighted and stand out from the remainder of the network, providing a clearer picture of his direct influence within the network.

We just created a graph that lays the foundation for a story, all in four simple steps. Imagine what you could do beyond this, using labels, shortest paths, edge coloring, and more. Remember, we haven't even ventured into any of the more sophisticated techniques, yet we have quickly created a useful network graph.

Summary

In this chapter, you were exposed to many of the available layout algorithms made available for Gephi, and received a brief overview for how they work, and how changing certain values can have a significant impact on your network graph.

You were then asked to step back and assess your graph needs, and think about which layouts might be most appropriate to perform your network analysis. Following this, you were given a table that laid out the various strengths and weaknesses of each layout type, to help you make a more informed layout selection.

You also learned how to go through a simple testing process, demonstrated using three different algorithms, and adjusting settings for each algorithm for it to result in an improved network graph. This was followed by some advice on the criteria for selecting an optimal layout, and some of the pitfalls to work around. Finally, we introduced the topic of graph aesthetics, and provided some simple steps to visually enhance a simple graph.

In the next chapter, we will explore network patterns and gain a better understanding of phenomena such as **contagion**, **diffusion**, **homophily**, and other network behaviors.

4
Network Patterns

One of the most critical roles of networks is their use in identifying various behaviors, regardless of whether they originate from social networks, disease tracking, idea diffusion, or any one of many other sources. There is a large and growing body of literature dedicated to network analysis that can be applied to a wide range of behavior across multiple realms, merging theory with real life examples to help you provide solutions to critical needs.

In this chapter, we will initially examine several of the most critical concepts, providing general overviews as well as external resources that examine each of these concepts more thoroughly. The topics covered in this chapter are as follows:

- Contagion and diffusion
- Clustering and homophily
- Network growth patterns
- Using Gephi generators
- Viewing a contagion network
- Viewing network diffusion
- Identifying homophily

After covering the theoretical foundations, we'll then move onto how to identify and apply these ideas using Gephi. The chapter will conclude with a section on traversing networks that will incorporate the previously noted concepts.

A significant portion of this chapter will be spent working with example datasets that can be used to illustrate various theories, demonstrate how Gephi can be leveraged to create and then to understand each of these network behaviors. So you are encouraged to join in using the same datasets used in the chapter and to replicate the steps used here in your own version of Gephi.

Contagion and diffusion

Contagion and diffusion are related concepts that are often best understood through network analysis. The use of network graphs can help you provide considerable insight into the potential spread of a disease as well as the success of a new innovation. This is done by exposing the structure of the underlying network. Densely connected networks can be effective in both of these realms, which can have both positive and negative effects, depending on whether we are viewing the diffusion of a positive innovation, or conversely, the spread of an infectious disease.

Contagion

One of the most intriguing and potentially valuable ways of using networks is to examine how disease transmission works within a network, and how the structure of a network can either promote or limit the spread of the disease. If the transmission pattern can be altered through some sort of intervention, such as vaccination or even simple avoidance (for example, not contacting a friend if there is a high likelihood of contagion), then the spread of the disease can be significantly reduced and perhaps stopped altogether.

We'll begin our discussion of contagion at a theoretical level by laying the groundwork for a practical approach later in the chapter, and using Gephi to demonstrate how network structures give rise to contagion levels, or conversely, how they might prevent further spread of a disease.

So what is the definition of contagion we'll be using in this chapter? Out of the multiple definitions using the Merriam-Webster dictionary, here are the two that best represent the concept for our purposes:

- The transmission of a disease by direct or indirect contact
- An influence that spreads rapidly

David Easley and *Jon Kleinberg* also allude to the similarities between diffusion and contagion in their book, *Networks, Crowds, and Markets: Reasoning About a Highly Connected World, Cambridge University Press* (published in 2010).

Easley and Kleinberg highlight the primary difference between the two when it comes to modeling:

> "...the biggest difference between biological and social contagion lies in the process by which one person "infects" another. With social contagion, people are making decisions to adopt a new idea or innovation...With diseases, on the other hand, not only is there a lack of decision-making in the transmission of the disease from one person to another, but the process is sufficiently complex and unobservable at the person-to-person level that it is most useful to model it as random."

In other words, contagion is often best expressed using random models, given the unpredictable contact patterns that often spread a disease. Diffusion (or social contagion), is typically the result of a network structure and the interaction between members of a network, and can thus be modeled using methods with a higher degree of sophistication compared to a random model.

Contagion, in its biological form, requires close physical contact to propagate, although there are some caveats to this rule. In many cases, direct contact is required, but in other instances, merely being in the same place where infectious germs remain from a prior occupant (a bathroom, bus station, escalator, and so on) is sufficient to spread the disease. Even in these cases, there are limiting factors that will halt the spread of the disease, at least for the moment. The most critical element here is time. Suppose two strangers ride the same train on the same day and occupy the same seat just 15 minutes apart. Infectious germs left by Stranger A might well survive long enough to infect Stranger B. Stranger C, who occupies the same seat 4 hours later, is highly unlikely to be exposed to the same germs, simply due to the difference in time. Here, we are witness to a bit of the randomness characterized by Easley and Kleinberg.

One of the ways in which the contagion can spread is through a simple branching network, where the individual carrying the disease enters a population and transmits it to each person he or she makes contact with. Note that there is always a probability associated with this event, as not everyone will contract the disease. The probability might range from a relatively low 0.10, with one of 10 contacts picking up the disease, to something much higher, contingent on both the infectiousness of the disease coupled with the immunity levels of the members in the network. In cases with a high level of infectiousness combined with relatively low immunity levels, the probability of each individual being infected can be very high. The inverse is true if there is a low contagion level paired with high immunity levels.

The branching network works quite simply. Let's assume a 30 percent (0.3) probability that members of the first individual's contacts will also get the disease. For simplicity, we'll assume this represents three individuals. This is the first wave in the spread of the disease. These three infected persons then go out into their respective (albeit somewhat random) networks, and further spread the disease to roughly one of every three persons they meet. This is the second wave of the disease. Finally, each subsequent wave is spread in the same fashion, making the branching process potentially infinite; although in practice, it will tend to die out well before this occurs.

For the next few graphs we used CmapTools, which is available at http://cmap. ihmc.us/. Let's track this initial scenario using a simple diagram to help you understand the spread of the disease through its first several waves:

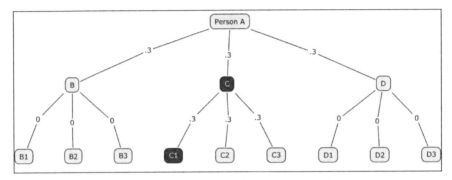

Contagion branching network with 0.3 probability

Notice how quickly the contagion fades in this instance, with just two of the 12 possible nodes getting infected. This obviously changes dramatically in the case of a highly infectious disease where the probability of transmission is 0.7, as shown in the following diagram:

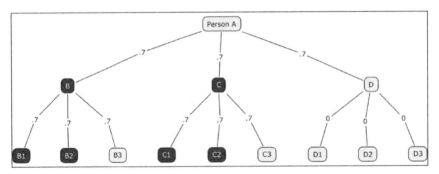

Contagion branching network with 0.7 probability

Instead of just two of 12 being infected, now half of the susceptible nodes have contracted the infection. This begins to illustrate the influence of individual nodes close to the source and demonstrates the downstream impact they can have. In this instance, even with a high transmission rate, those who come in contact with D have no chance of contracting the virus, given that D had some sort of immunity not present for either B or C.

Now let's move onto a brief discussion of three epidemic models discussed by *Easley* and *Kleinberg* in *Networks, Crowds, and Markets: Reasoning About a Highly Connected World, Cambridge University Press* (published in 2010), that provide further insight into the spread of disease and how network structure plays a critical role in the progression of an epidemic.

The SIR model

The **SIR model** offers three distinct stages for each node in a network: **Susceptible**, **Infectious**, and **Removed**. This can be viewed in temporal fashion, as follows:

A brief definition of each stage is provided here:

- **Susceptible**: This refers to the stage where an individual node could potentially be the recipient of an infection, as they neither have it currently nor do they have immunity. This does not mean that infection is inevitable, as that depends on other factors such as the strength of the virus, the immune system of the potential recipient, and the timing of contact with an infected node.

- **Infectious**: This simply describes nodes who currently have the infection and have the ability to transmit it to those in the susceptible stage. In the SIR model, those who have been in the infectious stage wind up as part of the removed population, as they cannot acquire the same infection for a second time.

- **Removed**: These nodes are those persons who have already been in the infectious stage and have now recovered. In the SIR model, they cannot be infected a second time and can therefore eventually bring the contagion process to a halt through their acquired immunity.

The SIS model

In a **SIS model**, the removed status has been replaced by a second instance of susceptible, as this model assumes the case that individuals are not immune from a disease simply because they were previously exposed to the infection. In this case, after leaving an infectious state, each member will become susceptible once again, which is represented as follows:

The single difference between SIR and SIS is the ability of previously infected persons to be reinfected; in other words, there is no immunity built up simply as a result of having had the infection. A SIS cycle has the potential to last almost indefinitely, as an infection can be passed back and forth through repeated exposure to infected individuals.

The SIRS model

A third case is presented that merges the first two models, resulting in the **SIRS model**, with a fourth stage where individuals have temporary immunity from the infection, but eventually re-enter the susceptible stage. It is represented as follows:

In this instance, persons coming out of the infectious stage are removed, as they are in the SIR model, but for only a finite time period. Once this period has ended, individuals revert back to the susceptible stage, where they can be infected for a second (or greater) time. We would anticipate that a contagion process will die off faster in this situation compared to the SIS model, but has the potential to run considerably longer than a contagion under the SIR model.

I hope this discussion has provided you with a fundamental understanding of how the theory behind contagion works, and how we might be able to use Gephi to understand the process further. Specifically, we can start down this path by working with dynamic networks in Gephi. A very quick approach will be to navigate to the **Generate | Dynamic Graph Example...**, which will create a relatively simple network. From there, we can choose to edit that file, or create our own dynamic dataset using time elements (start time, end time) for use in Gephi. We'll address this topic more specifically in *Chapter 8, Dynamic Networks*.

Diffusion

While contagion is often viewed through the lens of an infectious disease and other direct contact effects, diffusion can be thought of in a somewhat different manner. We'll use the following definition to best describe this process from a network analysis context:

Diffusion is the process or state of something spreading more widely.

Note how this is related to contagion, in the sense of something spreading (an idea, an innovation, and so on), but has a much broader definition that goes beyond the spread of disease. We should also recognize that while contact plays a role in the process of diffusion, it might not be the same sort of direct contact implied by contagion. For instance, the behavior within a network of Facebook friends can certainly enable a diffusion process through sharing and forwarding a particular post. No direct physical contact is required for this process to succeed.

We assume from our preceding example that one of these Facebook friends has recently contracted a flu virus. This virus will not spread through his or her Facebook network regardless of how many posts are shared, unless he or she also has direct physical contact with the same group of friends. This brings us to another critical distinction between the two processes: diffusion generally requires some sort of social contact or influence to take root, while contagion is dependent on physical proximity, regardless of whether others are part of your social or professional network. Diffusion can be witnessed in the spread of a specific good across a network. This might or might not be a physical product; it can just as easily be the spread of digital property (music files, videos, images, and so on) or even a concept or new idea. The Web has certainly aided the diffusion process in many cases, but is not the sole channel for propagation. Traditional media, advertising, word of mouth, and industry events are just a few other means for initiating a diffusion process.

The concept of preferential attachment, addressed earlier in the book, also plays a significant role in diffusion (as well as contagion). Networks that are defined by the presence of a relatively small number of influential hubs enable more rapid diffusion of many products or processes. For instance, when one of the large hubs promotes the latest cat video, it will soon be found in millions of Facebook feeds, regardless of whether the user is fond of cats. In contrast, try to picture this same process in a highly fragmented low density network. The diffusion process in this situation will have difficulty in establishing any momentum, and the process is likely to stop almost as quickly as it started.

Many of the ideas presented in this section are based on the work of *Easley* and *Kleinberg* in their book, *Networks, Crowds, and Markets: Reasoning About a Highly Connected World, Cambridge University Press* (published in 2010). Their work will help in providing a general overview of how network diffusion works, which will then be translated into examples using Gephi. The process of how diffusion takes place within networks can be fascinating, as it is frequently tied to both global and local structures within a given network. These structures can either promote or discourage diffusion, which we will demonstrate through some examples in the following sections.

Diffusion, as we noted earlier, is concerned primarily with the spread of ideas, innovations, and other concepts that do not necessarily require close physical proximity. Proximity can play a role, but it is generally not essential to the spread of something, quite the opposite of contagion. We might, in fact, find cases where physical location is critical—say the opening of an independent coffee house in Minneapolis, where the reputation of the store is only relevant to the customers living (or visiting) within a short distance of the store. So there can be a physical component to diffusion, but in this sort of case, it is likely to be a limiting factor that is dependent on network members in a small geographic area.

Contrast this with the spread of ideas and innovations in our twenty-first century world. Early adopters of the latest Apple or Samsung product might quickly become critical to the diffusion pattern of the product, with glowing reviews likely to lead to an accelerated adoption of the product, while a spate of negative reviews might well serve to limit the diffusion process. Similarly, ideas can also be spread rapidly via the Web, social media, texting, or other means of inexpensive, rapid communication.

You might have detected a physical element to diffusion that is not always addressed. Products or services that are inexpensive, or lightweight and easily shipped, are far more likely to have explosive diffusion patterns than large physical entities that are either immobile, expensive, or both. At its most extreme, think of the rapid spread of a simple video (probably involving cats) across the Web. The cost is low, access to the video is high, and thus diffusion is widespread and rapid, assuming the video is well-received.

In contrast, think of a spectacular new audio component (perhaps a revolutionary new speaker design) that has been developed in Boston and is available in just five high-end audio specialists at the outset. Perhaps all of the audiophiles in your personal network are very excited by this new product and wish to own it someday. The reviews might be spectacular, the desire to own the product is high, but the price, limited availability, and high cost of delivery beyond the Boston market will quickly restrict the diffusion of the product, at least until a comprehensive distribution system becomes available. Even then, the spread of the product will pale in comparison to the aforementioned cat video, where the cost of ownership is effectively zero, and where the distribution network (YouTube, Facebook, and so on) is already constructed.

We have thus established that the rapid diffusion of a product or service is not necessarily related to its quality, even in cases where an underlying peer network exists. Better products and innovations might well lose out to inferior ones, largely dependent on the ability of each product to access appropriate levels within a network and then to spread from there.

Now, let's take a brief look at what diffusion process might look like in theory, and then later in the chapter we'll examine this process using Gephi. Here's a case where we have the following criteria:

- Node B purchases a new product.
- Node G is considering purchasing the product, but needs to reach an aggregate threshold of at least 0.6 before making the purchase for himself/ herself.
- Each number on the chart indicates a relative influence level one node has on another. So we can see that G is influenced by B, D, and F, who are themselves subjected to influences from other network members.

Here's our network:

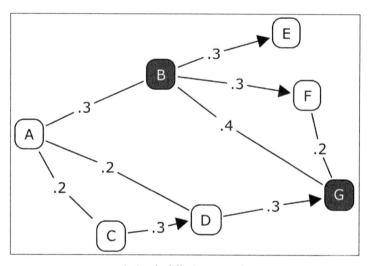

A simple diffusion example

Notice that based on the threshold level of 0.6, it is not enough for G to see that B owns the product. He also needs to know that either D or F also has purchased the item before feeling confident enough to also make the purchase. So G is dependent on the decisions of D and F as well as B. At least two of the three must own the product before G will elect to buy.

While this clearly represents a simplification of the diffusion process, it does illustrate an important concept that is crucial to both product adoption and more generally to the spread of information. We will return to this concept by building some examples in Gephi in the *Viewing Network Diffusion* section of this chapter.

Clustering and homophily

The two related concepts of clustering and homophily are essential components of network analysis in which they can provide key insights into network behavior. In simple terms, clustering refers to groupings of individuals (or entities) that are tied together by some common attribute (or multiple attributes). This can represent virtually anything, as long as it is effective in defining and differentiating individual clusters. The goal is to identify a common linkage that separates one group from another. This commonality might be based on geography, shopping patterns, age, type of vehicles driven, preferred genres of movies, and so on. It might well be a combination of these attributes that distinguishes clusters from one another. Let's take a look at an example.

Suppose we use the attributes identified earlier, and wind up with the following distinct clusters:

- Cluster 1 is composed primarily of Midwest Ford pickup drivers who shop at Target
- Cluster 2 is primarily East Coast Mercedes drivers who shop at Nordstrom
- Cluster 3 is made up of Chevy pickup drivers from Texas who shop at Sears

Each of these groups are self-identified using certain lifestyle attributes and are thus more likely to construct networks of others like themselves. If the preceding attributes clearly define each group, they will likely have little contact with each of the other clusters (although members at the fringe can form **bridges** to another cluster). Most of their interaction within a network is likely to occur at a **local** level, as opposed to a more **global** level.

There will also be cases where the clusters are still tangible, but perhaps less isolated from one another, with many members freely associating with the persons in different clusters on the basis of other shared attributes (religious beliefs, political affiliation, age, and so on). In this case, our network graph will show a greater degree of interconnectedness and will require fewer bridge members to connect disparate clusters.

In the first case, we have what is commonly known as **homophily**, a critical concept in understanding the formation of networks, the diffusion of innovations, and how information travels across a network. Miller McPherson, Lynn Smith-Lovin, and James M. Cook define homophily in their paper *Birds of a Feather*: Homophily in Social Networks as follows:

> *"Homophily is the principle that a contact between similar people occurs at a higher rate than among dissimilar people"*
>
> *– Birds of a Feather: Homophily in Social Networks by Miller McPherson, Lynn Smith-Lovin, and James M. Cook*

Homophily can actually inhibit the spread of ideas, innovations, and information due to its segregated structure. Information sharing tends to be within the clusters rather than between the clusters, thus limiting its flow. If the individual serving as a bridge between Cluster A and Cluster B fails to pass on specific information, the flow of that information will cease, at least for that portion of the network. Networks with high levels of homophily based on one or more attributes (gender, income, job status, and so on) are often said to be **assortative** on those elements, as in **assortative on income**.

In the second case, there are likely to be multiple contact points between clusters, leading to a greater sharing of information and innovation, and thus encouraging greater diffusion versus the network with a high degree of homophily. This can have a profound impact on information flow, product adoption rates, and other scenarios that are dependent on network communication. It is therefore critical to identify whether homophily exists, and if so, to what degree, in order to gain a more informed perspective about how communication will flow through a network. We can then begin to understand where barriers and potential failure points exist.

Let's take a closer look at how these concepts work in theory, and then later in the chapter we'll use Gephi to create some visual examples. We'll begin with the general principle of clustering.

Clustering

Clusters are certainly not unique to network graphs; they are a critical component in statistical analysis as well. There is even a specific set of methods devoted to their analysis, widely known as **cluster analysis**. However, the goal is the same, as it is in network analysis. We are simply attempting to understand how certain groups within our datasets are similar or different from one another (cluster analysis has methods that use either similarity or dissimilarity to build clusters) based on a single or, more typically, multiple attributes. These attributes can be in the form of observable physical characteristics, or they may be behavioral-based. In any case, they can be combined to form distinct clusters of individuals who form groups that can be further analyzed.

There is one essential difference between the two, even when the end result might be similar. In network graphs, the clusters require some sort of direct connection, which might or might not be true in traditional cluster analysis. When we view clusters in a network, they will almost invariably be based on the level of connectedness between neighbor nodes.

Our network graphs might have significant clustering, or perhaps the clustering is rather loose. In some cases, there might be no meaningful clusters at all, although as we will see later in this chapter clusters can be forced based on some common categorical attribute. These distinctions can have significant effects on the structure of a graph and certainly on the resulting visual display.

Let's refer to our very simple examples from the earlier section, where we used vehicle brand as a potential clustering attribute. This single distinction can create clusters that have little interaction with one another. To take the example a step further, we can use the population of pickup buyers in Texas, with Ford, Chevrolet, and Dodge representing the three vehicle brands most frequently purchased. These individuals can be very alike across multiple attributes—certainly geographic location, probably on average income level, perhaps very similar marital status, number of children, and so on. Yet they are often known to be fiercely loyal to the brand of truck they prefer, so it would be very unwise for marketers to treat them as a single group. The vehicle brand thus becomes a rational attribute to be used for clustering.

In a nutshell, whether we are using statistical analysis methods or performing network analysis, clustering is a critical concept in understanding information flow, product diffusion, and general behavioral patterns. In many cases, clusters will be closely related to one another and can potentially be aggregated for some purposes. In other instances, the clusters become so well-defined that it leads to the phenomenon known as homophily, which we will now discuss in some detail.

Homophily

Homophily refers to the likelihood that people with similar backgrounds, beliefs, or social status will tend to form groups that associate primarily within the group. This is often known colloquially as the **birds of a feather** phenomenon. Many studies have confirmed the widespread presence of homophily within networks, and it can certainly be observed anecdotally through casual observation of societal patterns. In this section, I'll walk you through a bit more on the theoretical side of homophily to be followed by some visual examples later in the chapter.

One of the key considerations with homophily, as mentioned previously, is its potentially profound impact on the rate of diffusion or even contagion. Groups that are so tightly knit as to be almost impervious to external influence are much less likely to adopt widespread innovations from outside the group. In many cases, there might be a lack of awareness of the latest developments, which of course will limit any sort of adoption rate.

Some of the most frequent sources of homophily in modern society come about through race and ethnicity, as individuals with these attributes in common might fail to venture beyond the comfort of associating with those who look, sound, and perhaps act most like themselves. *Wimmer* and *Lewis* have authored a paper on this topic (*Beyond and Below Racial Homophily: ERG Models of a Friendship Network Documented on Facebook*, 2010), available at `http://www.princeton.edu/~awimmer/ WimmerLewis.pdf`.

Networks with high degrees of homophily might be easy to spot, although this is not necessarily the case. It is possible for small portions of the network to exhibit this behavior, without the entire network being subjected to the same sort of pattern.

We will dwell on this subject more by showing some examples of homophily in the *Identifying Homophily* section.

Network growth patterns

Network analysis literature is filled with many examples of how networks grow over time. Multiple models have been developed to explain the growth of networks, as these patterns differ substantially depending on the sort of network we are analyzing. Network growth has been the subject of a great deal of research and analysis and will not be covered to the same degree in this book. In its place, I will provide an overview of some of the primary growth theories, and set the table for further exploration using Gephi later in this chapter.

What we attempt to understand through observing and predicting network growth is how networks form, how they are likely to grow, and what sort of patterns they exhibit as they are growing. Multiple models exist that attempt to predict network growth using different algorithms, ranging from extremely simple (random graph models) through much more sophisticated approaches that use concepts such as preferential attachment and popularity scores.

Many studies have been done proving that a few systems actually grow in a completely random fashion. So although the random graph models make a useful construct, they do not often mirror real-world networks, except perhaps in some of the contagion scenarios. In these cases, random public contact might occur without intent on the part of either party. We should not dismiss random models too quickly, as they can be used for certain situations; but we should also be aware that their application is limited, and that other approaches are able to simulate or predict the growth of networks far more effectively.

One way to begin exploring network growth is through the use of Gephi **generators**. These are simple tools that allow you to create different scenarios that can ultimately help you in understanding your own network data, and they can be used as building blocks for in-depth analysis of network patterns. The generators are available as a plugin (`Complex Generators`) from the Gephi marketplace and can be installed using the same process as other Gephi plugins. To install this or any other plugin, simply navigate to the **Tools | Plugins** menu and follow the process. Additional information can be found in the Gephi wiki and forums.

Now let's take a look at how these generators can be used to gain an improved understanding of network behavior.

Using Gephi generators

Gephi provides a wide range of network generators that can be used to better understand the formation and growth patterns forecast by some of the most prominent models in the network literature. These generators are valuable for building some knowledge for how different models work, and what happens to a network when we change various assumptions. In this section, we'll cover several of the most prominent models from the network graph literature, and then share examples from Gephi that will help further our understanding for how each model works.

If you're familiar with some of the network literature from *Easley* and *Kleinberg*, *Barabasi*, *Strogatz* and *Watts*, *Newman*, or any other good source, you will be familiar with most, if not all, of the following methods. Do not be concerned if you are not familiar with these sources. We will not be discussing the methods at any sort of deep technical level; that is both beyond the scope of this book and can be better learned from the creators and practitioners of the models. Many resources are provided in the *Appendix*, *Data Sources and Other Web Resources*, of this book.

The idea behind the various generators is to provide insight into how each of the methods work, using assumptions developed within each model. Gephi provides you with the ability to adjust different assumptions and to quickly view the results, helping to create a sort of interactive visual learning course without having to venture beyond the software. So with that minimal background, let's move into some of the generators, where I will provide a brief synopsis of the model and then share a sample output.

We'll begin with a simple **random graph** found by navigating to the **File | Generate | Random Graph...** menu location. This is the most basic of all network models that is built on the assumption that any single node has the same probability of connecting with any other node in the graph. We can adjust the probability level in Gephi as well as the number of nodes to be generated. The higher we set the probability, the denser the network will become. With a level of 0.05 and 50 nodes, I generated the first graph followed by a second graph with a 0.10 probability level (note that you must delete the first workspace prior to creating a new graph, otherwise Gephi will place them all in the same window). The first three of these graphs use the Force Atlas 2 model to effectively show the network patterns. Here, we are with just a 0.05 connection probability, as shown in the following diagram:

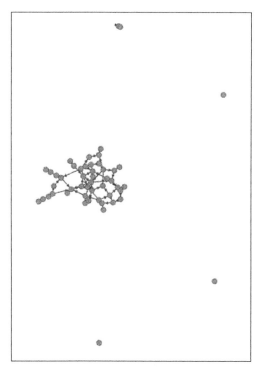

Random graph with .05 probability

Notice how the network is not fully connected — we have a single large component as well as a few nodes with no edges at all. Now, the following diagram illustrates the network with a `0.10` connection probability:

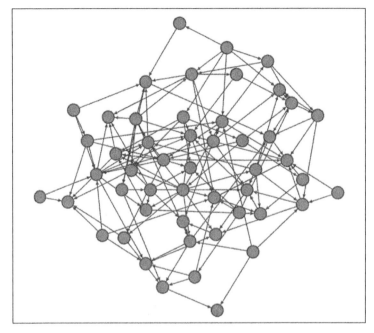

Random graph with 0.10 probability

Notice how the increased probability created far more connections between nodes, resulting in a much denser, yet still random graph.

Next, we'll take a look at the **Barabasi-Albert scale free** model (there are three other Barabasi-Albert models to play with), once again using `50` nodes, but added one at a time. Each new node will also have a single edge when it is created, in theory, which can be connected to any existing node in the network. What we would anticipate seeing with this model is the emergence of hubs with large degrees surrounded by many nodes with a lower-level of connectedness. While this doesn't fully comprehend all the nuances of **preferential attachment**, it takes us in that direction, with earlier nodes that have more opportunities to be connected to by later nodes, and thus to become hubs (high degree nodes) within the network. Let's take a look at the following diagram:

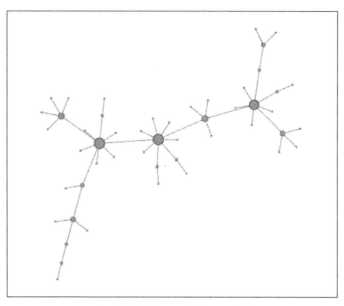

Barabasi-Albert scale free model

I elected to size the nodes based on degrees, making it easier to spot the network hubs. Here, it is easy to see the presence of multiple hubs in the network, akin to an airline industry hub and spoke model. It is interesting to see several secondary hubs that are often (but not always) directly connected to the primary one. One of the strengths of the Barabasi-Albert model is that it more closely models existing network structures, such as the Web, compared to any sort of random model. However, in this case, time of entry into the network is the single most critical growth criterion; we know from the real world that this is just one of many factors that determine the hub and spoke system seen here.

Another interesting category of models are the so-called **small world** networks made famous through the idea of six degrees of separation, where no two people on the planet, regardless of distance or dissimilarity are more than six degrees away from one another. While the number has varied in various experiments and real-world situations, the answer has not strayed far from the original figure. We are indeed living in a relatively small world, in spite of the physical distance between people.

We have three generators within this category: two from *Watts* and *Strogatz*, and one from *Kleinberg*. For this discussion, I'll work with the **Watts-Strogatz small world Alpha model**, although each of the three will illustrate the principle of small worlds very effectively. In this case, the number of nodes has been set to 50 for consistency with an average number of degrees equal to 4 and an alpha setting of 3.5. Small world patterns are often masked by the force-directed algorithms, so I have opted for a simple circular layout. Here's the result:

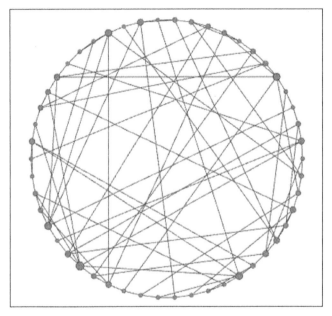

Watts-Strogatz small world model

Notice the difference in this model relative to both the random and scale free models shown previously. Even though I have once again sized the nodes to reflect their degree, the level of variation is much smaller than in the scale free model. In simple terms, there are no hubs in the graph, and in their place are a lot of well-connected nodes, and importantly, no isolated members of the network. Also, notice that many of the edges connect distant points on the graph rather than being restricted to more localized connections. This is the essence of small world models—member nodes are highly interconnected, have limited numbers (if any) of hubs, and are typically not subjected to a high degree of homophily, which would make traversing the graph far more difficult.

It is also important to understand the implications of a small world network for the diffusion of ideas, information, and innovation. Small worlds tend to be very effective at sharing and dispersing information and connecting persons who are physically remote. This obviously has a significant impact on information flow, whether it is trivial (cat videos going viral) or more serious (information about NSA surveillance). While a small world network clearly has profound consequences with respect to information flow, it typically has a smaller effect in spreading contagion given that the latter requires more direct physical contact than the former. However, there are still potential instances where a small world network can influence the spread of disease, often related to the ability to travel the globe far more easily than in previous eras. Today, individuals are more likely than ever before to have first degree relationships with others in another country or even on a different continent. As much as these relationships lead to overseas travel, the potential rises for the spread of once localized disease strains to be transmitted to new regions and to eventually impact a far larger population than was previously available.

Now that we have walked through several network models, we'll use Gephi to construct and analyze some contagion networks, where we can merge various network models with some contagion scenarios.

Viewing a contagion network

Now it's time to use Gephi for creating and viewing a network where we begin to understand the spread of a contagious disease. It is critical to view more than a single network instance to best understand the contagion process. We'll view a single network at multiple points in time, given the temporal nature of infectious disease, to understand how nodes act within a specific time window (the contagious stage of the disease) in spreading the infection. As we noted earlier, even then, the spread of the disease is not inevitable, as it is dependent on the probability of transmission throughout a network.

Let's outline the necessary elements we'll need to build a useful contagion network:

- A network of nodes with some level of contact within a given period: For our example, let's set the number of nodes to 50, so we have some ability to view the spread of the disease without making our network overly complex. We'll use the **Random Graph...** generator in Gephi as a proxy for the sort of random contacts a network of individuals might encounter in a single day.

- Several time-based (temporal) views of a single network: These views might contain the same member nodes in each case, or more realistically, an evolving network of nodes based on the time element. In this case, we'll take a look at a single network of contacts and assume a 72-hour period where each member node is susceptible to the disease. This will replicate the SIR model discussed earlier with each node falling into one of three states—susceptible, infected, or removed. We will also make the assumption that the duration of the infection is one day (24 hours), and any nodes that have previously been infected enter into the removed state after the infection period expires.

- A probability of disease transmission: This will be a number ranging between 0 and 1, with 0 representing no chance of transmission and 1 indicating a 100 percent transmission level. Let's set the threshold to 0.5 (50 percent) for our example.

This will give us a basic version for analyzing contagion within networks. For a more thorough discussion on contagion, there are many available resources, some of which are noted in the *Appendix, Data Sources and Other Web Resources*, of this book.

Let's start at the beginning of the 72-hour period, refer to this time as t_0, and assume that a single node is infected, as shown by the dark coloring within the node. Susceptible nodes will remain lightly colored, while removed members will be depicted with no shading (note that none exist at the outset).

Here, we see the network at t_0 as follows:

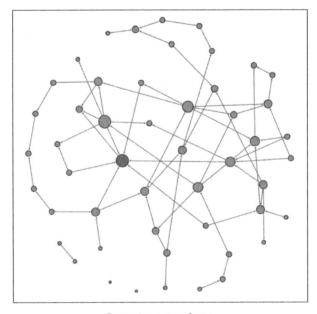

Contagion network at t_0

Note the single node in an infected state. This individual is well-connected within the network, which will hasten the spread of the contagion. In this instance, there are seven direct contacts (assume that all these represent contacts made at t_{+1}) of which approximately 50 percent will be infected. We'll assume that four of the seven are vulnerable to the infection, leaving us in this stage at the end of the first 24-hour period:

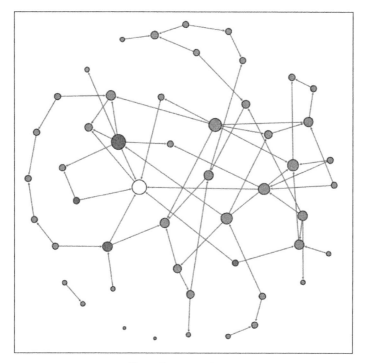

Contagion network at t_{+1}

The original node that kicked off the contagion process is now removed from the eligible population, having already been infected, while the four newly infected nodes become the new transmitters of the disease. This process will repeat itself in the second 24-hour period (t_{+2}) with the four infected nodes now immune and thus entering the removed state after having infected a new set of people:

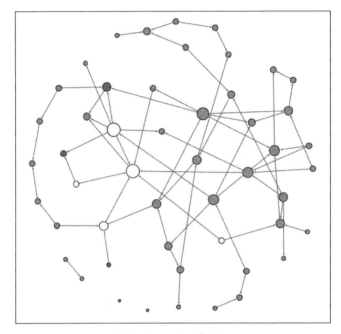

Contagion network at t_{+2}

This is getting interesting, as we can see that some of the previously infected individuals have a few physical contacts, limiting the spread of the contagion. A few new nodes are now infected, but the disease is not spreading rapidly due to the limited contact levels. Finally, let's see what our network looks like at t_{+3}:

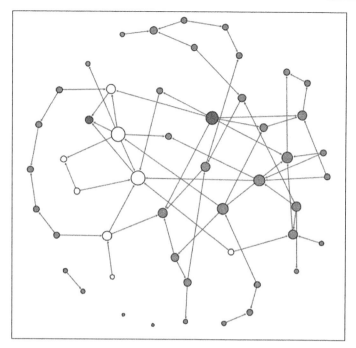

Contagion network at t$_{+3}$

Note how the relative lack of contacts for some individuals managed to limit the spread of the contagion in our small network example. In the real world, this is certainly a possibility, but there is also a very high probability that the contagion will accelerate through densely connected networks, resulting in rapid spreading of the disease. This should help you understand how the structure of a network is critical to the transmission of many things, including infectious diseases.

I hope this provided you with some insight into how we can use Gephi to illustrate a simple contagion network. While this was a simple manual example, Gephi can be used with more comprehensive datasets with defined time periods and node statuses at each of these times. Some examples of this process are provided in *Chapter 8, Dynamic Networks*.

Viewing network diffusion

While diffusion and contagion are not identical, there are certainly some shared elements we can leverage for our analysis prior to jumping into a visual assessment using Gephi. Remember, in our contagion discussion, the importance of physical contact coupled with the probability of transmission as critical elements in spreading the disease. With diffusion, we recognize that physical contact is not necessarily required for spreading information, but there is still a probability element at work, especially when product adoption is involved. I'll illustrate this briefly before we move onto the graphs.

Suppose a new tablet is planned for upcoming release, supported by a large marketing campaign and plenty of insider buzz about the virtues of the product. Some of your friends have talked about getting the new tablet, but you are unsure whether it's worth the investment, as you already have a perfectly capable unit purchased just 12 months earlier. What factors will sway you in one direction (purchase) or the other (don't purchase)? It might well be the behavior of your closest friends who will be the primary influence in your purchase decision. How does all of this relate to contagion? It relates through our use of probability. As with the contagion examples, there are probabilities associated with your decision to purchase or not to purchase. If many of your friends decide to buy the new tablet, it is more likely that you will also make this decision, as your collective probability has increased. In this sense, it is akin to the transmission of an infectious disease, albeit without (perhaps) the physical contact. A higher purchase probability leads to further spread of the new product, and the product sales continue to increase as it spreads further into the market.

Now it's time to see how this process can unfold using some examples from Gephi. As we did with our contagion illustration, we'll walk you through a rather simple example using a random network of 50 nodes; although in this case, we'll increase the connectivity level so that the network consists of a single giant component. Our case will be based on the release of a new cell phone that provides an attractive feature set that will influence some consumers to replace their old phones.

We will make some assumptions about our network:

- Our network will consist of 50 individuals who are all connected to at least one or the other node within the network. We'll again use the **Random Graph** generator in Gephi to build a simple network to illustrate the diffusion process.

- Each individual in the network will invest in the new phone only if at least one-third of their direct contacts also purchase the phone. For example, a person with four direct contacts, but just one who has purchased the phone, will not be influenced enough to purchase the phone themselves. However, if two or more of his/her friends already have the phone, then he/she will also make the purchase.

Let's begin to examine the diffusion process for this product. We're using the **Out-degree** measure to define who the primary influencers are within this network and sizing the nodes to reflect this influence. Our initial graph will reflect t_0, when a few early adopters have elected to purchase the new phone. These adopters are identified using darker shading, as shown in the following diagram:

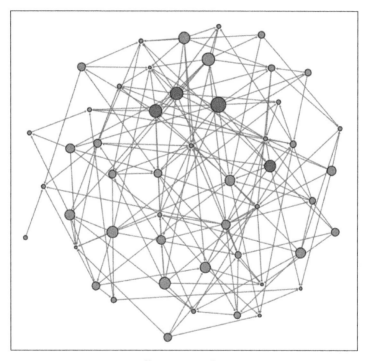

Diffusion network at t_0

As alluded to earlier, we see four early adopters who appear to have significant influence levels within the network based on their number of out degrees (as depicted by node size). Just how influential they are remains to be seen as we iterate through time periods. For the sake of this discussion, let's assume that each snapshot represents a weekly interval, as potential buyers need some time to consider their purchase likelihood. For this example, we will show all purchasers in a cumulative manner, as they will be unlikely to consider a new tablet for another year or two.

One week later at t_{+1} several new purchasers have appeared, as at least one-third of their direct contacts have purchased the phone previously:

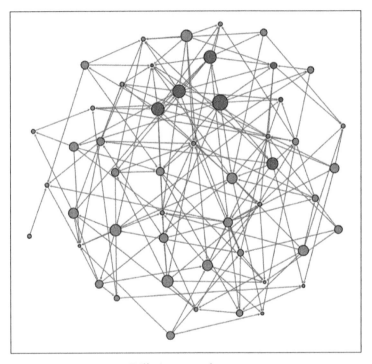

Diffusion network at t_{+1}

Four new buyers have appeared, while others have yet to purchase the phone, opting to wait for a higher proportion of their friends to make a purchase. Now let's take a look at t_{+2} to see how many incremental buyers have been sufficiently influenced by their friend's purchase decision:

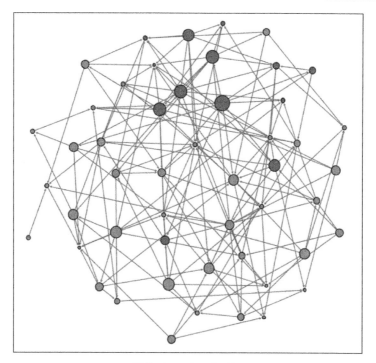

Diffusion network at t_{+2}

Another four people have elected to purchase the new phone based on their friends' behavior, including two buyers with more distant but still direct connections. After just two weeks, nearly 25 percent of the network members have elected to buy this phone; while this might not equate to the diffusion level of a viral video on the Web; it does appear to represent a successful level of product adoption through the diffusion process.

This represents a very basic diffusion example; there are additional factors that can be employed in displaying the diffusion process, many of which can be discovered through resources listed in the *Appendix, Data Sources and Other Web Resources*. Also, as we mentioned in the discussion on contagion, some more dynamic examples of diffusion will be shared in *Chapter 8, Dynamic Networks*, which employ datasets with time elements.

Network clustering

Earlier in this chapter, we discussed the concept of clustering in a network, and some of the ramifications for network structure and information flow. In this section, we'll use Gephi to provide you with some illustrations of networks with varying degrees of clustering, and add some further discussion on how Gephi can be leveraged to identify and measure clustering.

In the interest of clarity, I would like to take a moment to define clustering. When I refer to clustering in this section, it indicates the patterns that exist within a network, not the practice of creating clusters from the data. While the two instances are frequently related, this section is devoted to understanding why these patterns exist, and how they might affect the flow of information within a network. Later in this book we'll examine how to create clusters or partitions within the network through the use of defining characteristics in the data. These topics will be addressed in *Chapter 7, Segmenting and Partitioning a Graph.*

The best way to detect clustering within a network is to provide some visual examples of networks with varied levels of grouping, ranging from virtually none at all (a random network), all the way to a network with a high proportion of completed triangles, and confirming the presence of significant levels of clustering. Our key statistics to detect clustering can be found in the **Statistics** tab. We'll now use Gephi to present three examples that show detailed networks on low clustering, moderate clustering, and heavy clustering. This should help you quickly convey what we are looking for when we speak of clustering within a network.

For these examples, we'll use one of the **Erdos-Renyi** generators, which is found by navigating to the **File | Generate | Erdos-Renyi G(n,m) model** option. In each case, we'll set our network to 50 nodes while changing the number of edges from 100 to 200, and finally to 300. In doing so, we should anticipate higher levels of clustering as the number of edges grow. We'll begin with the graph of 50 nodes with just 100 edges—a rather sparse network:

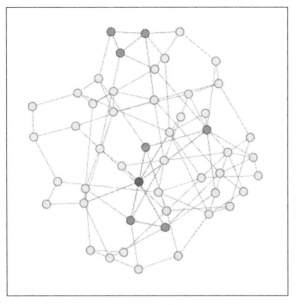

Erdos-Renyi network with low clustering

Note the presence of several colored nodes, indicating either one or two completed triangles. The vast majority of nodes have no complete triangles — the friends of a given node are typically not friends with one another. The average clustering coefficient for this network turns out to be just 0.022, which means that just over 2 percent of possible triangles are actually realized. When we increase the number of edges to 200, the network changes dramatically, as shown in the following diagram:

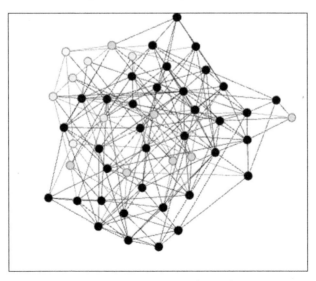

Erdos-Renyi network with significant clustering

We now see a much denser network, since the number of edges has doubled. This doubling has had an even more pronounced impact on clustering, as the average clustering coefficient has now grown to 0.164. One of every six possible triangles is now complete, compared to the one in 45 as seen in our first graph. The dark nodes indicate at least three completed triangles per member; note that there are just a couple of areas of the graph where the member nodes don't reach this threshold.

Finally, we'll take a look at the same model with 300 edges:

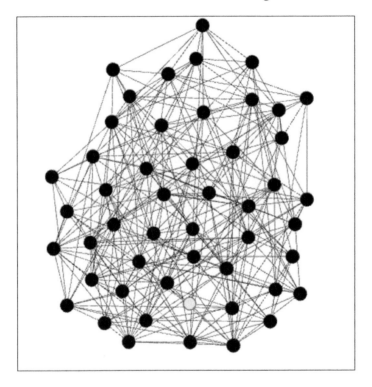

Erdos-Renyi network with high clustering

Our network is now growing quite dense with many members connected to each other. Note just a single node (at the center bottom) that falls short of the three completed triangle criteria from the prior graph. Being consistent with these patterns, we now have an average clustering coefficient of 0.253 — one of every four possible triangles is complete.

We have used the clustering coefficients to tell us when clustering is present, but this has not shown us which nodes form communities based on the clustering patterns. For this, we can turn to a couple of options. Several Gephi plugins exist that can be used to detect clusters based on connection patterns and community structures. The Chinese Whispers plugin is a very capable option if we choose this path. For this example, we'll simply use the **Modularity** option found in the **Network Overview** section of the **Statistics** tab. After running this function, we can then apply the results as colors to our graph and get a very nice look at where the clusters exist. Let's take a look at our final Erdos-Renyi network:

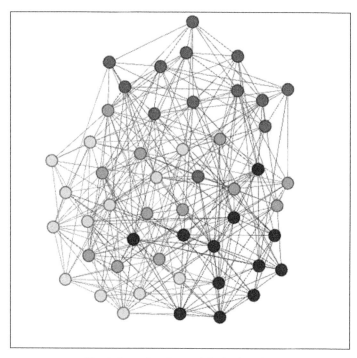

Clustering using the modularity function

Now we can see four distinct clusters ranging from light to dark. We see some limited overlap, but we can now easily view clustering patterns in the network. Cluster 4 (the darkest nodes) occupies the lower-right position, while Cluster 3 (the dark gray nodes) is dominant at the top of the graph. These relative positions might change depending on the algorithm used, but should remain visually distinct.

This last point is particularly important to understand our data; each algorithm will depict the data according to its particular settings. Even within each layout selection, we have multiple options for setting spacing through attraction and repulsion settings. This topic is covered in more detail in *Chapter 3*, *Selecting the Layout*. It is essential that you experiment with different settings so that your data conveys the story it was supposed to tell, and network clustering is a component of this process. If there are natural clusters within the network, graph viewers must be able to detect them. Otherwise, the graph conveys an incomplete if not an inaccurate story, which is something to avoid if at all possible. Better to not tell the story at all rather than be misleading.

Identifying homophily

As we noted earlier, homophily is an extreme form of clustering, where groups within a network are more likely to be highly interconnected within the group, but remain largely disconnected from the outside world. This can be driven by many factors such as geography, religious or political preferences, or perhaps some very specific shared interests that are restricted to a small segment of the overall network. In this section, we'll employ Gephi to illustrate a few examples of homophily and highlight the impact it has within the scope of the entire network.

What is critical to remember about homophily is the way it can restrict the flow of information, innovation, and even infection within a network. Since many individuals within specific groups have little exposure beyond the group, there is an increased probability that they will not have access to all the latest information and that they might be more reluctant to adopt new technologies (at least until others in their group do). On the positive side, they might be at lower risk for acquiring infectious diseases, especially if the homophily is related to physical patterns (remote geographic location, limited exposure to public places, and so on).

Now that we fully understand the importance of homophily within a network, it is time to identify specific cases within network structures. For this exercise, we will return to Gephi, and use some fictional small networks I have created for this purpose:

- Network A will represent a very homogenous small town population where a significant majority of the people have shared characteristics, resulting in very low homophily

- Network B will be a cross section of a mid-sized urban area where many residents have the same shared values, but where some smaller groups differ significantly on religious grounds and thus do not interact significantly with the majority of the residents
- Network C will be a subset of a large urban population that is home to multiple ethnic, racial, and religious groups that have tended to form their own enclosed communities

Here is Network A:

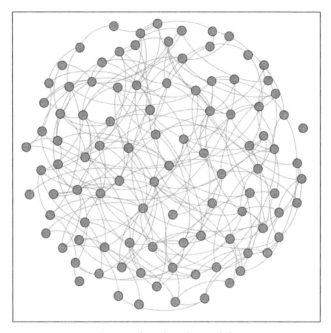

A network with no homophily

Notice the general connectedness across the network with little in the way of obvious groupings or clusters. The shared characteristics of this population have resulted in a homogenous network. Now let's take a look at Network B, where the population base is a bit more diverse:

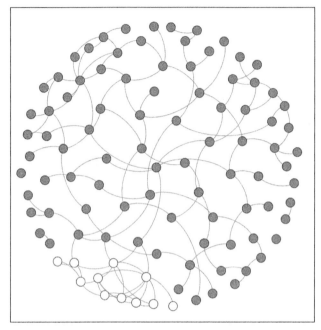

A network with minimal homophily

Here, we begin to see some homophily at the lower left of the graph, which is shown by the white nodes. This cluster of individuals is highly connected within the small group (based on their religious affiliation), but many of its members have no connections beyond their local neighborhood. Information flowing into this part of the network will have to pass through the two or three individuals with some level of connectedness to the remainder of the network.

Finally, our big city network, where many diverse groups coexist, is shown as follows:

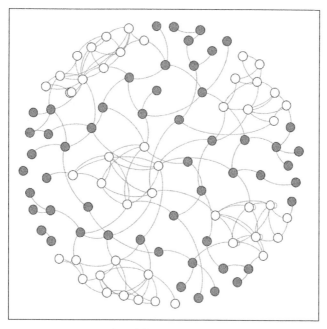

A network with high levels of homophily

We now see some serious homophily with five distinct groups that are each densely connected within their own neighborhoods, but have little in the way of external linkages. These groups have tended to self-segregate based on religious, racial, and ethnic characteristics. Information flow or product adoption now has a much higher friction level as it must pass through the influencers who are connected beyond the local clusters in order to reach other individuals within the group.

Summary

In this chapter, you have seen numerous examples of some of the primary patterns that are fundamental to the study of network graph analysis.

We began the chapter with theoretical discussions on the critical processes of contagion, diffusion, clustering, homophily, and network growth. A number of network growth examples were created using the `Complex Generators` plugin, providing a fundamental understanding of how to use this tool to construct and analyze multiple network models.

In the last few sections of this chapter, our focus was on implementation of some of these concepts using the Gephi workspace. We first created a contagion network that viewed the progression of an infection over a three-day time period, followed by a simple diffusion process that tracked product adoption within a small network. Finally, we addressed network clustering and homophily, showing some examples that illustrated relative levels of each of these within a network.

Our next chapter will be devoted to mastering Gephi filters, a powerful set of tools that can be used to provide focus and develop insights when working with large datasets.

5
Working with Filters

Filters are an essential component in Gephi, yet can be challenging to use compared with some of the other Gephi features. That's why we're devoting an entire chapter to the use of filters, one that will spend a minimal amount of space on theory before providing many examples on how to take full advantage of the power of filtering.

So why is filtering so critical for successful network analysis and graph creation? The simple explanation is that filters help to reduce the complexity and scope of large datasets, making them easier to navigate through and understand. The better answer is that filters can help improve our ability to tell stories and communicate with our data, as they allow us to focus on the critical elements in the network. This chapter will familiarize you with Gephi filters and what they can do, and then use multiple examples that demonstrate how to apply the filters and what the results look like in our networks. We will build on this knowledge at the end of *Chapter 6, Graph Statistics,* and begin employing filters on the statistical measures.

In this chapter, we will examine the following few key elements that are related to filtering:

- Advantages of filtering
- Primary filtering functions in Gephi
- Using simple filters
- Working with complex filters

Let's begin with a quick discussion of the filtering theory.

The filtering theory

You might be wondering why we should filter our network graphs in the first place. After all, it is possible to view entire networks using Gephi, and even to further navigate the same graphs using interactive tools. That's all well and good, but if you have been exposed to one of the hundreds (thousands?) of examples of overly dense, hairball-like graphs with no clear meaning, I believe you will quickly come to appreciate Gephi's ability to reduce visual complexity through the use of filters.

One of the beauties of filters lies in their ability to reduce complexity while not affecting the underlying data structure. All we are doing when we filter is removing unnecessary clutter from various stages of our exploration, including the final output. Filtering permits us to reduce the amount of guesswork and speculation about patterns and relationships by removing peripheral elements, thus permitting us to focus on the pieces that matter the most to our story. Think of a complex novel with more than 200 characters; should each character receive equal billing? Of course not. Yet when we produce graphs where it is difficult to tell the important members from peripheral actors, we have done our viewers a disservice.

Some elements can certainly be differentiated through adjusting their size, color, placement, and so on, but filtering provides a clarity that is difficult to achieve through any other means. By removing nonessential items from our field of vision, we also reduce the complexity and confusion that might impair the cognitive ability of viewers to interpret the graph. End users cannot draw conclusions about the elements that are not in the graph.

Filtering is also powerful from an analysis standpoint, as it enables you, as the graph builder, to be more easily exposed to patterns in the network, making it simpler to determine which elements belong in a finished graph. Rather than attempting to tell a single story from your network dataset, filtering can well lead you to multiple smaller insights that can contribute to a more compelling (and visually coherent) narrative.

These are the reasons we should filter our graphs, especially when they have any degree of complexity beyond the simplest of networks. With that said, let's transition to how we can use Gephi to build both simple and complex filters. Our first step is to become familiar with a wide range of filtering options that can be used alone or in tandem with other functions. Once we have become familiar with these functions, we'll begin using them on a dataset that details the interactions between students within a specific primary school environment.

Primary filtering functions in Gephi

Gephi filters are categorized into several groups, shown as individual folders in the **Filters** tab. Within each of these folders are multiple filtering selections that can be used on their own as simple filters, or combined to create complex filters. Primary filter categories include:

- `Attributes`: This folder houses many options that enable filtering on nodes, edges, partitions, clusters, and various graph measures such as eccentricity and various centrality levels. In addition, the user-defined attributes (such as a new column) can be found and acted on from this folder.

- `Edges`: This filter is applied strictly to the connections within the network.

- `Operator`: This filter allows you to execute a few functions on the graph.

- `Topology`: This filter offers a range of options where you can use graph measures such as degree ranges to filter the network.

Here's a screenshot showing the primary and secondary filtering folders:

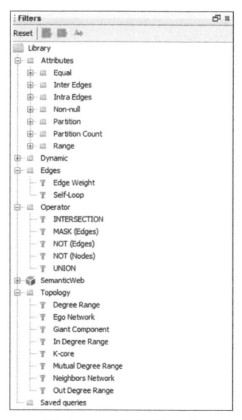

Filtering options in the Filters tab

Let's take a more detailed look at these folders so that we acquire enough understanding to spend time working with them on our example network. The next few sections separate the filters into groups just as they are laid out in Gephi. Not every filtering option is covered here. Additional options exist for **semantic** and **dynamic** filtering. While we won't explore them here, you should note that the dynamic filters can be used in instances where we have a time-based network where node and edge values are dynamic. The semantic filters can be used while working with RDF data structures such as SPARQL. For more information on RDF, you can visit the site `http://www.w3.org/RDF/`.

The following functions will nonetheless provide you with a powerful toolkit for navigating your network graphs.

Attributes

The **Attributes** filter allows you to query your graph based on the specific values within the network, including ID, Labels, Weight, and Modularity Class. This set of tools is highly useful when you wish to focus on a specific element of a group of values within the larger network. We'll provide basic instructions here for how you can expect these individual filters to operate, and then we'll work on them later in the chapter using some of the most essential ones on an actual dataset:

- The **Equal** function operates much as you might anticipate. Several options are available to take advantage of; for nodes, we can look for specific values based on `Id`, `Label`, or `Modularity Class` (assuming that you have clustered or partitioned your data). If we are looking to learn more about edges, then we can likewise use the `ID` and `Label` values, while also being able to specify the edge weight value to filter by.

- **Inter Edges** can be used to focus only on those edges that connect nodes within various partitions or clusters. This is particularly effective when the focus is on connections inside a group, and could certainly be used to shed light on networks with high levels of homophily. As is the case with other edge functions, one of the most compelling uses for this filter is to help clarify the connection patterns in an otherwise dense network.

- **Intra Edges** plays the opposite role to the **Inter Edges** functionality, highlighting only those connections that occur across groups. This will obviously be useful in cases where we are less interested in within the group communications, but are highly drawn to understand patterns between groups, and to determine which nodes are critical to these paths.

- The **Non-null** condition simply helps to hide missing values from the network graph, allowing us to focus on populated variables only. Options here are the same as for the **Equal** function we just discussed, giving us the ability to remove both nodes and edges that have missing values.

- The **Partition** filters are especially adept at creating custom views of individual partitions or clusters within the larger network, making it possible to quickly create subset versions of the entire network. Not only does this help in making the network more navigable for analysis, it also leads to visual results that can be far easier for viewers to comprehend.

- The **Partition Count** filter works on partitions as well, but does so using the counts within each partition, as opposed to the number that identifies each group. If our goal is to learn more on partitions with few members, the threshold can be set to remove larger groups from the graph, leaving us with only the smaller partitions being viewable. The opposite is true as well, if our focus is on heavily populated groups.

- With the **Range** filter condition, we have the capability to extend some of what was made available in the **Equal** filter. For instance, we can now specify a range of edge weights to display (say from 2 through 5). This can also be used to display a range of partitions in the same fashion, by differentiating this tool from the other partition filters.

Edges

A pair of edge filters exists beyond those already discussed in the *Attributes* section, which gives us the ability to further highlight desired patterns in the network that are mentioned as follows:

- If our goal is to examine or highlight a range of connection strength, then the **Edge Weight** filter is a highly useful tool. With this filter, all edge weights within specified minimum and maximum values can be highlighted, making it quite simple to draw attention to critical network paths.

- The **Self-Loop** filters can be applied in cases where a node connects with itself. This filter requires a subfilter (equal, partition, not equal, and so on) to activate the filter. We can then use these conditions to focus our attention on those nodes either with or without self-loops.

Operator

Several operator functions exist that can help us to build more complex filters. In our section titled *Working with complex filters*, described later in this chapter, we'll explore the practical use of these functions through a series of examples. In this section, our focus will be on providing a theoretical construct to help you understand when and how you might put each of these operators to use.

- The **INTERSECTION** operator enables the construction of highly complex filters using multiple conditions to narrow a network dataset. This can be thought of as resembling a database query where multiple conditions must be satisfied to return a set of records.

- **MASK (Edges)** can be used to customize the edges that are shown within a network graph. The filter provides four possible criteria via a set of radio buttons. These selections include **any**, **both**, **source**, and **target**.

- **NOT (Edges)** is used to remove certain edges from a view, either for practical or perhaps cosmetic reasons. As with the other operator functions, you must choose another filter for applying this criteria. For instance, we could elect to hide all of the edges that go across groups (inter edges), or conversely, all those within a group (intra edges).

- **NOT (Nodes)** can be employed to remove specific nodes from the network graph, and can be applied using other attributes that group the data, such as a class or other categorization. When used in this fashion, all nodes that belong to a specified group will be hidden from the view.

- The **UNION** operator is used to combine multiple conditions within a single data attribute. For example, in the case where we have categories from 1 through 25, we could use a union query to display both categories 1 through 5 and 20 through 25 while hiding the remainder. However with the other operator functions, we need to use separate filters such as **Equal** or **Partition** to build the union query.

Topology

Some of the most interesting filtering options are found in the **Topology** folder of the **Filters** tab. This is where you should go when you wish to learn more about the behaviors within the network, as opposed to focusing on highlighting specific elements within the network based on their specific group or position within the network. In this section, you'll learn more about how to navigate the network using a variety of filters that examine network structure and the role played by specific entities within the network.

- One of the starting points to understand influence within a network is to focus on the importance of specific individual nodes within the network. In Gephi, this can be done using the **Degree Range** filter, which enables filtering based on the number of connections each node possesses. In an undirected network, we are indifferent to the direction of the connection; in fact, it plays no role whatsoever. If the network is directed, then we can wish to defer to the **In Degree Range** and **Out Degree Range** options to better understand the patterns of influence within the network.

- Using the **Ego Network** function allows us to easily understand which other entities a single network node is connected to, at the first, second, third, and max degree levels. This allows us to see how the network is accessed by a specific individual working through the network and illustrates the possible paths required to access the second or third degree connections.

- The **Giant Component** filter enables users to hide portions of the network that are not part of the giant component or largest part of the network. In the case of a fully connected network, this filter will have no effect, but in other cases it will help to drive visual focus on the largest component in the network.

- We previously noted the **In Degree Range** filter, and how it can be useful to determine the levels of influence within a network. In a directed graph, this filter helps us to set thresholds that expose the nodes with the highest numbers of inbound edges from other nodes. This is a critical element for understanding which nodes serve as hubs and are relied on by other members for information or indirect connections.

- The **Neighbors Network** filter can be used in a similar fashion to the **Ego Network** filter, but with the ability to move beyond a single node. Thus, we can examine the neighbor network for a specific group within a network, rather than a single member, and extend it to include first, second, and third degree connections.

- The **Out Degree Range** filter lets us examine the degree to which nodes connect to other nodes; a sort of reverse hub effect if you will. While nodes with high levels of out degrees (relative to In Degrees) are typically not the influencers in a network, they might serve valuable functions as transmitters of information, acting as a conduit to many external information sources. The ability to isolate these nodes can help to understand the network structure and how information flows between members.

Using simple filters

For our purposes, we will define simple filters as consisting of a single filter placed on an element or attribute for the purpose of reducing the visual complexity of a network graph. The filter could be used to limit or highlight nodes, edges, partitions, or clusters in an effort to better understand and view structures within the larger network. To that end, we will devote this section to illustrate multiple examples for using simple filters to produce meaningful results that can be easily understood by the end users.

Even the so-called simple filters can help us uncover many intricacies in a network graph, particularly in cases where the network is too large to be easily deciphered by the naked eye. The following pages of examples are intended to walk you through the filtering process and provide an idea for what's possible even if you venture no further. Once again, we'll be using the primary school network to illustrate the power of simple filtering. This network can be found and downloaded from `http://www.sociopatterns.org/datasets/primary-school-cumulative-networks/`.

Let's start by looking at the entire network, colored by classnames:

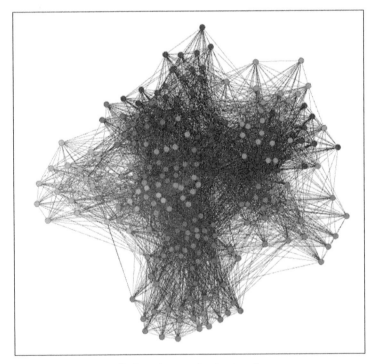

Entire primary school network

Even though this is not a large network, being composed of just 236 nodes, it still presents a visual challenge, in part due to the high degree of connectedness within the graph. We could simply choose not to show the edges, but we would then lose much of what makes the network unique. So our goal in the next few sections is to illustrate the value of filtering, not just for visual clarity, but also because we might well wind up seeing unanticipated patterns.

Using the Equal filter

We'll employ a host of filters to begin navigating the graph, starting with setting the gender attribute to female, by following these simple steps:

1. Navigate to the **Filters** | **Attributes** | **Equal** filter, and select the gender attribute.

2. Drag the gender attribute to the **Queries** space in the lower half of the **Filters** tab.

3. Set the value to F and run the **Select** and **Filter** options using the available buttons.

Your query settings should look like this:

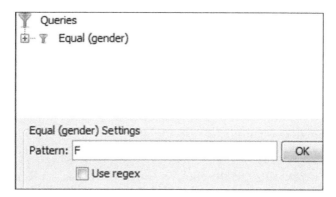

Filtering on gender using the Queries window

Here's our result after applying the filter:

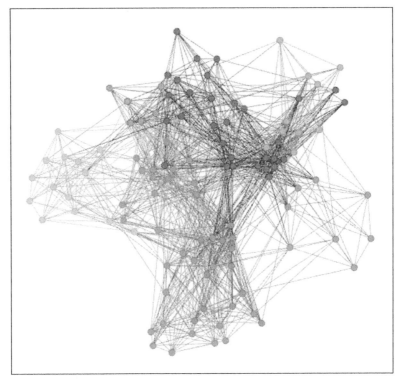

Primary school network filtered on female gender

While we haven't discovered anything too significant yet, the network has been thinned a bit which makes it somewhat easier to interpret. There are a couple of spots in the graph with very high density that might be worth investigating, but there is more we can do to query this network.

Let's remove the current filter (right-click on the filter and select **Remove**) and replace it with an instance where we become more selective with the data. Follow these steps to replicate the process:

1. Navigate to the **Filters | Attributes | Equal** filter and select the `classname` attribute.

2. Drag the `classname` attribute to the **Queries** space in the lower half of the **Filters** tab.

3. Set the value to 3B and run the **Select** and **Filter** options using the available buttons.

Here's our result:

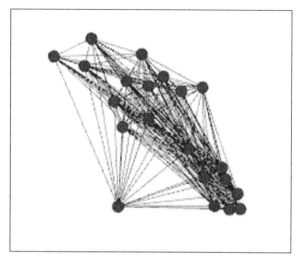

Filtering on classname equals 3B

Now, we have something we can really focus on, as we have completely removed all the remaining classnames from the display. Notice the high degree of connectedness within this group, as well as the single node at the bottom-left, positioned some distance from the other classmates. This might provide a clue that this individual is more likely to be adjacent to some other classes, or perhaps acts as a bridge between classes.

Applying the regex function

Let's move on to another example using the same approach with a single difference. Certain Gephi filters enable the use of the **Regular Expressions (Regex)** function, which permits wildcards as part of the filter criteria. You probably already noticed this in the prior examples, and now we will take advantage of its capabilities. If you wish to learn more about using regex, visit `http://www.regular-expressions.info/`.

The only change we need to make is to replace the 3B value with 3 (3 followed by a period (.) symbol), followed by checking the **Use regex** checkbox. Now our filter will seek any instance where the classname starts with 3, which should return both 3A and 3B (think of this as similar to a LIKE statement in a database query). This will enable us to view the entire third grade to understand how much interaction occurs both within and across the two classes. Here's our graph:

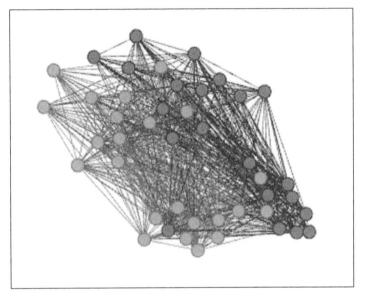

Filter with classname equal to 3. using regex

Filtering edges

Let's switch from the **Equal** filter to the **Inter Edges** option, which will give us the opportunity to examine how nodes in one class link to those in another. To do this, we're going to remove the existing filter, and then apply the new one using the following steps:

1. Navigate to the **Filters | Attributes | Inter Edges** filter and select the classname attribute.

2. Drag the classname attribute to the **Queries** space in the lower half of the **Filters** tab.

3. Set the values to 1B and 2B by clicking on their respective boxes and then run the **Select** and **Filter** options.

This will give us a look at the level of interaction between classrooms 1B and 2B—a single grade apart but presumably located in close proximity to one another:

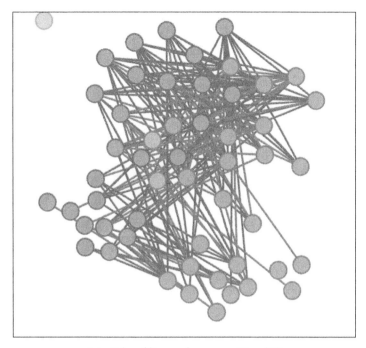

Inter Edges filter on classnames 1B and 2B

It is quite easy to see that a considerable degree of interactivity occurs across these two classrooms. Notice also that this image is merely a subset of the entire graph, and the only portion with edges on display. There are some approaches that will also remove the remaining nodes from view, which will be covered in the next section on complex filters. For now, we can zoom in for better focus on our selected classes.

We have just seen the level of connectedness across these two classes, but what about within each class? To answer this question, we will simply replace the **Inter Edges** filter condition with **Intra Edges**, using the following steps (remember to remove the existing filter first):

1. Navigate to the **Filters | Attributes | Intra Edges** filter and select the classname attribute.

2. Drag the classname attribute to the **Queries** space in the lower half of the **Filters** tab.

3. Set the values to 1B and 2B by clicking on their respective boxes and then run the **Select** and **Filter** options.

Let's see what happens when this filter is applied:

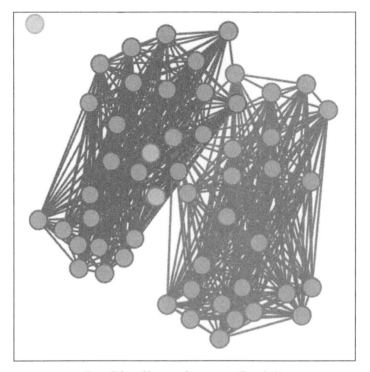

Intra Edges filter on classnames 1B and 2B

Now we get an idea for how dense each class is—at first glance, it appears that connections within each class are much stronger than those across the classes. This can be verified using various graph statistics, which we'll introduce in *Chapter 6, Graph Statistics*.

Using the Partition filter

The **Partition** filter is another valuable tool that makes it very easy to select multiple values within an attribute. We'll demonstrate this in the following example. We'll begin by removing the existing filter, and then follow these steps to apply the partition conditions:

1. Navigate to the **Filters** | **Attributes** | **Partition** filter and select the `classname` attribute.

2. Drag the `classname` attribute to the **Queries** space in the lower half of the **Filters** tab.

3. Set the values to 4A, 4B, 5A, and 5B by clicking on their respective boxes and then run the **Select** and **Filter** options.

This will offer a view of the higher grade levels in the school and provide a first look at their patterns with respect to one another. Let's have a look at the resultant graph:

Partition filter on classnames 4A, 4B, 5A, and 5B

Here we get more interesting results, where there is some obvious overlap in the center of the graph composed of multiple classname members. Also of interest are the members at the lower-right and upper-left of the network, who appear to be less likely to interact with students from classes beyond their own.

Working with the Topology filters

To this point, our focus has been driven primarily by class levels. Now it's time to shift our focus to individual student behavior free from the somewhat artificial constraints of grade and class structures. This might also be a better way to understand critical behaviors within the network that are potentially being masked by group affiliations.

With that in mind, let's set our next filter using the following steps:

1. Navigate to the **Filters | Topology | Degree Range** filter.
2. Drag the filter to the **Queries** space in the lower half of the **Filters** tab.
3. Use the slider control to adjust the filter, moving the left slider to a value of 80 (or alternatively, type the value manually). Then run the **Select** and **Filter** options.

Our goal here is to reduce the viewable network to the most highly connected nodes so that we can observe who is most influential without having to cut through the visual clutter of seeing every member of the network. This will dramatically reduce the scope of the graph—your results should look like this:

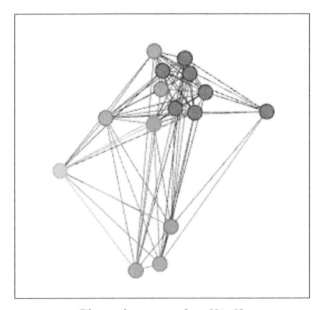

Filter on degree range from 80 to 98

This simple filter reduced our graph from 236 to just 15 nodes. There are two immediate benefits to this approach. First, we can now easily identify the most highly-connected members of the network and simultaneously identify which classname they belong to, assuming that we have elected to partition the graph based on classname (you can read more on partitioning in *Chapter 7, Segmenting and Partitioning a Graph*).

Secondly, we can also detect connections between these influential members, which will shed a little insight into clustering patterns in the network. It does in fact appear that a majority of these nodes are connected with one another, which some of our statistical tests in *Chapter 6, Graph Statistics*, should pick up. In addition, we will learn how statistics can be recalculated after filters have been applied.

Let's go through two more quick examples before we move on to more complex filters. Our first example simply adjusts the filter settings from the previous example, as we seek to learn more about the least connected members of the graph. Use the slider to adjust the filter to return nodes with degree ranges between 18 and 30, and view the results:

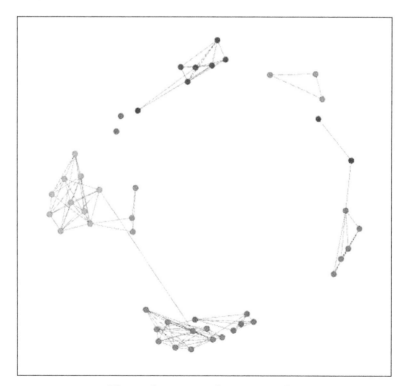

Filter on degree ranges between 18 and 30

As you might anticipate, the nodes with the lowest levels of interaction with the network are positioned around the perimeter of the graph. There are a couple of interesting patterns worth investigating from these results, with three of the classes having clusters that appear to be highly connected within the group, but are likely to have few external connections. While these don't appear to be perfect cliques where every node is interconnected, the patterns are still intriguing and can lead us to some interesting conclusions.

Our final example focuses on a single member of the network and his connections to others. Using the data laboratory, we have identified `Node 1551` as the most highly connected member of the network, with a degree range equal to `98`. This makes him a worthy candidate for further exploration as we attempt to understand his entire neighbor network and where they reside.

We're now going to explore the ego network for Node 1551. An ego network is simply the network of nodes that are connected to a single selected node. At a depth of one, we will see only the direct connections of the selected node, while a depth of two will show us all the second-level connections (the so-called **friends of friends' network**). To achieve this, we can employ the **Ego Network** filter, which can be applied using the following steps:

1. Navigate to the **Filters | Topology | Ego Network** filter.
2. Drag the filter to the **Queries** space in the lower half of the **Filters** tab.
3. Type the value `1551` in the **Node ID** box and leave the **Depth** setting equal to `1`. Then run the **Select** and **Filter** options to see the first degree ego network for this node.

Here are the results, with Node 1551 manually resized for easier interpretation (you could also manually recolor for a similar effect):

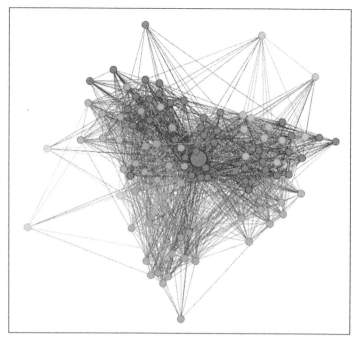

Ego Network for Node 1551

Now we have an instructive view into the extent of Node 1551's influence across the network. While a majority of the connections are relatively close by, there are also some outliers at the perimeter of the graph, an indication that this particular student has interacted with a wide range of other students across multiple grades and classes. This might lead us to further investigate the reasons, if any, for this pattern. A similar analysis can be performed for any other node by entering the node ID in the filter.

By now, you should have a firm grasp of what can be done using simple filters. The benefits of filtering can be enormous, especially when we are encountered with dense networks that are difficult to decipher to the networks that are easily deciphered. Now the time has come to step up to complex filters where multiple conditions are combined in a single query.

Working with complex filters

Complex filters, for our purposes, are defined as filters with two or more conditions placed on some combination of nodes, edges, partitions, or clusters, once again for the purpose of focusing on a specific set of elements within a larger network. Using multiple filters in Gephi is not always easy or intuitive, so we will spend some extra time in this section to walk through several examples in order to expose both the complex filtering approach and the potential for further use of complex filters in your own graphs.

Applying multiple filter conditions

Let's start with some relatively simple examples, complex only in having more than a single filter. In this case, we will create one filter and then use a second condition as a subfilter to the first. Here are the steps:

1. Go to the **Filters** | **Attributes** | **Equal** filter and select the `classname` attribute.

2. Drag the filter to the **Queries** space in the lower half of the **Filters** tab.

3. Type the value 3B in the **Pattern** textbox and click on the **OK** button. You might also need to rerun the **Select** and **Filter** processes.

4. Now repeat step 1 using the `gender` attribute and drag it to the subfilter area of the initial filter.

5. Enter the value F in the textbox and click on **OK**. Our settings should look like this:

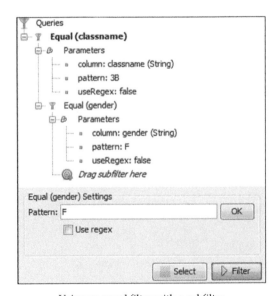

Using an equal filter with a subfilter

We should now see the following result in your graph window:

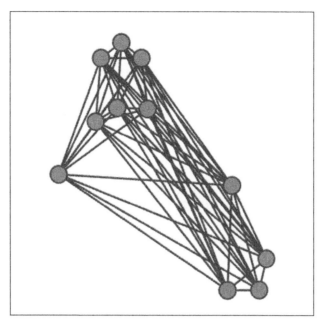

Nodes filtered by classname equals 3B and gender equals F

We now have a graph that has been quickly reduced to just 11 nodes of the original 236 by merging two simple filters. From here, we can easily change the `classname` value or the `gender` value that allow us to filter the network in a rapid fashion. This filter could also be saved for later use by right-clicking on and selecting **Save**, which will park the filter in the **Saved queries** folder. Let's move to another example; this time we will cover an example that combines three separate filters into a single query by using the subfilter capability.

Using subfilters

This time we'll really narrow our graph down by merging three filters as follows:

1. Go to the **Filters | Attributes | Partition** filter and select the `gender` attribute.

2. Drag the filter to the **Queries** space in the lower half of the **Filters** tab.

3. Select the **F** value by clicking on the adjacent rectangle and click on the **Select** and **Filter** buttons. You'll now see only female members of the network.

4. Go to the **Topology | Degree Range** filter and drag it to the subfilter section of the gender filter we just created. Now adjust the value to a minimum of `60` by using the left slider or by entering text.

5. Navigate to the **Operator | NOT (Nodes)** filter and drag that to the subfilter area of the degree range filter we just created.

6. Go back to the **Partition** filter and select `classname`.

7. Drag `classname` to the subfilter area of the **NOT (Nodes)** filter.

8. Run **Select** and **Filter** using the usual buttons.

Here's what our filter should look like:

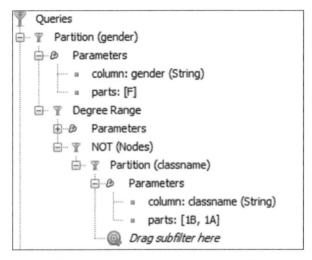

Complex filter that combines gender and degree range excluding the classnames 1A and 1B

We now have a filter that identifies all highly connected female members of the network who are not in classnames 1A or 1B. Here's our result:

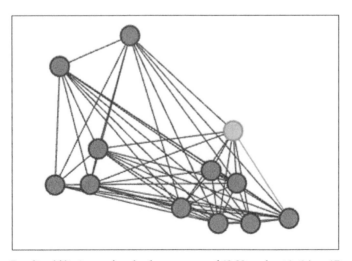

Results of filtering on female, degree range of 60-98, and not in 1A or 1B

You can see how quickly we whittled the network to just 12 nodes by combining these three conditions. From here it's also easy to tweak the settings—perhaps we would like to view only the 10 most connected female students. Simply increasing the degree range threshold will enable us to see these results refreshed with the new conditions. In fact, if we increase this value from 60 to 62, we are left with just nine students who meet all three criteria.

What would happen if we hadn't nested these criteria in a single query, but had chosen to isolate each filter? You can probably guess what the results will look like. Here are the three filter conditions we just presented, but now they act as standalone queries:

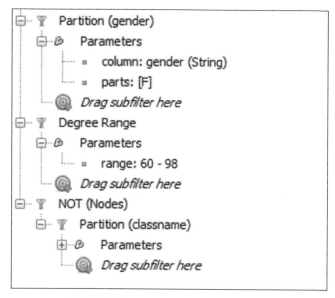

Individual filters not nested in a single query

To create this query, simply follow the same steps we previously used, with one exception. Rather than nesting each filter inside another as a subfilter, this time add each one as its own query, as shown in the preceding screenshot. Run them one at a time by clicking on the **Select** and **Filter** buttons.

First, we'll run the **Partition** filter with the value set to F, which results in the following graph:

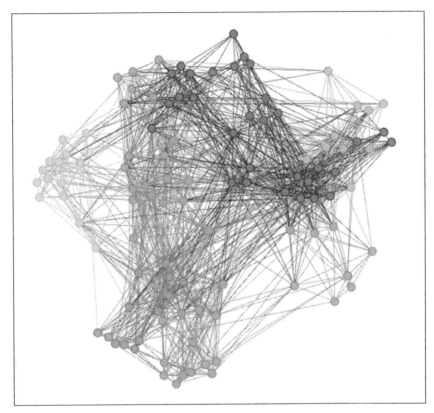

Filtering on partition equal to F

As you might have anticipated, the network has been reduced to roughly half by hiding all nodes with gender equal to male.

Next, we'll filter on **Degree Range**, to identify all network members ranging between 60 and 98 degrees. Make sure the lower value is set to 60, and then filter the results to see the following output:

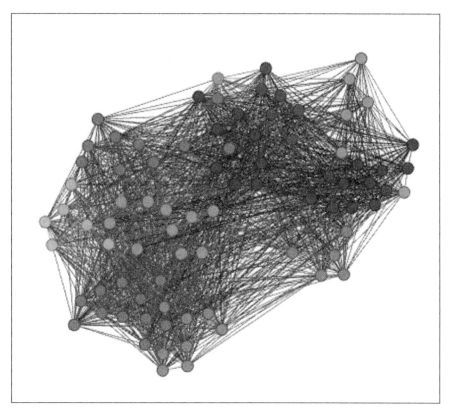

Filtering on degree range between 60 and 98

Now you are seeing only those nodes with a degree level of 60 or greater, including both male and female members. The prior filter is effectively overwritten by the new condition, rather than combining them as we previously saw. To verify that this is the case, go to **Data Laboratory** and view the results to confirm the presence of both male and female students.

Let's apply our third filter — the **NOT (Nodes)** operator that excludes classnames 1A and 1B. You should see the following results:

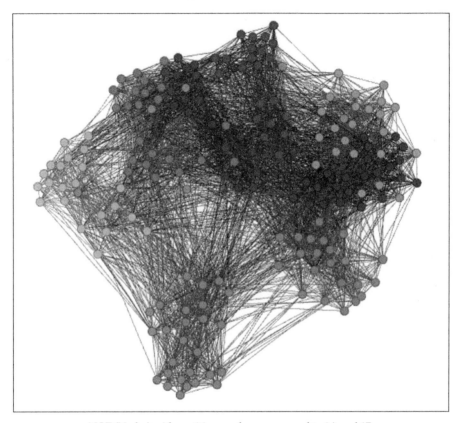

NOT (Nodes) with partition on classname equal to 1A and 1B

Not only do we have both genders visible in our dataset, but also students from the entire degree range from 18 through 98. The only missing members are those from classnames 1A and 1B, which can be confirmed by viewing the **Data Laboratory** results.

So while these individual filters can obviously not be used in the same manner as the nested versions, they do have a considerable value. If you wish to filter your network across many conditions then simply set those up in the **Queries** window, and then you have the ability to toggle through an array of filters to learn more about your network. Think of it in the same way as a statistician might work with single variable crosstabs to learn more about a dataset before moving on to a higher level of complexity.

Working with Mask and Intersection conditions

Now let's tackle our remaining examples, starting with an instance where we will focus on the ego network of an individual student. To complete this example, we'll work with the **INTERSECTION** filter, found in the **Operator** folder within the **Filters** tab, as follows:

1. Apply the **Ego Network** filter found in the **Topology** folder of the **Filters** tab. Follow the usual process of dragging the filter to the **Queries** tab, and then setting **Node ID** to 1551. Run the filter to get the initial results. This might appear a bit messy at this point, but we're going to take care of that in a moment.

2. Next, locate the **MASK (Edges)** filter found in the **Operator** folder of the **Filters** tab. Things get a bit trickier here, but we'll recap our steps at the end of this section. Drag the filter to the **Queries** tab as a standalone filter. Then add the Id filter from the **Equal** folder. Make sure you select the node version, rather than the edge filter. Add this to the subfilter area of the **MASK (Edges)** filter and set the value to 1551, just as we did in our initial filter (we need these values to agree with one another). By the way, your graph will still look a bit untidy at this stage.

3. Next, repeat the process we just did with the Id (Node) filter by dragging it to the subfilter section of the first Id filter. Set the value to 1551 yet again. Now your graph should look quite different—a network with many nodes (98 to be specific) but with no connecting edges. To make the edges appear, we need to create an intersection between our filter conditions.

4. To complete the process, drag the **INTERSECTION** filter from the **Operator** folder down to the **Queries** tab. Make sure it is standalone at this point. Then drag the original filters one at a time into the subfilter area of the **INTERSECTION** operator. Set the **MASK (Edges)** setting to **any** by selecting the corresponding radio button, and run the **Select** and **Filter** processes. If you have taken a look at an intermediate stage, you might have seen something along these lines, with extra nodes that are not part of the ego network:

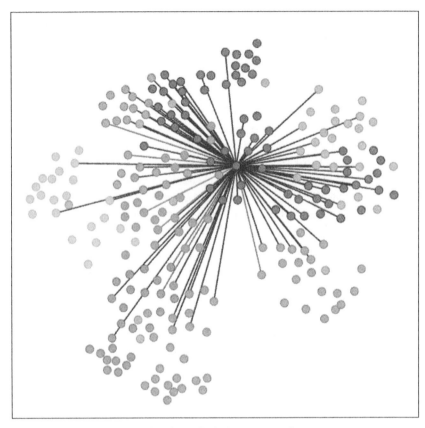

Ego Network with masked edges, intermediate stage

Your finished graph will resemble the following graph, with the remaining nodes filtered out of the process, and all first degree connections displayed like this:

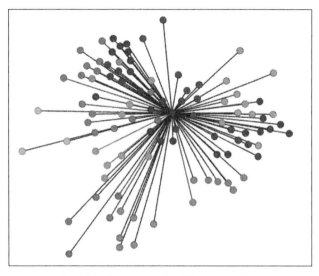

Completed ego network with masked edges

Here's a screenshot for how your complete query will appear:

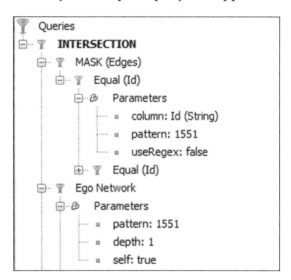

Intersection of masked edges and ego network

Remember to set the second (redundant) `Equal (Id)` value to make sure that the filter operates as expected. This might seem slightly quirky at first, but once learned, it becomes simple to apply to many other examples.

Working with the UNION operator

Now that we have run through a fairly complex example using the intersection logic, we'll end the chapter with an instance using the **UNION** operator. If you think of intersections as being parallel to the use of AND constructs in database queries, then unions are much closer to the OR condition. One notable difference is the requirement that union queries to get based on a single data attribute, where intersections derive their power from merging conditions across multiple attributes.

Given that this example is easier to follow than the last, we'll first introduce the filter conditions of the filter that we are creating, and then view the results. Here's how we want our filter to appear, which can be achieved by performing the following steps:

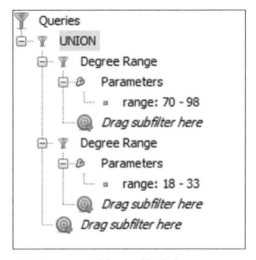

Union query with low and high degree ranges

To create the filter, follow these steps:

1. Go to the **Filters | Topology | Degree Range** filter and drag it to the **Queries** tab.

2. Repeat the same process by dragging the second filter to the **Queries** tab as a standalone instance.

3. Set the first **Degree Range** filter to a minimum value of 70.

4. Set the second filter to a maximum value of 33.

5. Go to the **Filters | Operator | UNION** filter and drag it to the **Queries** tab as a standalone item.

6. Drag each of the two filters to the subfilter area of the **UNION** operator, similar to what we did with the intersection example.

7. Run the filter using the **Select** and **Filter** buttons.

Your result should look like this:

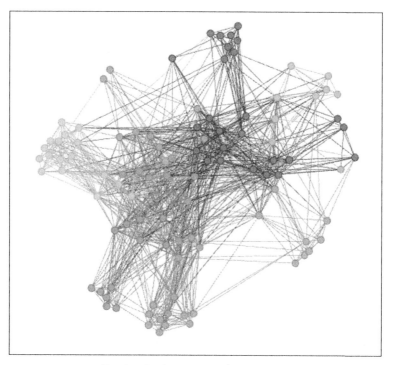

Results of union query on degree ranges

We now have a graph that shows the least connected members of the network, as seen near the perimeter of the graph, and the most highly connected nodes concentrated in the center. The results can be verified in the data laboratory, where we see no nodes with degree values greater than 33 or less than 70. We could follow a similar process using other data attributes such as classname.

I'm sure that you have also thought of some additional applications for complex filters using your own datasets, and it is my hope that these examples will provide both a springboard and reference for some of these processes.

Summary

We covered four main topics in this chapter that will enable you to use Gephi's powerful filtering capabilities to great advantage.

In the first section we explored the purpose of filtering, explaining its benefits and why you should strive to use it for your network analysis in Gephi. We then moved on to describe many of the available filtering functions in Gephi that help you apply good filtering principles.

The last two sections were devoted to help you to apply both simple and complex filters using Gephi. Through multiple examples, we looked at some of the very simple, single filter instances before capping the chapter with some more complex examples using subfilters, intersections, and unions.

In the next chapter, *Chapter 6, Graph Statistics*, we'll work with many of the available statistical functions available in Gephi and learn how to apply filtering in tandem with network statistics.

6
Graph Statistics

While much of the work we do with graph analysis is visually oriented, there are still some critical ways to assess networks that rely more heavily on calculated measures. These measures can help us to add some hard numbers to our existing graph and begin to compare elements both within a network as well as across networks.

Graph statistics come in many flavors and can be used to assess multiple aspects of a network, giving us additional support beyond the visual analysis we might already have done. In this chapter, we'll take a tour through many of the statistical measures available in Gephi in the following order:

- We'll start with a general overview of graph statistics and learn how and why they are critical to understanding the structure of our network.

- Next, we'll focus on interpreting many of the statistical measures using the Gephi **Statistics** tab.

- Finally, we'll spend a significant portion of the chapter working with some network data, using the statistics to illustrate structural differences between networks. For this section, we will again use the primary school network data used in *Chapter 5*, *Working with Filters*.

Let's begin with an overview of some of the primary methods used within the field, with a focus on those that are available within Gephi.

Overview of graph statistics

There are a number of directions we can head toward when we seek to understand the patterns and behaviors within a network. Here are a few of the key questions we might wish to understand:

- What does the overall structure of the network look like? Is it densely connected, or is the network rather sparse?

- Does our network have a high level of randomness, exemplified by few distinct patterns? Or are there very pronounced groups within the network that exhibit advanced levels of clustering?

- Do we see evidence of high degree hubs in the network, as in the case of the Web, with many smaller nodes surrounding the hubs?

- Are certain nodes critical within the structure of the network, perhaps acting as bridges between otherwise disconnected groups?

Each of these questions (and more) can be answered using graph statistics. Our job in this first section of the chapter is to better acquaint ourselves with which statistics to use and when to measure the various behaviors and structures of a network.

Network measures

Gephi provides many statistics that help us to assess the overall structure of our network, including measures for density, path length, hub detection, and overall connectedness. These measures can provide tangible numbers to help support an initial visual assessment of the network, and can also lead us to explore facets of the network that might have been less than obvious from a visual perspective.

We'll walk through several statistics and explore how you can use them to explore your own networks at a relatively macro level. Later sections will then delve into the patterns within the network, as measured by various centrality and clustering statistics.

Diameter

The concept of diameter in network analysis is very simple; it refers to the maximum number of connections required to traverse the graph. Another way to look at it is knowing how many steps it takes for the two most distant nodes in the network to reach one another. In practice, there will be more than a single pair of nodes that fit this description, but the concept remains the same.

Understanding the diameter of the graph helps us begin to comprehend the structure of a network; a graph with a diameter of three will often be less complex than one with a diameter of seven, although this is not always true. Similarly, if we know that a single node has an eccentricity level of four in a network where the diameter is seven, it lets us know that the node is likely quite central to the network.

Eccentricity

Eccentricity refers to the number of steps required for an individual node to cross the network. This number is limited by the diameter of the graph; for example, a graph with a diameter of seven will have nodes with a maximum eccentricity level of seven.

When used to compare nodes, eccentricity can help provide some context to assess the relative position and influence of nodes within a network. While not a substitute for the various centrality measures, eccentricity can nonetheless provide some clues into the relative importance of individual nodes within the network.

Graph density

Graph density is a measure of the level of connected edges within a network relative to the total possible value and is returned as a decimal value between zero and one. Graphs with values closer to one are typically considered to be dense graphs, while those closer to zero are termed as sparse graphs. What constitutes dense versus sparse will vary depending on the type of network data being studied, so it might not be appropriate to compare numbers between very different network subjects. Nonetheless, this is an important measure to develop an understanding for how an individual network is structured, and might help identify gaps or holes within the graph.

Average path length

The average path length (abbreviated as **Avg. Path Length** in Gephi) provides a measure of communication efficiency for an entire network, by measuring the shortest possible path between all nodes in the network. An overall number is calculated for the entire network, with lower numbers giving an indication that the network is relatively more efficient, and with high average numbers signifying a relatively inefficient graph for information flow.

This number will necessarily be less than the network diameter, as that value represents the maximum path length between nodes.

Connected components

When we have a network where more than one component exists, the **Connected components** tool can be used to provide us with a simple read on the number of distinct components within the network. When our network is fully connected, a value of 1 will be returned, so there is little need for this calculation. However, in very large networks it might be difficult to visually determine whether the network is fully connected, so we can use this function to ascertain the number of components.

Erdos number

The original Erdos number definition was based on the number of connections other network researchers had with Paul Erdos, the most prolific (published) mathematician in history, with more than 1,500 papers to his credit. The number that bears his name provides an indication of the collaborative distance between other mathematicians and Erdos. For example, an Erdos number of 1 indicates a direct collaboration with Erdos, while a value of 2 indicates that someone collaborated with one of Erdos' own collaborators, and so on.

In Gephi, this statistic is applied more generally, by specifying a base node (an Erdos proxy), and then determining the Erdos number for all other nodes in the network. Those directly connected to the base node have a value of 1, followed by the nodes which are connected to those with a 1, which have a value of 2, and so on. To work with Erdos numbers in Gephi, be sure to install and activate the `Social Network Analysis` plugin.

HITS

The **Hyperlink-Induced Topic Search (HITS)** function is based on the work by *Kleinberg*, and it calculates two separate values for each node. The first, termed as **Authority**, provides a measure for how valuable information stored by a particular node is, while the **Hub** number measures the quality of the links to and from that particular node. These measures can help to identify or confirm the roles played by critical members within the network.

Edge betweenness

The edge betweenness statistic provides a glimpse into how often specific edges reside within shortest paths between network nodes. This can help us to illustrate the most efficient paths for traversing a network by identifying the most frequently used paths. As with many of the statistics, the number can be returned in raw nominal form (say 10 or 12), or as a normalized value between zero and one. Normalized values allow us to make comparisons between networks to gauge relative edge betweenness importance levels, while non-normalized numbers are highly dependent on the size and structure of each network.

To work with this measure in Gephi, be certain that you have the `Edge Betweenness Metric` plugin installed and activated.

Centrality measures

The role of centrality within a network and its member nodes is part of what we generally attempt to understand. There are many ways to measure centrality, each with its own algorithm. Generally speaking, each of these approaches will help us understand a specific type of centrality, as opposed to offering competing versions of the same measurement.

Think of the various ways in which we might wish to understand centrality in a network:

- We might begin by measuring how central a specific node is relative to the entire network. Is the node in question highly connected and centrally positioned within the network, or is it on the fringes with just a few connections? This is probably the first and most obvious of the centrality measures, but there are several other options.

- Is a node surrounded by highly connected neighbors, without necessarily being directly linked to large portions of the network?

- Is a given node most likely to be connected to other key members of a network, thus affirming its status as an important player, or are most of the connections with members on the fringe of the network, thus reducing the influence level?

- Does a node form a bridge between otherwise unconnected portions of the network, even though it might otherwise appear to be unimportant to the network structure? This can be measured by how often a node appears on the shortest path between other nodes.

These are the four critical questions to address when we are applying centrality measures, and each has one or more methods in Gephi to help supply definitive answers. Let's take a look at these methods, first in theory, and then through some actual applications later in the chapter. We will include the standard statistical calculations used for each measure, but it is not critical that you commit these to memory. The definitions are provided for those of you who wish to further understand or explore the mathematical constructs further, but we will not spend additional time on the formulas within this book.

Degree centrality (undirected graphs)

Perhaps the simplest approach to measure centrality is found in this form, where we assess importance through the number of direct connections (degrees) one node has to other nodes. This approach is applicable in undirected networks only, but does have corollary measures (In-degree and Out-degree) designed for directed networks.

The assumption with degree centrality is that the number of connections is a key measure of importance or influence within the network. In an undirected network we do not have the luxury of determining whether one node exerts more or less influence in a relationship; we merely see that they are in fact connected and as such are weighted equally. As anyone familiar with the structure of the Web is aware, this is not always the most accurate way to determine influence, but it likely provides a good proxy for relative importance in a network structure.

Note that there are two ways in which we can measure each of these centrality methods:

- The first, and most obvious way is to use the nominal degree figure, such as 49, 32, or 18 degrees. While this is informative within the context of a single network, it doesn't allow for comparisons between networks. Larger networks are quite likely to have more nodes with a higher degree measure, yet these nodes might not be as important as a node with a lower degree level in a smaller network.

- The second, slightly more informative approach, albeit more complex, is to normalize the number based on the maximum potential degree level. Using the same three numbers, and assuming a network of 200 possible direct connections, we can then calculate the relative centrality of each node. This then provides us with the numbers that are better suited for comparison to other networks, as all nodes will have a decimal value between 0 and 1.

In-degree centrality (directed graphs)

If the graph has directed edges, we have the ability to go beyond the simpler degree measure and split it into **In-degree** and **Out-degree** measurements. These two measures can inform us whether a network is highly reciprocal (In-degree and Out-degree measures are quite similar) or not. Referring back to the Web example, a site such as Google has a very high In-degree measure, as millions of external sites link to Google. Most of these sites will have very few inbound links of their own and will therefore have very low levels of In-degree centrality. This will lead us to conclude that the Web is primarily a unidirectional network, characterized by a small proportion of hubs with high levels of In-degree connections, while the bulk of sites are weighted far more heavily to Out-degree links.

Out-degree centrality (directed graphs)

Another important measure for directed graphs is the measure of the number of Out-degrees, defined as connections flowing from a selected node to a range of other network members. We have already noted that a high level of Out-degrees relative to In-degrees will often tell us that a particular node is not thought of as a direct information source. This same node can however provide paths to a variety of critical sources, serving as an information aggregator or hub for others.

Closeness centrality

Closeness centrality represents an interesting case, wherein the selected node might actually be poorly connected in a direct sense, yet is still highly influential due to the proximity of well-connected neighbors. Consider the case of someone who is seen as a gatekeeper to an important and influential person; this individual might have relatively few first degree connections, but is still well positioned due to the presence of a high proportion of highly connected nodes as direct connections.

Eigenvector centrality

When nodes are highly connected to other nodes with high levels of influence, the result will be a high-level of Eigenvector centrality. In this case, it is not simply being connected to many other nodes that is critical, but being connected to the most highly influential nodes is paramount. Google's page rank, the famous algorithm used by Google Search to rank websites in their search engine results is a variation of this approach, taking into consideration the connections between sites and weighting their relative importance in terms of web searches, page hits, and other criteria.

Betweenness centrality

The betweenness centrality presents us with a rather unique case, identifying nodes that might well be poorly connected as defined by other centrality measures. In cases where these nodes offer the most direct path between otherwise disconnected clusters, we have what is often termed as a bridge. Being a bridge is not a necessary precondition to have a high betweenness centrality score, but it is often the case that these nodes will rank as critically important using this measure.

Clustering and neighborhood measures

Another key aspect of network graph structure is the level at which nodes group together into various clusters or groups, defined by some shared characteristics or behaviors. These common characteristics might come about as the result of a wide variety of social or geographic factors, including education levels, race, gender, profession, and so on. Gephi provides a few key statistics to help us assess the relative levels of clustering within a network that we'll discuss in the following sections.

Clustering coefficient

With the Clustering coefficient, Gephi provides us the ability to measure the level at which the nodes are grouped together, as opposed to being equally or randomly connected across the network. Scores on this measure will have an inverse correlation with other statistics, including several of the centrality calculations, particularly when we are speaking at the global level (the entire graph). We can also measure this statistic at a local-level, to understand the influence of a single node within its own neighborhood.

This calculation is based on calculating the number of closed triangles (triplets) relative to the potential number of triangles (triplets) available in the network. When we speak of triangles in network graph terminology, we are referencing the connections between the nodes that form complete triangles; in essence, this measures the degree to which your own friends are also friends with one another. In network science language, this could be termed a clique of size 3. High clustering coefficient scores reflect a network where this is most likely true. One might anticipate a high score from tightly knit social groups or clubs (church membership for example), whereas geographically remote networks might be expected to produce lower scores.

At the local level, the measurement determines how likely a single node's neighbors are to form a complete graph (clique). If all possible edge connections are made, the local clustering coefficient would have a score of 1.0, reflecting a graph where all available connections have been created.

Number of triangles

Another way to determine the connectedness and clustering patterns within a network is by measuring the number of triangles present, a measure that provides the nominal count of triangles that are part of the clustering coefficient calculation. This is simply a summation of all possible triplets (connections between three nodes with two or more nodes connected) in an individual node's network, regardless of whether we have a **closed triplet** (with three edges) or an **open triplet** (two of three edges are present). To calculate the clustering coefficient, we need to understand what proportions of the triplets are closed (complete).

Modularity

One more approach to measure clustering in a network is through the application of the modularity statistic, which attempts to assess the number of distinct groupings within a network. This can be done simply by using this statistic, or through the use of one of the Gephi plugins geared to parse nodes into distinct groups. The Chinese Clusters tool can be used for this purpose, as well as the MCL, MCODE, and Girvan Newman plugins. The end goal for any of these algorithms is to group nodes based on the strength of their relationships. Nodes that are highly connected are likely to wind up in a common cluster, regardless of which algorithm is employed. Yet each approach will return slightly different results depending on the size and structure of the network as well as the statistical thresholds employed.

Link Communities

The Link Communities function can be used to understand how individual nodes connect to multiple communities or neighborhoods within the graph. This gives us a slightly different view of the network compared to the most clustering or partition approaches, which force each node into a single grouping. In the communities' case, each edge connection is identified with one or more communities, creating a more complex but potentially more insightful mapping of the network and its relationships.

Neighborhood overlap and embeddedness

The idea of embeddedness and overlap are part of a larger area of network analysis termed as **social cohesion**. While these are not exactly synonymous with traditional clustering, they are certainly related concepts. The basic premise is that rather than neatly defined clusters or partitions, most networks will have nodes with connections into multiple groups or neighborhoods. We can then measure the embeddedness level of specific edges to help determine the neighborhoods where a given node has the strongest associations.

Note that a node can still be connected to other more distant nodes and their respective neighborhoods, but if this is a random or singular connection, the resulting level of embeddedness will be lower.

Interpreting graph statistics

Now that we have discussed all of the measures available in Gephi and provided a brief overview of what they can do, the time has come to understand what the raw numbers signify. Each of these measures provides statistical output that needs to be interpreted in order to understand each and every network and to be able to make accurate comparisons between networks.

Fortunately, many of these measures provide normalized output, that is, values that reside on a zero to one continuum, facilitating easy comparisons between different networks. We'll spend a little time on the interpretation basics before moving on to the actual application of many of these statistics to our working network.

Interpreting network measures

When we are examining the various network statistics in Gephi, our goal is to understand the general structure of the network. There are a few simple questions we need to answer using these functions:

- How large is our network, measured by how many steps it takes for the two most distant nodes to connect to one another?

- On average, is our network closely connected, with perhaps a few outliers, or do a high percentage of the members reside many steps away from other nodes?

- Is the graph relatively dense (that is, many connections between nodes) or would it be considered sparse, with few connections relative to the size of the network?

- Does the network have large hubs with many smaller surrounding nodes, or is there a more random structure to the graph?

- Do we see clearly defined groupings, or is the network highly connected in many directions?

These are all key questions to address as we begin to more fully understand the structure of the network, and they can all be answered using some of the statistical tools we just reviewed.

Before we take this any further, it is critical to understand that all statistical measures are calculated relative to the network we are working on. This means that we cannot literally compare statistics from one network to another, although we might be able to make some of these comparisons in a relative sense. All statistics will be subject to external variables such as the industry or situation being studied, the definition of connectedness (are we measuring collaboration or simple interaction), the time span being studied (if applicable), and a host of other considerations.

So with those caveats in mind, let's move on to a basic understanding of what we are looking for as we interpret each of the available statistics.

One of the simplest measures to understand is **diameter**, which is merely a measure of the distance between the two most distant nodes in the network. However, even this rudimentary statistic has some subjectivity involved in its interpretation. Let's consider two networks, each with a diameter of six. Simple, right? At least until I inform you that Network A has 200 nodes, while Network B has 2,000. This begins to alter our perception about the structure of each network relative to the other. Network A suddenly seems inefficient compared to Network B, which should at least pique our interest into why these two different size networks require the same number of steps to fully traverse.

Eccentricity is closely related to diameter, as it essentially measures the diameter for each node within the network, versus a single network-based number. Every node in the network (assuming they are all connected) will have a value between 1 and the diameter value, with 1 being highly unlikely. In the case where each of our two networks has a diameter of 6, it would be very interesting to learn how many individual nodes match these criteria. If there are just a few nodes at the edges of the graph with an eccentricity value equal to 6, then there is perhaps little to be gleaned from this information. If, however, 10 percent of nodes in Network A have an eccentricity measure equal to the graph diameter, compared to just 3 percent in Network B, then we can safely assume that the relative structures of the two networks likely differ to a considerable degree.

If we wish to understand the role played by a single node in the network, we can apply the Erdos number calculation to see how all other nodes connect to this single member. In a sense, this is related to the eccentricity calculation we just discussed, although we are now looking at the inverse—how many steps does it take for all other nodes to connect to a single selected member?

The **graph density** statistic gives us critical feedback on the structure of the graph as measured by the proportion of edge connections relative to the total available number. As you would expect, this will return a value between 0 and 1, with higher values indicative of a dense graph where a majority of available connections have been completed. This is another measure where there is some room for subjective judgment, even though the returned value is based on a mathematical calculation. Take the earlier example of a collaboration network versus a simple interaction (Facebook, for example) network. The collaboration network requires that two or more individuals work together on a paper or project; this is a more challenging criteria compared to the simple acknowledgement that James (and James' friends) is a friend or acquaintance. Therefore, we would anticipate a lower graph density statistic for the collaboration network, given the more demanding connection criteria.

The most appropriate situations to compare graph density measures would be when the types of connections are similar, as in the case of Collaboration Network A versus Collaboration Network B, or Facebook connections versus Twitter connections. Either of these scenarios would furnish us with an apple to apple comparison where the various statistics could be fairly compared.

Average path length can provide insight into the general structure and connectedness of a network. If we reference the average path length for a graph, and find it to be very close to the network diameter, then this is an indication that the graph is inefficient from a communication standpoint. If this is the case, it may well be due to the presence of multiple clusters in the network (homophily) that add friction to the process of traversing the graph.

On the other hand, if the Average Path Length measure is well below the diameter, then it is likely that the network is efficient, and information can easily flow across the graph. We do need to be cautious in making this assessment, particularly if certain paths are heavily dependent on one or more bridge nodes to facilitate connections. In this case, the removal of a single pivotal node may have significant negative consequences on the network as a whole.

The HITS algorithm, as noted earlier, creates both the Authority and Hub statistics, which might or might not provide different values for each node. In the case of our primary school network dataset used in *Chapter 5, Working with Filters*, identical values are returned using this approach—an indication that no individual member is considered more authoritative than any other. In other words, the weighting is equal for all nodes, leading to values that are aligned with the hub statistics. If we had a directed network, the results would almost certainly be different. We still see differentiation within the hub statistic—a finding that is consistent with the degree measure produced earlier—but we have no way of determining the direction of the links; so no additional value comes out of the Authority number.

HITS is similar to the **PageRank** method for assessing web pages, with higher authority scores indicative of a page that is linked into by many hubs (In-degree connections), while the hub calculation is based on the number of outbound links (Out-degree connections).

Edge betweenness is an approach that helps to sort out the paths that are most often taken to minimize travel across the network. In the normalized version, this measure will reside somewhere between 0 and 1, with a score of 1 indicating that all nodes must travel via that particular edge to reach a desired node or nodes. Conversely, scores near 0 signify that there are other more efficient paths to use to make the shortest journey between two or more points. In the case where a small number of paths carry very high values (that is near 1), there is a risk that if these connections are lost, the network will become more fragmented and communications across the graph will suffer.

Now that we have a more complete understanding of how to interpret and apply generalized graph statistics, we can move onto the various node-based centrality measures and understand how to interpret their output.

Interpreting centrality statistics

Centrality statistics provide the framework to compare the roles played by various nodes within a single network. Given that every node is resident in the same graph, we are able to judge these statistics on equal footing, as all nodes (at least in theory) have the same opportunities. In practice, as we have already seen from our school network, some members might be better positioned than others based on constructs such as grade level, physical location, and so on. If these structures influence the network significantly, we still have the ability to compare results within smaller groups such as individual classes.

Let's take a look at how we might construe the meaning of the statistical results provided by each of the centrality algorithms.

Degree centrality

Degree centrality, as noted earlier, is the simplest of the centrality measures, as it calculates a result based only on the number of connections possessed by a given node. This number does not inform us about the strength of each connection, nor does it tell us the importance of any connections. So when we look at results and see that Node 1551 has 98 direct connections, and Node 1609 has merely 18, we can probably assume that this indicates a dramatic difference in their respective levels of influence in the network. However, in cases where the difference is of a much lower magnitude, we would not be so comfortable making this claim and would certainly want to support it through some of the more sophisticated measures to follow.

In-degree centrality

When we have a directed graph, **In-degree centrality** provides a more robust measure of influence compared to a simple degree measure. This measure tells us how likely other nodes are to seek out a single node, whatever the reason might be—charisma, money, perceived influence, knowledge, or some other attribute that makes this member an attractive target for others. Let's assume from our earlier case that we have a directed graph, and we discover that Node 1551 has an In-degree measure of just 18 (implying an Out-degree number equal to 80). Let's also assume that Node 1552, with a total of 90 degrees, has an In-degree value of 50. Now who seems to play a more influential role in the network? A simple undirected degree measure would have told us that 1551 was marginally more important, while our In-degree number portrays a vastly different story. In this case, 1551 would appear to be a social butterfly who seeks out others, while 1552 is perceived as someone who provides greater influence, power, or prestige.

Out-degree centrality

Out-degree centrality, as we just touched on, might well indicate someone who reaches out to others for more information, influence, or prestige; or in the case of the Web, it could be an indication that many small sites have high connection levels to hubs such as Google or Yahoo!. This is especially the case when there is a significant imbalance between the Out-degree and In-degree measures. Certainly, it is possible for individuals to have relatively even profiles in this respect, although this is generally not the case when networks are dominated by a small number of hubs, be they individuals, websites, or some other entities.

Closeness centrality

With **Closeness centrality**, we begin moving toward a more sophisticated measurement of centrality; in this case defined by the effort required (as measured by path length) to reach all other nodes in the network. As noted earlier, we might well have a number of graph members who score low on other measures such as degree centrality, but who still exercise influence based on their position within the network. It is often the case that a single node scores highly on each of these measures; if an individual has enough degree connections, she/he will likely have fewer long path connections to other nodes, resulting in a lower (that is, more connected) score on this statistic.

In terms of output, each node will have a measure higher than 1, with lower values indicating greater centrality. Members of the network located at the outer edges are highly likely to have high relative scores, as they require more steps to reach all other nodes in the network. A final note on Closeness centrality is that our network must be completely connected in order to run this measure, otherwise we get an infinite result.

Eigenvector centrality

Eigenvector centrality takes Closeness centrality a step further. Instead of being most concerned by the number of steps required to reach all other members of the network, our focus is on the importance of the connections. This is measured by understanding whether individual nodes have a high proportion of their connections to influential members, which boosts their own standing. This is calculated on a 0 to 1 continuum, with values near 1 indicating the highest levels of centrality. In our school classroom network, values range from 0.1 to 1, indicating vastly different levels of influence within the network.

Eigenvector centrality is likely to show a positive correlation with Degree centrality and Closeness centrality, although the relative correlations will of course change depending on the network structure.

Betweenness centrality

Betweenness centrality plays a unique role in understanding how information, influence, and even diseases flow within networks. Unlike the other centrality measures, which are largely predicated on direct connections and/or proximity to others with many connections, betweenness measures how important an individual node is for others traversing the network. Specifically, this measure tells us how often a given node lies on the shortest path between two other nodes.

It is quite possible, and often likely, that a member with a very high betweenness centrality score has very low numbers on all of the other centrality calculations. This will be highly dependent on the network structure and is far more likely to be true in networks with higher levels of clustering.

From here, let's transition to a discussion on the meanings of the various clustering statistics, and how we can develop a better understanding of the aggregation patterns within the network. These measures will help to bridge the gap between statistics that examine the network in its entirety and the centrality calculations, which were focused on the role of individual members within the network.

Interpreting clustering statistics

Clustering statistics are crucial to our understanding and interpretation of network behavior, and specifically, how individual nodes interact and form groups, or clusters. This is the third and final series of graph statistics that begins with the concept of overall network structure as embodied by measures such as diameter, path length, eccentricity, and edge betweenness. Our second series of statistics was focused on centrality, and how individual nodes are related to the network as a whole. When we look at clustering behaviors, we are synthesizing the first two series through the study of how individual nodes work together to shape the internal structure of the network. These measures will help close the loop to understand why certain networks have very high (or low) diameters relative to the number of members, and help us to understand how individual nodes manifest high (or low) centrality scores.

We'll begin with a discussion of how to interpret the **clustering coefficient** score, followed by brief overviews to understand triangles, modularity, Link Communities, and finally embeddedness.

Interpreting clustering coefficients

The global clustering coefficient is based on the concept of triplets: three nodes often in close proximity to one another, connected by two or three edges. In the case of two connections, the triplet is referred to as an open triplet, while if all three nodes are connected with one another, we have a closed triplet, also referred to as a triangle. The derived statistic is simply calculated by dividing the number of closed triplets by the total number of triplets (open and closed), resulting in a coefficient value between 0 and 1.

An interesting observation can be made about clustering coefficients—they are often inversely correlated to the number of degree connections possessed by a single node. Part of this is easily explained—those nodes with many connections spanning a network are likely connected with many others less likely to have the same behavior (most networks show a wide degree range from low to high). This is certainly the case in our school network, where the most highly connected members have rather low clustering coefficients, while those nodes that tend to stay closer to home with their links sport much higher values. The idea of having your own friends connect to one another (thus forming closed triplets) is more likely to happen in smaller, more cohesive groups, and this is ably demonstrated by the school network example.

Number of triangles

The **Number of triangles** statistic is simply a nominal count of all the available triangles generated by a node's degree connections. As you might have anticipated, this is strongly positively correlated to the number of degree connections, although the literal rank order might change slightly. Used in tandem with the clustering coefficient value, we can back into the number of closed triplets each node has in their personal network; just allow some rounding error differences.

Modularity

The **Modularity** statistic places individual nodes into an aggregated group or cluster based on shared characteristics. This is a simpler approach compared to plugins expressly designed for clustering and partitioning, but it can nonetheless help in understanding the network and provides a very easy means to do so when combined with filtering methods. Output for this function is simply an integer value starting at 0.

Link Communities

With the **Link Communities** statistic, we can begin to understand deeper levels within the network that might go undetected if we rely on traditional clustering or partitioning approaches. This statistic will group edges into communities based on similar patterns, applying a single number to every edge in the network. These communities can encompass a single edge or can be composed of dozens of edges that follow similar paths.

Embeddedness

Embeddedness refers to the level at which specific edges tie nodes into neighborhoods across the network. If a given edge connects two nodes across the network in a solitary fashion, then we will expect the embeddedness score to be quite low, perhaps approaching zero. This suggests that these two nodes have relatively little in common, despite their direct connection, which might be simply incidental. The fact that the two nodes have been positioned far apart from one another by a layout algorithm confirms this belief.

Higher embeddedness scores can help direct us toward an understanding of secondary neighborhoods that a given node is linked with, which might be far less evident through a simple inspection of the network layout. We would still anticipate the highest scores to be strongly correlated to the close physical proximity of similar nodes; however, some moderately high scores might point us to other associations or neighborhoods that are important to an individual node.

Application of statistical measures

In this final section of the chapter, we're going to apply many of the statistics we've just reviewed to our school classroom data and begin to gain a greater understanding of the network beyond our earlier visual assessments. Even better, we will use the power of filtering in tandem with the graph statistics to begin using Gephi in an even more sophisticated fashion. We'll start this section with some fairly straightforward examples, and then move on to more complex analysis using the available filtering options.

Basic statistical applications

We're going to work once again with the primary school dataset as we will illustrate the practical application of many of these statistics. We'll proceed in the following order:

- The first section will apply some of the network-oriented measures that will inform us about the general structure of the graph

- Our second section will view several of the centrality statistics and compare how individual nodes are classified

- We will close out by taking a look at a few of the clustering statistics in order to gain a better understanding of how individual nodes form groups based on their behaviors and location within the graph

Let's begin by checking out a few of the network-based statistical measures, and what they tell us about our primary school data. We'll work through each of these statistics by providing the calculated values from the school network graph, and follow with discussions on the overall meaning of each measure. Before we begin, it might be helpful to see the network as follows:

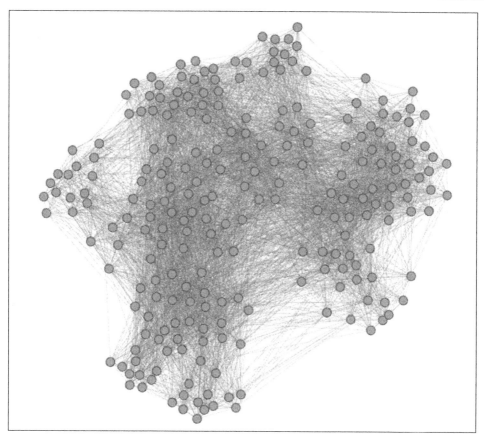

Primary school network

Network statistics

The several measures discussed in this section will provide a lens into the general structure of the network — its size, density, and efficiency will be examined as ways of understanding the composition of the graph. These statistics will help lay the groundwork for the more detailed centrality and clustering measures to follow. Remember that each of these statistics (and many others) can be found in the **Statistics** tab within Gephi. For most, all that is necessary is to click on the **Run** button. For a few others, you will need to specify whether your network is directed or undirected.

Let's see what results we get for some of the critical network statistics. You should be able to easily validate these numbers in your own Gephi instance.

Network diameter

The maximum steps required to cross the network is three, which would seem to indicate a network without a lot of clustering. This seems to be a fairly low value relative to the total number of nodes (236).

Eccentricity

About 20 percent of the nodes have an eccentricity value of 2, with the remaining 80 percent requiring three steps to reach the furthest member of the graph. This provides further confirmation that this network is relatively evenly distributed and easily traversed by all nodes. We do not have any outliers at the fringes of the network who require four or five steps to cross the graph (this would require a higher network diameter, of course).

Graph density

About 21 percent of nodes are connected with one another, based on the output value of 0.213. This is neither an exceptionally high number, nor could it be considered very low. If we reflect on the parameters of this network (grade levels, individual classes), the number appears to make sense in its context. The next step would be to compare this with the same measure from a similar network to judge whether this value is within an expected range (as it seems), or if this network is typically well connected or poorly connected.

Average path length

It takes nodes close to two steps (1.86) on average to reach any other node in the network. This feels like a reasonable number given the prior measures we have discussed. If our graph density figure was considerably higher, we would then anticipate a lower average path length, as a higher proportion of members would have first degree connections.

Edge betweenness

As expected in a well-connected network, there are often multiple paths available to reach specific nodes, resulting in only a few edges with very high values; for instance, 97 percent of all edges have values below 0.5, with the range running between 0.34 and 1.0 The literal translation is that there are just 3 percent of cases where more than 50 percent of all nodes must travel along a single path to reach another node most efficiently (that is, shortest path). This informs us that we have a very robust network for information flow, and that even if a number of links were broken, the network would still be well-connected and efficient.

So what have we learned about the structure of this particular network?

- Overall, it seems safe to assume that this is generally a tightly knit network with minimal variation, as determined by eccentricity levels
- The network appears to be well-connected judging from the graph density measure, but it does not seem to be especially dense

Next, we'll look at a handful of centrality statistics from the same network, and determine what sort of story they are telling us about the behavior patterns of individual nodes inside the graph.

Centrality statistics

We previously talked about the use of centrality statistics for understanding the role played by each member of the network. In this section, we will also see how these measures help to define aggregate patterns within the graph and begin to understand how these individuals interact with one another. Our analysis will be based on four key centrality approaches: degree, closeness, eigenvector, and betweenness.

Degree centrality

There is a considerable variation in the degree ranges within this network (from 18 through 98), as is the case in the majority of network graphs. This is not an extreme variation in the sense of measuring nodes on the Web, but given the total potential number of degrees ($n-1 = 235$), it does represent a significant variance. To help illustrate these differences, let's have a look at a graph where we have colored the nodes based on degree level—darker colors being indicative of higher degree counts:

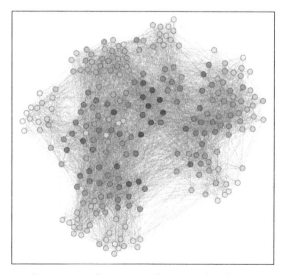

Degree centrality expressed using node coloring

We can now see how the high degree nodes tend toward the center of the graph, while those with low degree values are forced to the perimeter; a typical pattern for many layout algorithms. It is also evident that many of the high degree members are in close proximity to one another, an observation which will prove consistent with the lack of significant clustering in this network. This fact will also influence some of the other centrality measures.

Closeness centrality

This is a much tighter distribution (1.583 through 2.209) than we saw for degrees, largely attributable to the generally close-knit structure of this network. As you can recall, the eccentricity level for all nodes was either 2 or (mostly) 3, an indication that there are no far-flung outliers residing at a great distance from the center of the graph. In cases where there was a greater distribution of eccentricity, we would anticipate a more dispersed distribution of values for this statistic. Visually, this is what we see, again coloring the values based on the statistic, with higher closeness scores (that is, greater distance) indicated by darker nodes:

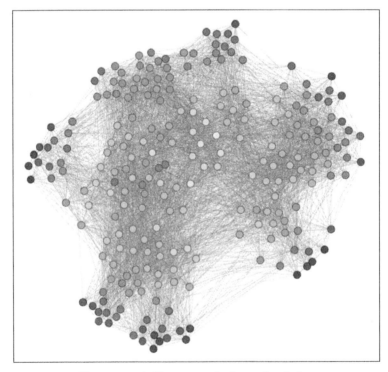

Closeness centrality expressed using node coloring

Remember that this is a sort of inverse measure—higher values indicate more distant levels of proximity to other members of the network. So the same nodes that had fewer direct connections are also associated with higher closeness measurements, which should come as no surprise. Those in the center of the graph can more easily travel to all other nodes in the network (on average), while members on the perimeter cannot do so quite so easily.

Eigenvector centrality

In contrast to the narrowly distributed values within the closeness centrality statistic, we see a far greater range for the eigenvector measurement (0.108 through 1). Now we are attempting to understand the relative importance of connections to gauge whether influential members are likely to be connected with other members of similar standing. Likewise, this measure will tell us whether nodes with lower influence are more likely to be connected with their peers. In this case, both of these patterns appear to be true, giving us a wide range of values. Our example looks like this:

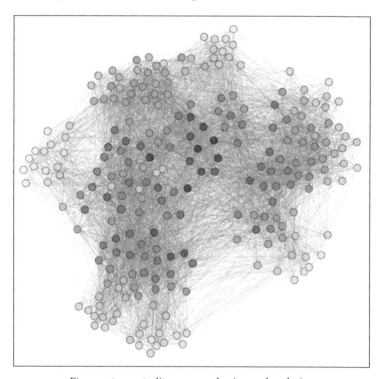

Eigenvector centrality expressed using node coloring

Here, we have a diagram that resembles, but differs slightly from the degree centrality image shown a moment ago. As expected, the higher levels of centrality are concentrated in the center of the graph, with a general progression toward lower levels as we approach the perimeter. Influential nodes are surrounded by other influential nodes, with the inverse also true, that is, low degree members are largely enmeshed with similarly behaving nodes.

Betweenness centrality

There is a rather large spread in betweenness centrality from top to bottom (2.7 to 396.7), with a few nodes having values near zero located around the perimeter of the network. At the other extreme is a total of 8 nodes with betweenness measures of 300 or greater. These members are important players that help to connect diverse portions of the network, although we don't have any that fill the classic role of a bridge between clusters. A view of this statistic seems to confirm what we have already learned about the network:

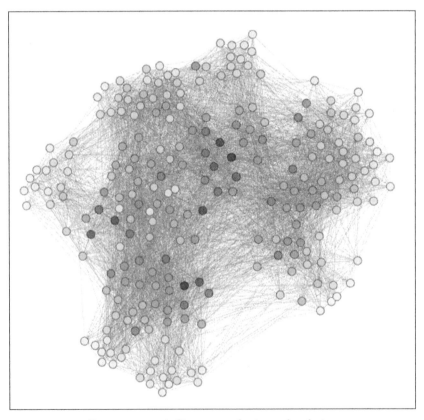

Betweenness centrality expressed using node coloring

As expected, nodes at the perimeter have very low betweenness scores—there is nowhere to go that requires traveling through these members. However, we can detect a handful of critical members that facilitate network traversal, and notice how they are spread out to a much greater degree than we saw for some of the other measures. This is actually quite logical, as it would make little functional sense to have two nodes with very high betweenness properties sitting adjacent to one another; this would be highly redundant. Instead, we can see a more scattered pattern with one or two high scoring nodes strategically located within the graph, which help to create a more efficient network.

Based on these statistics, we can safely conclude the following:

- There is a high level of differentiation across individual nodes, as shown by the variance in degree level
- The most highly connected nodes tend to associate with one another, while lower degree members primarily link to similar sorts of nodes
- There is considerable differentiation in betweenness centrality, even though the network does not require bridge nodes

Our third and final section will examine a few of the clustering measures available in the **Statistics** tab, and what they can tell us about the behavior patterns within this network.

Clustering statistics

Our aim in interpreting the clustering statistics is to comprehend larger behaviors taking place within the network, to see if there are identifiable patterns that tell a significant story. Conversely, the lack of any evident clustering behaviors can also tell a story about the network. We'll analyze five key statistics in the context of our school network to unearth any patterns, beginning with the clustering coefficient.

Clustering coefficient

As we discussed earlier, this is a measure that determines the percentage of available triplets that are fully closed. The statistical measures are 0.502 for the network, and 0.338 to 0.877 for individual nodes. In the case of our school network, the total network number is almost exactly half closed, with the remaining 50 percent still open—two of three edges are connected, but the third edge is missing.

Is this a high or low number? Again, this is somewhat subjective as well as dependent on the individual network, but it does seem to be a rather high figure. If we reflect back to what this network is measuring, this should not come as a complete surprise; we are not looking at long-term relationships or collaborations, but simply interactions between individuals within and across classrooms. The number will almost certainly grow if we restrict it to a single grade level or classroom, as it will reflect the proximity of members throughout the course of a day.

When we examine patterns at the individual member level, we see a wide range from less than 35 percent up to nearly 90 percent of all triplets being closed. Remember that this statistic is inversely correlated to the number of degrees and it begins to make sense. Nodes with relatively few connections are considerably more likely to have a high percentage of closed triplets, while the lowest coefficients come from some of the most aggressively connected members of the network.

Number of triangles

There is a very wide range of triangles from the minimum (96) to maximum (1,616) number of triangles at the node level. At first, this variance seems extreme, but if we step back and look at a couple of other statistics, these numbers make complete sense. First, consider that our degree ranges ran from 18 to 98, and second, remember that many of the most popular nodes are connected with one another (the same is true for the least popular ones). This creates a geometric effect that favors the most highly connected nodes, at least in terms of the number of available triplets. However, as we learned from the clustering coefficient figures, a majority of these triangles will remain incomplete.

Modularity

The **modularity** statistic splits this graph into five distinct clusters, numbered from 0 through 4. Doing some simple math tells us that each cluster will average close to 50 nodes. This might be satisfactory for our purpose, or if we need further splits, we can employ one of the dedicated clustering algorithms. A quick way to determine if this number is adequate is to color the graph using the modularity class, as we have previously done with the centrality measures.

Link Communities

This network has many Link Communities ranging in size from a single edge to well over 100 edges. What this tells us is not clear from a purely statistical viewpoint, but it can help us decipher interactions between multiple nodes, as defined by their connecting edges. In fact, the two most prominent communities in this graph account for greater than 20 percent of all connections, providing a new insight about the common behaviors that might be less clear if we rely solely on node-based statistics.

Embeddedness

Our final clustering-oriented statistic to measure is embeddedness, which will aid us in understanding the depth at which nodes are affiliated with specific groupings. This measure can help explain how specific nodes or groups of nodes cooperate with one another beyond simply being superficially connected. In our school network, we have an average embeddedness level of 24.6 with individual edge values ranging from 0 to 64. If we examine the data further, it tells us that those edges with very low counts (infrequent interactions) are found at the lowest embeddedness levels; conversely, the highest scores typically correspond to frequent interactions between two nodes.

In the first case, this would represent the sort of superficial connection just referenced; perhaps this contact was random or incidental to a certain time and space. As the frequency of contacts between two parties grows (and with it, the embeddedness score) we can be fairly certain that this is not a random pattern, but something more purposeful and structured.

Now that you have learned how to work with a variety of useful statistics, it's time to take them to the next level by combining them with the powerful filtering capabilities in Gephi. We'll look at a number of graphs in this section so that you get a feel of both, the visual output of the various statistics as well as the multiplicative power delivered by the filtering capabilities of Gephi.

Filtering using graph statistics

We spent a lot of time with filtering in the previous chapter prior to diving into graph statistics. Now we have an opportunity to combine these two powerful features in Gephi, as we can employ most of the statistical measures we have just reviewed as filters to help refine our graph output. This capability gives us considerable power to learn more about our network and drive attention to the most important aspects of the graph. We can also probe to understand the statistical variation within the network which might provide some surprises that would otherwise go unnoticed.

We'll use multiple graphs in this section to help illustrate the impact of combining statistics with filtering. So let's begin by working with some rather simple examples before stepping up the complexity level and showing some of the impressive capabilities of Gephi.

Let's begin with a simple case where we wish to focus our attention on only those nodes that meet a specified betweenness criteria; so we can better understand which nodes are most critical to connect sections of the network. If you recall, our betweenness levels ran from near zero all the way to nearly 400. We're going to follow a few steps to set a filter for only those nodes with betweenness levels above 250. While this number is slightly arbitrary, it is designed to identify the top 5 percent to 10 percent of the influential nodes. Refer to the paper *Identifying High Betweenness Centrality Nodes in Large Social Networks*, Nicolas Kourtellis et al, 2014, for more insight into identifying the impact of betweenness centrality.

This should give us a good sense for which members are most adept at connecting other nodes. Perform the following steps:

1. Open the **Filters** tab in the Gephi workspace.
2. Navigate to the **Attributes | Range | Betweenness Centrality** attribute.
3. Drag the filter down to the **Queries** area.
4. Set the lower range to 250 using the slider control or type the value manually.
5. Click on **Select** and then **Filter** to get the results.

The original network of 236 nodes has now been dramatically reduced, as shown in the following graph:

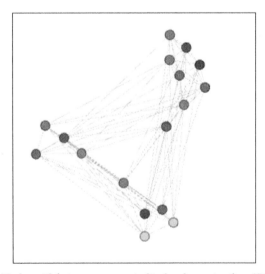

Nodes with betweenness centrality levels greater than 250

We now see the 17 most influential modes in terms of their ability to connect to others in the network. We can of course manipulate the filter to further reduce this group by raising the threshold, or to expand it by reducing the lower bound of the filter.

If you have been working along with these examples, you will have noticed many other statistics that are now available for filtering purposes. In addition to the various centrality measures, we now have the ability to look at hubs, triangles, neighborhoods, eccentricity, embeddedness, and communities, among others. We can also begin to apply some of the more advanced filtering techniques we worked with in the last chapter, giving us incredible power over the network. Let's take a look at a few of these possibilities.

We'll begin by merging the betweenness measure with a specific classname in order to understand which members are most likely to be the bridges within a given class. We're going to assume that you have already applied the previous filter. If not, you can start by following the last process of setting the **Range** filter using betweenness centrality:

1. Set the lower bound of the range to `150`.
2. Run the **Select** and **Filter** processes to verify the new setting.
3. Navigate to the **Attributes | Partition | classname** variable.
4. Drag this filter to the **Queries** window, as a separate filter and not a subfilter.
5. Click on the **2B** option in the **Partition Settings** window.
6. Go to the **Operator | INTERSECTION** filter.
7. Drag this to the **Queries** window, again as a separate filter.
8. Move each of the prior filters under the **INTERSECTION** query as separate subfilters. Repeat steps 3 and 4 by dragging the **classname** filter to the subfilter area of the original classname filter.
9. Apply the filter by running the **Select** and **Filter** processes.

We now have a new result that has merged our two filters by requiring a betweenness centrality of at least 150 combined with membership in classname 2B. I took the liberty of adding node labels, so we can see who these individuals are:

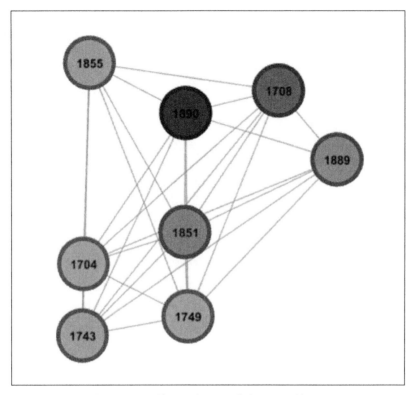

Intersection of betweenness and classname filters

If you wish to see additional details, simply navigate to **Data Laboratory**, which will now show only the results for these 8 nodes. Of course, if you wish to reduce this set, or apply the logic to a different classname, then simply adjust the filters we just created. Be sure that your two classname filters match; otherwise you'll be staring at a blank graph window.

While it might seem that setting these filters requires a lot of steps, it really becomes much simpler the more you go through the process. However, a great way to avoid having to repeat all of these steps is to save your queries after they have been adjusted to your satisfaction.

To do this, perform the following steps:

1. Go to the top of the query (the **INTERSECTION** level in this case) and right-click on it.

2. Select the **Save** option, and your complete set of filters will be saved into the **Saved queries** folder.

3. You can test that the save process works by removing the existing filters from the **Queries** window, followed by dragging the saved query to the vacated space. Apply the usual select and filter steps, and you will see your expected results in the graph window.

Saving your complex filters can be a great way to save time and effort and will allow you to create many queries that can then be easily substituted for one another.

It is time to move on to our next example. This time around, we'll work with some of the clustering output we've already created using the statistical functions. Here's our scenario we would like to answer. We already know that the network is divided into specific classnames, based on the grade levels and assigned classrooms within the school. What we really want to know is whether this paints an accurate picture of how the school functions during a typical day. Do students tend to associate with others in their classrooms, or at least within the same grade level, or are there informal structures that are better predictors of information flow? To answer this, we will utilize the Modularity Class calculated earlier and intersect those values with some of the more formal attributes such as classname.

Let's take the following steps to construct our filter to test the above questions:

1. Navigate to **Attributes | Partition | Modularity Class** in the **Filters** tab.

2. Select and drag this filter to the **Queries** window.

3. Set **Modularity Class** to 3 by clicking on the color rectangle next to the 3 value.

4. Now create the classname filter, as we did in the prior example by going to **Attributes | Partition | classname** and dragging that selection to the **Queries** window above the modularity filter.

5. Select the 1B, 2B, 3B, 4B, and 5B values by clicking on the corresponding rectangles.

6. Create a subfilter within the classname filter by repeating steps 4 and 5.

7. Drag an intersection operator to the **Queries** window and then add each of the prior queries (modularity and filter) as subfilters within the intersection filter.

8. Run the **Select** and **Filter** processes.

Our theory here is to see whether we will find evidence of multiple classes from the B portion of the classnames winding up within a single modularity. If this is true, then we might regard the modularity value as being more predictive of network behavior than the more formal constructs of grade levels and classnames. Let's find out whether this is true by looking at our filtered graph, which we'll color by classname using the **Partition** tab and **classname** field:

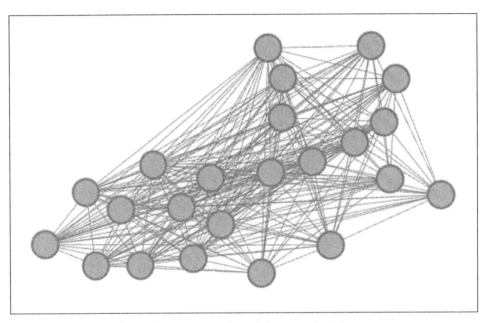

Intersection of modularity and classname for B classes

Our returned graph shows a single color corresponding to classname 5B. This means that not a single member from 1B, 2B, 3B, or 4B is classified within this modularity class. It looks like classname might in fact provide a strong proxy for network behavior. What happens if we expand our filter to include classname 5A to see if any of these students wind up in the same modularity class? Let's have a look:

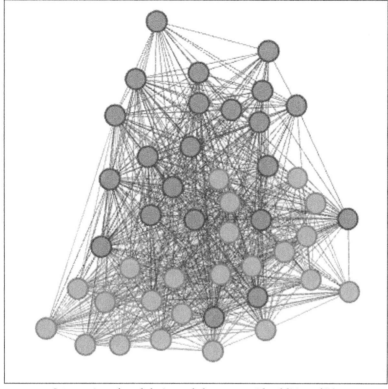

Intersection of modularity and classname with addition of 5A

We now see that Modularity Class 3 also contains many members from 5A as well as 5B, an indication that the grade level is in fact a very strong predictor of network behavior, at least based on how the modularity algorithm has classified the network.

Our next example will filter on a combination of nodes and edges to get to our desired result. Suppose we want to understand the relationships within a modularity class for nodes that score high on the hub measure we saw earlier in the chapter. We can do this by using a partition filter for the modularity class and a range filter to set the hub threshold. Now what if we wanted to also limit the number of edges based on a certain threshold, such as the embeddedness statistic? We can do this as well using the range filter, so we'll wind up with a query that filters both nodes and edges all at once.

Here are the steps to follow:

1. Navigate to the **Equal | Modularity Class** filter and drag it to the **Queries** window.

2. Set the value equal to 2.

3. Repeat this process as a subfilter to the original modularity filter and set it 2 for the second time.

4. Navigate to the **Range | Hub** filter and drag it to the **Queries** window; be sure it is a standalone filter rather than a subfilter.

5. Set the minimum range level to 0.005.

6. Go to the **Range | Embeddedness** filter and drag it to the **Queries** window, again as a standalone filter.

7. Set the embeddedness minimum value to 50 using the slider control or by typing a text value.

8. Add an **INTERSECTION** operator to the **Queries** window.

9. Now drag each of the three queries to the subfilter area of the **INTERSECTION** filter.

10. Run the **Select** and **Filter** processes to apply the entire filter.

We now have a custom view that shows only nodes from Modularity Class 2, with a Hub value of greater than 0.005, and with edge embeddedness levels greater than 50. Here's our result:

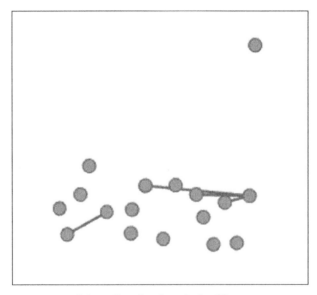

Intersection of node and edge filters

These examples scratched the surface of what can be done by filtering using statistical measures. There are many other conditions and combinations which you can apply to your own networks, perhaps using these instances as templates for knowing how to proceed. While we noted that filtering on these attributes is not always easy or intuitive, I believe you will come to appreciate the power that statistics and filters deliver to your own network analysis.

Summary

In this chapter, we covered many of the most critical graph statistics, dividing them into three basic categories: network, centrality, and clustering measures. In the first section, we walked through brief overviews of what each of these statistics can provide for analyzing networks in Gephi.

The second section focused on the interpretation of each of these statistics, when and where they are useful, and what sort of numerical output to anticipate in each case. This was followed by examples of actual applications of these statistics using our primary school network graph.

We closed the chapter with multiple examples showing how graph statistics and filtering can be used together for advanced analysis of any network graph. These examples provided step-by-step instructions that can serve as templates for additional statistical filtering.

We'll now move on to *Chapter 7, Segmenting and Partitioning a Graph*, where we will explore the multiple methods to improve our graph by identifying common node characteristics.

7
Segmenting and Partitioning a Graph

Being able to view a network graph and understand the component parts is a critical aspect of network analysis. There are a number of approaches we can take to do this, including the use of clustering algorithms, data partitioning, or simply through the creative application of colors and sizing of specific portions of the graph. The end goal is typically the same — to tell an effective story through the use of visual elements.

- We'll begin by exploring the various partitioning and clustering options available in Gephi
- We'll then share several examples using some of the clustering and partitioning tools
- In the final section, we'll walk through some cases where we take a more free form approach to visual clustering, using variations in size and color to direct the audience's attention

Let's begin with a tour through some of the many available clustering and partitioning options that are part of the Gephi core or available through a host of plugins.

Partitioning and clustering options

Before moving into specific methods to partition our network graphs, we should understand why we choose to do so. There are at least two main reasons for segmenting our graphs in this fashion:

- To highlight patterns in the data based on underlying statistical or behavioral patterns. This can be especially essential when we have a dense network where patterns are not obvious to the naked eye.

- To make a network more visually attractive through the use of size and coloring options.

Note that these two are not mutually exclusive aims, but can be used to great advantage together. So the end goal of the efforts taken for partitioning or clustering should be to enhance the viewer's ability to interpret the graph. Clustering methods will do this through specialized algorithms that interpret network patterns into distinct groupings (clusters) of similar nodes. Partitioning is typically more manual, but also seeks to deconstruct the network into meaningful groupings based on categorical data.

With this in mind, Gephi provides multiple options to segment a network graph, which includes the following selections:

- The **Partition** tab enables the segmentation of a graph using a variety of attributes or statistical measures applied to both nodes and edges. As we will see in a moment, partitioning differs in approach from clustering, even when the end goal might be the same.

- Sizing and coloring options can be created using the **Ranking** tab. A typical approach is to have scaled coloring based on a measurable attribute, with darker colors corresponding to higher values. The same approach can be applied using node size to scale values according to their degree level.

- Manual sizing and coloring is an option in cases where we need to step outside of categorical or value-based partitioning. For instance, we might have five individual nodes we wish to focus on; Gephi enables custom coloring or sizing for these cases. This can be useful when we wish to draw attention to a specific set of nodes based on some salient characteristic.

- The **Chinese Whispers** clustering plugin is a community detection algorithm that provides you with the ability to customize a number of parameters. The goal of this method is to find groups of nodes that broadcast the same message to their neighbors, hence the use of the Chinese Whispers children's game as the title.

- **Markov Clustering** is one more option available as a Gephi plugin. This is an easy-to-use plugin that does not require a lot of intervention, although a few settings can be adjusted. With **Markov Clustering**, the approach is based on a comparison of random walks (a succession of random steps of varying lengths) to actual patterns found within the graph, resulting in the identification of clusters where patterns vary significantly from a simple random walk expectation.

At this point, let's clarify a significant difference between partitioning and clustering. While the aim of both is to separate a network into easily understood groups, each approach goes about this in different ways. When we partition a graph, it is typically through an arbitrary selection of one or more attributes or measures, an **a priori** segmenting of the network. This enables us to see how nodes or edges are categorized across a specific dimension. On the other hand, clustering is typically performed by an algorithm—we might have the ability to adjust the settings, but the individual method analyzes the network data to create clustered groupings. We can also reference the concept of **community detection**, where overlapping (or non-overlapping) communities are defined based on their connection patterns. In the case of overlapping communities, the resulting graph might be more complex than in either partitioning or clustering, as individual nodes might be members of multiple communities. The **Link Communities** statistic can also provide insight into these patterns.

One instance where the partitioning and clustering approaches interact is when we use a clustering method to classify the graph, and then elect to display it using the **Partition** function. This gives us the ability to create clusters using one or more algorithmic approaches, followed by the ability to partition the graph using data attributes or the newly created cluster values. The partition method makes it very easy to select the color scheme for our network groups, regardless of whether they are manually defined partitions or algorithmically created clusters.

The Partition tab

We're going to start this section with the **Partition** tab, often located above the **Layout** tab in the Gephi **Overview** window. This is a very powerful option in Gephi, as it can be quickly applied using many different fields in a network dataset. These fields can be part of the source data—perhaps gender, class, country, or any of a long list of values that can be used to visually segment your graph display.

Like many other options in Gephi, it is quite simple to change the partitioning variable—just navigate to the **Partition** tab and select a new attribute (you might need to refresh these on occasion by clicking on the green colored refresh icon). In most cases, this will be done using the **Nodes** option, but there might be instances where you wish to perform partitioning using edges.

As noted above, the primary goal of partitioning is to visually segment a network to help identify patterns based on categorical or integer-based attributes. Be careful not to use this approach when too many possible values are available, as it will only cause visual chaos, as 30, 40, 50 or more distinct colors might be introduced to the graph. The best use of partitioning is when you have a handful of possible values— anywhere from two to perhaps 15 or 20. Anything beyond this point might lead to confusion rather than clarification.

The Ranking tab

The **Ranking** tab allows value-based manipulation of the graph that employs both color and sizing options. This method can be highly effective to create visual segmentation based on numerical values, including both data attributes (such as number of games played, number of visitors, and so on) as well as calculated attributes (degrees, centrality measures, and more).

Unlike traditional partitioning, you will not be able to examine categorical variables in this fashion, so you might wish to utilize the two approaches as complements to one another.

Manual settings

Gephi provides users the ability to manually adjust virtually any aspect of a network graph, including resizing and recoloring graph nodes. This can be an effective route to choose when just a few modifications are needed to tell a specific story. In some instances, categorical or computational clusters might fail to tell the story we are seeking, forcing us to shift to more manual methods. Whatever the use case, Gephi provides the requisite tools to aid in customizing our graph. The next section will demonstrate these capabilities using a simple example.

Chinese Whispers

The **Chinese Whispers** algorithm, named after the children's game, is a useful plugin that can help to segment your graph by identifying similarities (and differences) across network members. The results are returned as specific clusters, with each node in a graph assigned to one of the groupings. For a detailed understanding of the methodology, here is the link to the paper describing the approach: `http://wortschatz.uni-leipzig.de/~cbiemann/pub/2006/BiemannTextGraph06.pdf`.

In simple terms, the algorithm is used to partition undirected, weighted graphs. Similar to the children's game of the same name, the goal is to understand which nodes are able to broadcast the same message to their neighbors. Nodes with very similar patterns are then grouped into clusters based on these similarities.

There are a couple of limitations to the approach:

- Component boundaries cannot be crossed. If your graph has a single giant component with no secondary components, then the algorithm works as designed.

- Nodes with no edges are removed from the clustering process, leaving any such nodes outside of the partitioning structure. These nodes are simply unclustered and are referred to as singletons.

In the next section, we'll demonstrate the value of the Chinese Whispers approach in helping to develop stories based on network patterns.

Markov clustering

This plugin is based on the work of *Stijn van Dongen*, with his thesis available at `http://www.micans.org/mcl/`. This approach uses the theory of random walks in determining how the graph should be clustered. Two operators known as **expansion** and **inflation** are used to simulate the random walks. At a simple level, a random walk should have low probability of crossing from one cluster to another, resulting in a graph with natural splits based on the existing network structure. We won't dive into the mathematical constructs here (refer to the preceding link for more details), but will view some examples later in this chapter.

One caveat with the Markov approach—it can be very demanding computationally, so be certain to tweak your settings appropriately for the network in question, or prepare to receive memory errors. We'll look at this a bit more while running through some examples later in this chapter.

Partitioning and clustering examples

Over the next few sections we'll walk through multiple examples using a single dataset, starting with the basic partitioning approach, followed by each of our clustering techniques discussed a moment ago. We'll then conclude the section with a recap of what we learned from these examples.

Partitioning

In the next several pages, we will look at some partitioning examples using a new dataset, which is a network derived from some historical baseball data, specifically involving the Boston Red Sox. This dataset covers all seasons from 1901 through 2013 and has a handful of string attributes that can be used for partitioning purposes. There are also a number of numeric variables that can be employed for filtering and other uses, but these are not available for partitioning. Here are the steps to get started:

1. To download the data files, go to this location: `https://app.box.com/ s/177yit0fdovz1czgcecp`.

2. Import the files using the Gephi **Data Laboratory** and the **Import Spreadsheet** functionality. You will wind up with a node table of 1,668 records, and an edges table of more than 51,000 rows.

We'll work with multiple partitioning options so that you become familiar with more than one approach. Before we get into any of the partitioning examples, we should take a look at how the network sets up on its own. I will let an ARF process run for about 25 minutes to achieve the following graph, but depending on your preference (and CPU) another layout type might be preferred. I find the ARF layout ideal for visualizing relatively sparse mid-sized networks like this one as it seems to make node clusters highly visible.

Here's my initial instance of the network:

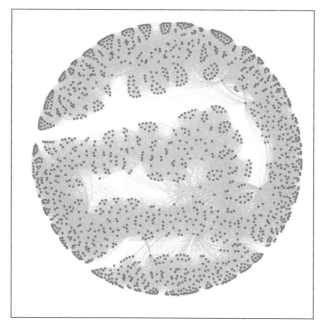

The Red Sox player network

So we have a much more complex network than we used in the previous chapters, but one that is nonetheless manageable, with fewer than 1,700 nodes. Still, this complexity level could prevent us from learning more about the network unless we elect to partition it into meaningful pieces. Let's run through a few examples for fun. If you want to follow along, just remember that you might need to reset the colors after each iteration, using the **Reset Colors** rectangle icon in the **Overview** window (you can find this icon at the bottom-left of the graph area). This will return the nodes to a single default color — the color currently seen within the rectangle. Also note that I am sharing each of these using the **Preview** window, which gives us more refined imagery.

For the first case, we'll look at the **Decade** attribute, which informs us in which decade a player first played for the Red Sox.

 Note that the **Partition** tab will display decades ranked by proportion, as opposed to their data order.

Gephi will also select the colors for you, although you can modify these individually after the update has been applied. So select the **Decade** attribute from the **Partition | Nodes** tab, click on the **Apply** button, and have a look to see the following output:

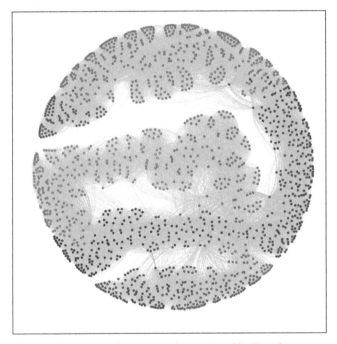

The Red Sox player network partitioned by Decade

We now have a graph that is visually segmented into 12 groups, each representing 5 percent or more of nodes in the network. As noted a moment ago, the color legend appears in the partition window and allows you to manually edit by selecting a specific rectangle and right-clicking to load the color palette.

What if we prefer something other than Decades as our partitioning variable? Let's suppose that our goal is to understand birth country patterns. This can be easily done by selecting the **birthCountry** attribute in the **Partition** window, as seen in this screenshot:

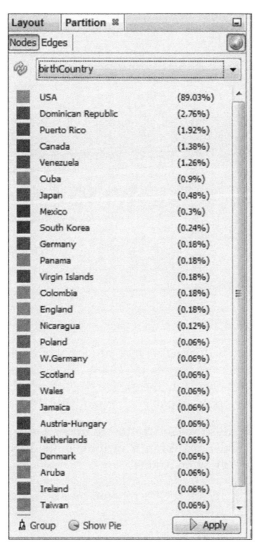

Partition results using the birthCountry attribute

Applying the settings will update the legend and graph colors to look like this:

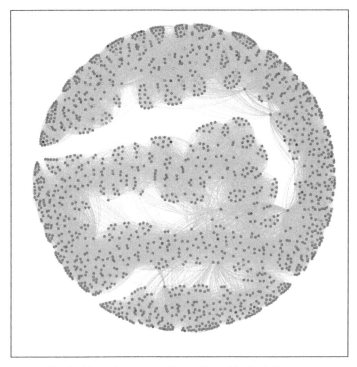

The Red Sox player network partitioned by birthCountry

We now have a graph that is dominated by a single color, as close to 90 percent of all the players in the network were born in the United States. This pattern would change significantly if we were to select only the most recent decades which have seen a major increase in the proportion of players born outside the US.

Let's have one more look, this time in an effort to understand calendar month birth patterns. To do this, select the **birthMonth** attribute in the **Partition** window, and click on **Apply** to see the following results:

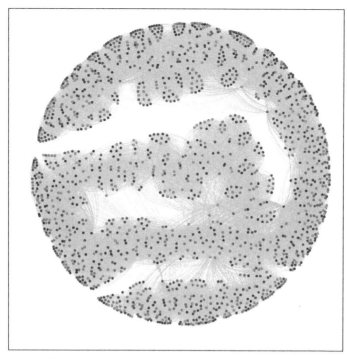

The Red Sox player network partitioned by birthMonth

Now we can see that August (8) and September (9) appear to be the dominant birth months for Red Sox players throughout their history, while June (6) is the least likely month to produce major league baseball players, at least for the Red Sox organization.

I think you have the idea by now that partitioning in Gephi is a straightforward yet powerful process that can help us to quickly spot some patterns in our network. Go ahead and play with some other attributes if you wish, and adjust a few colors to get a feel of that process.

We'll now move on to adjusting the graph using the ranking functions, working on numerical rather than categorical attributes.

Working with the Ranking tab

The **Ranking** tab, as noted earlier in this chapter, enables us to segment our graph based on the numerical values derived from data attributes and statistical measures. This method provides different results than the partitioning approach just discussed. Partitioning works on categorical values and colors the node values according to a specific value in that data field. Ranking takes a different approach by examining numerical values, and colors or sizes these values on a sliding scale without distinct breakpoints (although this can be implemented using the **Spline** settings, as detailed here).

To adjust the distribution of the size settings automatically, use the **Spline** option in the **Ranking** tab. This function provides multiple settings to size the nodes according to some predefined distribution curves, which can also be customized by moving the *x*- and *y*-axis settings in the **Spline Editor** window.

Let's look at some illustrations that are using ranking, which can then be contrasted with the examples we saw in the prior section. We'll continue using the same network graph of Red Sox players.

Using color and size options

In cases where we intend to create custom partitions, Gephi offers the ability to use color and size options to help visually classify a network graph. This process would not fall under the usual guidelines for partitioning (or clustering, for that matter), but is simply an automated or manual means to customize your network to highlight specific patterns.

Let's suppose that we wish to draw special attention to specific elements in the graph that are not addressed through the use of partitions. You might have noticed already that partitions apply only to non-numeric elements. In this particular case, many of our most interesting data fields are integer-based, including the number of games played, home runs hit, or total bases earned. Fortunately, Gephi provides the ability to replicate partitions by ranking our graph nodes according to numeric values. We'll walk through some examples of this, sharing the resulting graphs.

A bit of a caveat before we begin—if your field type is BigInteger, you will be unable to follow this process. To rectify this, you can either make a copy of this field in the data laboratory, setting the type to Integer, or you could also recast the column (using the Recast column plugin) to the integer type.

For our first instance, let's assume that we wish to see which players played the most seasons in a Red Sox uniform. Follow these steps to create a graph that is sized based on the tenure:

1. Go to the **Ranking** tab (often at the upper-left of your screen) and select the **Nodes** tab.

2. Choose **Seasons** (or whatever your equivalent integer-based field is named) from the listbox.

3. Apply the sizing based on the values in the data. In this case, we have a minimum of 1 and a maximum of 23. To be consistent with good data practices, we should size the area of each circle using the radius, as opposed to the circumference, which equates to roughly a 5:1 ratio in this example (as the circle with size 1 has a radius of approximately 0.57 while the circle of size 23 has a radius of 2.7 approximately). So we'll use a minimum value of 4 and a maximum of 20 for better visibility while maintaining the 5:1 ratio.

4. Apply your settings.

You should wind up with a graph that resembles the following screenshot:

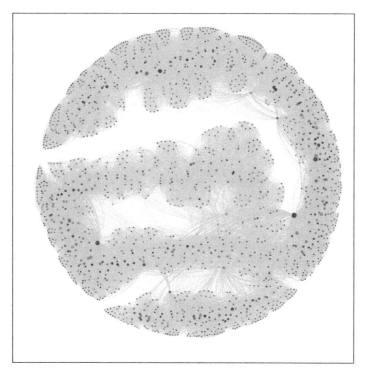

The Red Sox player network ranked by seasons

We can now see a handful of nodes that stand out from the remainder of the graph based on their career longevity, as measured by seasons played. A similar approach could be applied to any integer-based data attribute in the network. One of the nice aspects of this approach is that it lets us see how our graph can change based on the application of measurable data attributes, as opposed to the categorical approach delivered by partitioning.

Let's view one more example before moving onto manual partitioning. In this case, we'll follow the same procedures we used a moment ago, replacing Seasons with 3rd_Base. Make sure your field has integer values or create a copy that does. Follow the same steps as before, but this time adjust the sizing to a minimum of 0.5 (0 is not allowed even when the data value is zero) to 44, based on the high value of 1,521. This should provide great clarity within the graph for which players had the greatest number of games at the third base position, as shown in the following screenshot:

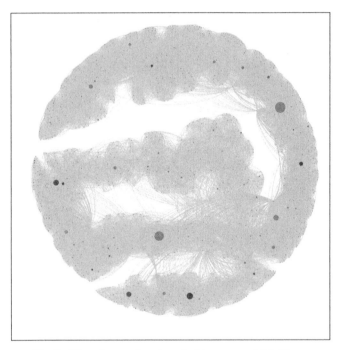

The Red Sox player network ranked by games at third base

Now we can see very clear results, with most of the graph receding to the background while a mere handful of nodes are very prominent. This provides us with great insight into who played most often at that position, without having to deal with a lot of visual clutter. This could also be considered something of an alternative to filtering, with the difference of seeing the remainder of the graph in the background. We should also note that we could have used coloring to rank the games played—typically as a gradient ranging from light (lower values) to dark (higher values).

Manual graph segmentation

We have already seen two ways in which we can visually partition a graph in Gephi using built-in functionality to work on either categorical or numeric values. Let's take a brief look at a third method, one which involves a bit more manual effort to create a specific look for our graph. We'll return the graph to its original state by resetting the size and color values, resulting in an unembellished graph where all nodes have identical appearances.

For this example, let's assume that we wish to focus the reader's attention only on players who began their tenure during the 1980s. We already know that we could do this using the partitioning approach working with the Decade variable, as illustrated earlier in this chapter. That approach will give the 1980s nodes a unique color, but we want something more to draw attention to the member nodes who meet this criterion.

Here are the steps we'll follow to arrive at our goal:

1. Go to the **Filters | Equal | Decade** filter and drag it to the **Queries** window. You should be familiar with this process from *Chapter 5*, *Working with Filters*.

2. Enter the value 1980s and run the **Select** and **Filter** processes using the appropriate buttons. This will take our graph to an intermediate stage where only nodes that correspond to the 1980s decade value will be displayed, as shown in the following screenshot:

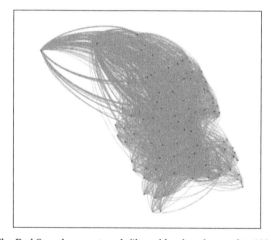

The Red Sox player network filtered by decade equal to 1980s

3. Use the **Rectangle selection** tool from the workspace toolbar—it's represented by a dotted rectangle icon—to select all the nodes displayed on the graph. By the way, this selection will also limit the visible nodes in the data laboratory, allowing you to calculate new statistics or other actions only on the chosen nodes.

4. Recolor these nodes using the **Reset colors** icon on the toolbar.

5. Increase the node size using the **Reset size** icon on the same toolbar — a value of 10 should be sufficient. This results in the following output:

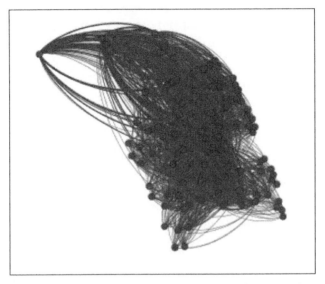

The Red Sox player network filtered and colored using decade equal to 1980s

6. Remove the filter, and then open the graph in the **Preview** window to see the final result; make sure the edges color is set to use the source value:

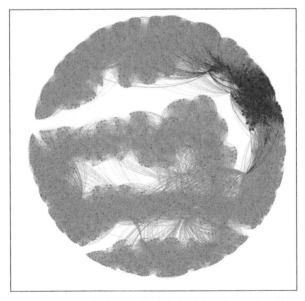

The complete graph showing highlighted decade equal to 1980s

We now have a graph that begins to tell a story by drawing immediate visual attention to the items of interest.

We have just highlighted a few powerful methods to partition or otherwise visually segment a graph using existing or calculated data values. It's now time to take a look at another approach, wherein various Gephi plugins work to create clusters derived from the intersections of these variables and their values. The next few sections will examine some clustering approaches and the visual results they yield.

Using the Chinese Whispers plugin

The Chinese Whispers plugin is an easy-to-use tool that creates distinct clusters from the values in our network dataset. Several options are provided that will affect the outcome of the algorithm and the resulting cluster structure. In this section, we'll first examine the available options and then work with our familiar Red Sox player network to show how the results differ depending on the settings chosen. You'll find the Chinese Whispers plugin on the **Clustering** tab.

Let's start by examining the available options, as shown in the screenshot:

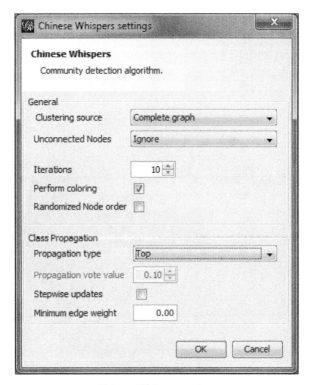

Chinese Whispers options

Starting from the top, here are the choices:

- For the clustering source, either a **Complete graph** or **Visible graph** setting can be selected. These are somewhat self-explanatory, based on whether any filters are being applied to limit the visible portion of the network.

- We can choose how to treat unconnected nodes in the case where there are multiple graph components.

- The number of iterations can be adjusted in an effort to increase accuracy. Coloring and node order options are also available.

- Four propagation options exist — **Top**, **Distance**, **Log Distance**, and **Vote**. We'll examine how they differ using the example illustrations.

- We can also select a minimum edge weight and stepwise updates.

My recommendation is to play with these settings on your own graphs to better understand the impact of each selection. We'll vary a few of these settings in the following examples to help you gain a feel of their application. Changing the propagation setting is the primary means for returning different results, so that's what we'll play with in the following example.

Now let's return to our base graph, with all nodes treated equally. This will give us a clean slate to start applying the clustering. For our first example, we'll use the complete graph with 10 iterations and a **Top** propagation type. We'll have the algorithm performing the coloring as well, since that will save us a step. Here's our result:

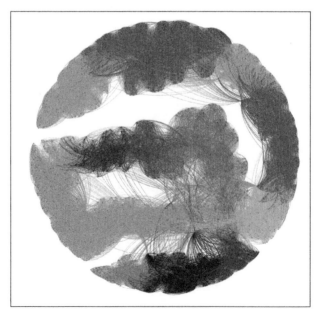

Chinese Whispers using top propagation

These settings segmented the graph into 14 distinct clusters, colored accordingly. The **Top** method creates clusters based on a summation of neighborhood patterns. It would be interesting to see how closely these clusters correlate with the **Decade** variable, as they appear to follow a roughly similar pattern.

Now let's apply the **Distance** setting for the propagation type, and see how our graph differs:

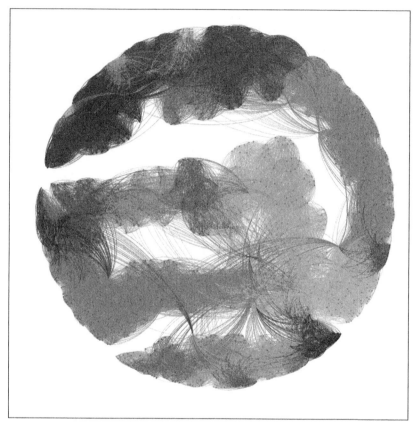

Chinese Whispers using distance propagation

Now instead of 14 clusters, we have 42; a significant increase that might deliver a higher degree of precision for this particular network. Individual clusters range in size from just 7 nodes all the way to 104 members. The distance setting differs from the top method by looking at individual neighbors and reducing their level of influence. In this case, it feels as though the algorithm might be detecting relationships (players who played together) at a more granular-level as opposed to the broad neighborhood-based patterns of the first approach.

What if we use the **Log Distance** option? Interestingly, this returns us much closer to the first instance, as we now have 17 clusters to work with, ranging in size from 15 to 214 members. This makes sense considering that taking a log of individual distances will minimize the extreme influence of specific nodes in the network. Here's what our graph looks like using the log distance:

Chinese Whispers using log distance propagation

A cursory examination reveals that the clustering patterns for the **Log Distance** option resemble those from our initial top propagation.

The fourth and final method uses the **Vote** method, which works the same as the top approach with the exception of the use of a numerical parameter for creating class changes. In this case, setting the propagation vote value to `0.01` yields a 14 cluster result, just as we previously saw with the **Top** method. If we increase this value to `0.02`, the resulting graph still has 14 clusters, but at `0.03`, the number of clusters is reduced to just 7. At values between 0.02 and 0.03, the number of clusters will range between 7 and 14, contingent of the specific value.

If you have been following along with these examples, or using your own data in a similar fashion, you will have noticed the speed of the Chinese Whispers process. This encourages us to test and tinker with the settings to customize the number and size of clusters identified in the network.

Remember that the end goal of using a clustering approach such as Chinese Whispers is to better understand patterns and relationships within your network. For the Red Sox network we just used, each setting provided significantly different results in the number and size of clusters. There is no absolute right or wrong answer in this case — you should take a closer look at your network structure before determining which settings provided the most satisfactory results. In the above examples, I would perhaps stick to the lower-end of the cluster scale, as shown by the first and last examples (14 and 17 clusters, respectively), as the 42 clusters might be over-segmenting the network and separating nodes that should remain together.

We'll now examine an alternative clustering approach using the Markov Clustering plugin.

Using the Markov Clustering plugin

Another clustering option is found in the **Markov Clustering** plugin, which differs in approach from Chinese Whispers, but should yield generally similar results. We'll walk through a similar process to illustrate how to use this method. We're going to return to the primary school network for this example, as the Gephi version of this algorithm seems most effective with relatively smaller datasets, at least working with the moderate CPU and memory settings on my personal machine.

To start, select the **Markov Clustering** option from the **Clustering** tab, and click on **Settings** to see the default screen:

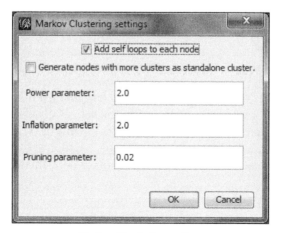

Markov Clustering options

We'll start with the default settings and then customize them to see the difference in our graph results. Here's what the defaults yield, with the edges removed from view for better visibility:

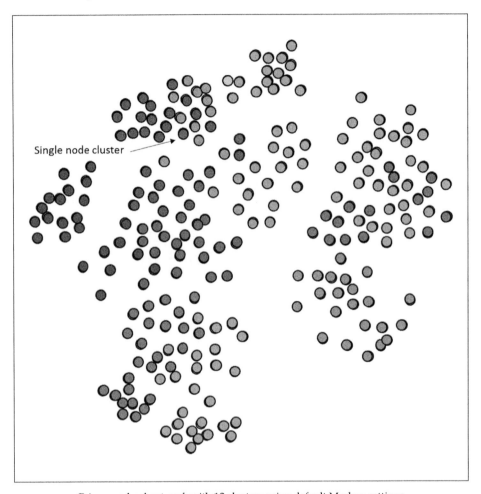

Single node cluster

Primary school network with 12 clusters using default Markov settings

No great surprises here, as the 12 generated clusters line up reasonably well with node placement on the graph, suggesting that the school classes are highly predictive of cluster structures. There are a few spots where we might be able to improve results, such as the upper-right area which shows considerable overlap between two clusters. Note that we also have a single node cluster near the top of the graph.

Now let's adjust the settings to increase or decrease the number of clusters. There are a few ways we can achieve this goal:

1. Raise or lower **Power parameter**
2. Raise or lower **Inflation parameter**
3. Adjust **Pruning parameter** to be more or less selective in determining clusters

Lowering the **Power** and/or **Inflation** parameters will yield a higher number of clusters, assuming the pruning level is left untouched. Let's start there, by changing each value from 2.0 to 1.8, while leaving the pruning parameter at 0.02. Our new graph looks a bit different, with 18 clusters, versus the 12 we had a moment ago:

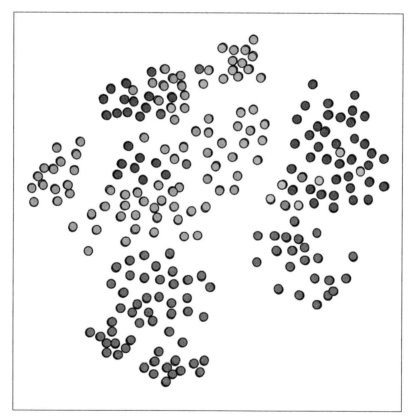

Primary school network with 18 clusters using reduced power and inflation values

If you recall the graph results from our original example, you might remember that the graph had only a single cluster with just one member. In our new graph, there are five cases with a single node. Perhaps this is representative in some fashion, but it feels as though we have possibly gone too far in segmenting the graph. Let's see what happens when both the power and inflation parameters are returned to the original level while the pruning parameter is lowered to 0.015. This should result in slightly larger groups, thus decreasing the number of clusters.

Our network now has just seven clusters using this approach—we have made it easier for nodes to join existing clusters:

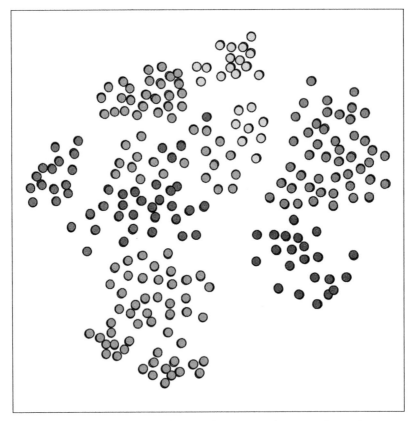

Primary school network with seven clusters using lower pruning setting

Our smallest cluster is now composed of 22 nodes, a far cry from the single member present earlier. We might have gone too far in the opposite direction, although the graph results display minimal overlap between clusters, generally a good indicator. Let's make one more attempt, this time setting the pruning parameter to 0.175, splitting the difference between our original and revised levels.

As anticipated, our new graph has fallen between the 7 and 12 cluster graphs, yielding nine distinct clusters in this case. What is most interesting is the return of a single cluster with just one member, providing a good illustration for just how sensitive the network can be to small parameter adjustments.

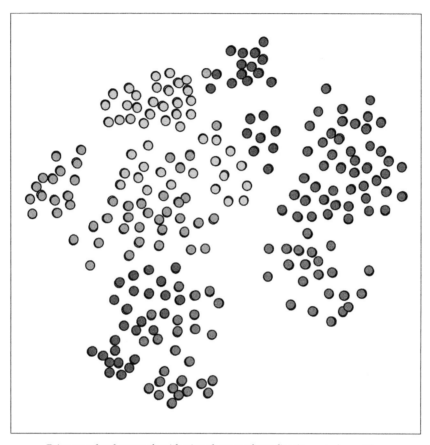

Primary school network with nine clusters after adjusting pruning setting

The Markov Clustering method is another useful tool for understanding network behavior using a clustering approach. I recommend you to adjust the settings and test results on each network you analyze, as opposed to simply relying on the default settings. Trust your eyes when comparing any clustering or partitioning results, and adjust the settings until you see something that makes visual sense.

Summary

In this chapter, you witnessed a variety of approaches that will help you to tell better stories using Gephi and network graphs. Here's a brief recap of the five approaches we examined.

We began with partitioning, and learned how to use both existing data attributes as well as calculated values. Our next step was to illustrate the use of ranking in sizing and coloring graphs for visual impact.

Manual editing of graphs was also explained, where we used filtering to make this process both more effective and efficient to highlight portions of a graph.

The Chinese Whispers plugin was used in a series of examples to illustrate the power of applying clustering methods to a graph.

We concluded with a series of illustrations using the Markov Clustering method and learned how to adjust settings to improve our graph output.

In our next chapter, *Chapter 8, Dynamic Networks*, we'll begin to look at how to create time-based visualizations using Gephi. We'll also learn how to create time intervals and use existing ones to create dynamic network graphs, and begin to understand how to implement individual node and edge values that change over time.

8
Dynamic Networks

Dynamic Network Analysis (DNA), is an emergent field within the larger area of network analysis. At its simplest level, DNA adds a time element to the usual network structure, facilitating temporal analysis of the data.

There are many potential variables introduced when we add a time element to the network. Relationships between network nodes may strengthen, weaken, or even disappear as time unfolds. We may also witness physical movements in the network, the entry of new members, or the removal of existing nodes for a variety of reasons. In short, the network becomes increasingly complex.

What we can deduce from the preceding definition is that dynamic networks afford the possibility for greater exploration compared to traditional networks. We can see how networks are likely to evolve, witness the appearance and disappearance of links, and understand how a network changes (or is likely to change) over time. Here's what we'll cover in this chapter:

- When to use DNA
- The process of preparing data for DNA analysis in Gephi
- How to implement and view graphs within Gephi
- How to create GEXF files outside of Gephi

Let's begin by discussing when we should use dynamic network analysis.

When to use DNA

There are a host of potential applications for DNA, including the following:

- Social media analysis, where friends and contacts are frequently changing

- Communication networks, such as corporate e-mail systems, where evolving patterns emerge over the course of days and weeks

- Political networks that change over time as entities gain or lose power

- Terrorist cells with frequent changes in structure driven by increasing membership and evolving network connections

- Disease modeling, where contagion rates can force rapid changes in the status of nodes within a network

In short, any network with relatively frequent changes over time will be a good candidate for DNA. Networks with infrequent or very slow changes (perhaps tenured faculty at a university or power grid infrastructure networks, to name just two examples) are often adequately addressed by static networks, as temporal analysis adds complexity while shedding little additional insight into network behavior.

There are two distinct types of DNA that can be created, as described here:

- A dynamic topological network, where member nodes can change positions, and appear or disappear at specific time intervals. This approach can be used to observe network growth achieved via new entrants, and to witness changes in structure due to movements within the network. If your wish is to see changes to an overall network, this is probably the direction to pursue.

- A network with dynamic attributes is different, with the focus being on changes to the nodes themselves, rather than the structure of the network. In this case we might observe the degree of growth of specific nodes across multiple time intervals. This approach is somewhat more challenging to implement, as it involves repeating each node at multiple stages rather than the customary single instance, which will require your source data to have a somewhat different structure. We'll take a look at how to do this later in the chapter.

It is important to note that the two types highlighted above are not mutually exclusive. They can be combined to detail the evolution of complex network behaviors where nodes and relationships emerge and vanish, but also change in stature over time.

Our first look will be focused on the processes needed to create common topology-based examples of dynamic network analysis. Later in the chapter, we'll take a similar walk to develop and create projects for attribute-based DNA.

Topology-based DNA

Let's begin our exploration with the dynamic topology approach, using the following as our guidelines. We'll begin with an example instance before moving on to creating our own working examples using a few simple steps:

1. We'll start by exploring the concept of DNA using the graph generators familiarized in *Chapter 4, Network Patterns*. We'll begin with the dynamic graph example, which will be used to illustrate a very simple example of a dynamic network.

2. Next, we'll start preparing the data for use in a DNA project, which will allow us to leverage Gephi's built-in capabilities to create time intervals that facilitate dynamic networks.

3. Then we'll move on to the process of implementing, and ultimately working with, a dynamic network analysis example in Gephi.

4. Finally, we'll end the section with a discussion on what we learned from our example and how we might apply this process to other network datasets.

So without further delay, let's look at a very basic example of DNA as provided using the dynamic graph example from the generators menu.

Generating a dynamic network

To begin this process, navigate to **File | Generate | Dynamic Graph Example** from the Gephi menu system. Selecting this option will create a network with 50 nodes and somewhere upwards of 50 edges (this will vary somewhat randomly). In your workspace, you should see something simple along these lines:

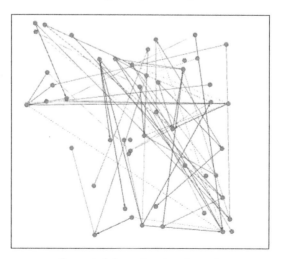

Generated dynamic network graph

This particular graph has 50 nodes and 64 edges, a small, sparse network that will nonetheless illustrate a simple instance of DNA quite effectively. At first glance, this looks like any other network we might see in Gephi, but there is something hidden in the data that is not present in the static graphs. For a quick illustration of how the data differs, take a look at the **Nodes** tab in the **Data Laboratory** window:

Label	score	Time Interval
n0	<[2003.0, 2012.0, 2]; [2013.0, 2019.0, 1]>	<[2003.0, 2032.0]>
n1	<[2003.0, 2012.0, 1]; [2013.0, 2015.0, 0]>	<[2003.0, 2024.0]>
n2	<[2000.0, 2008.0, 1]; [2009.0, 2010.0, 4]>	<[2000.0, 2024.0]>
n3	<[2007.0, 2012.0, 2]; [2013.0, 2021.0, 3]>	<[2007.0, 2032.0]>
n4	<[2006.0, 2015.0, 1]; [2016.0, 2016.0, 3]>	<[2006.0, 2026.0]>
n5	<[2003.0, 2004.0, 0]; [2005.0, 2007.0, 2]>	<[2003.0, 2023.0]>
n6	<[2002.0, 2003.0, 2]; [2004.0, 2005.0, 3]>	<[2002.0, 2027.0]>
n7	<[2004.0, 2005.0, 0]; [2006.0, 2010.0, 4]>	<[2004.0, 2024.0]>
n8	<[2003.0, 2011.0, 0]; [2012.0, 2017.0, 4]>	<[2003.0, 2030.0]>
n9	<[2002.0, 2010.0, 1]; [2011.0, 2013.0, 3]>	<[2002.0, 2029.0]>
n10	<[2004.0, 2011.0, 4]; [2012.0, 2013.0, 3]>	<[2004.0, 2030.0]>

Time intervals for dynamic networks in the Nodes tab

Understanding time intervals

Take a look at the **score** and **Time Interval** attributes, where each node has more complex information sets. If you are familiar with XML, or have become acquainted with **GEXF** (a graph-based variant of XML), you will recognize the data layouts for these attributes. If not, don't worry, as it will be quite easy to understand. What we see here is quite basic—starting with a time interval value that shows when each individual node enters or exits the network, say **[2004.0, 2024.0]**. In this example, node **n7** will appear in the graph in 2004 and remain visible through 2024.

The **score** attribute will also change in this case, giving us a preview of dynamic attributes, which will be covered in greater detail later in the chapter. For node **n7**, we see the values **[2004.0, 2005.0, 0]; [2006.0, 2010.0, 4]**, which translates to a score of **0** in the period between 2004 and 2005, followed by a score of **4** for 2006 through 2010. No information is provided for the years through 2024 in this case, although that could also be added.

Now take a look at the **Edges** tab, specifically the **Weight** attribute in the following screenshot. Notice the higher level of complexity here, as the relationships between nodes change over time, alternately strengthening or weakening of their respective connections.

Weight
<[2010.0, 2012.0, 1.0); [2012.0, 2014.0, 2.0); [2014.0, 2016.0, 3.0); [2016.0, 2018.0, 5.0); [2018.0, 2020.0, 5.0); [2020.0, 2022.0, 6.0); ...
<[2010.0, 2012.0, 3.0); [2012.0, 2014.0, 3.0); [2014.0, 2016.0, 4.0); [2016.0, 2018.0, 4.0); [2018.0, 2020.0, 5.0); [2020.0, 2022.0, 6.0); ...
<[2010.0, 2012.0, 1.0); [2012.0, 2014.0, 3.0); [2014.0, 2016.0, 3.0); [2016.0, 2018.0, 6.0); [2018.0, 2020.0, 7.0); [2020.0, 2022.0, 8.0); ...
<[2010.0, 2012.0, 1.0); [2012.0, 2014.0, 4.0); [2014.0, 2016.0, 5.0); [2016.0, 2018.0, 6.0); [2018.0, 2020.0, 7.0); [2020.0, 2022.0, 7.0); ...
<[2010.0, 2012.0, 1.0); [2012.0, 2014.0, 3.0); [2014.0, 2016.0, 4.0); [2016.0, 2018.0, 4.0); [2018.0, 2020.0, 5.0); [2020.0, 2022.0, 6.0); ...
<[2010.0, 2012.0, 1.0); [2012.0, 2014.0, 4.0); [2014.0, 2016.0, 3.0); [2016.0, 2018.0, 6.0); [2018.0, 2020.0, 5.0); [2020.0, 2022.0, 8.0); ...
<[2010.0, 2012.0, 1.0); [2012.0, 2014.0, 4.0); [2014.0, 2016.0, 3.0); [2016.0, 2018.0, 6.0); [2018.0, 2020.0, 7.0); [2020.0, 2022.0, 6.0); ...
<[2010.0, 2012.0, 2.0); [2012.0, 2014.0, 2.0); [2014.0, 2016.0, 5.0); [2016.0, 2018.0, 6.0); [2018.0, 2020.0, 6.0); [2020.0, 2022.0, 7.0); ...
<[2010.0, 2012.0, 3.0); [2012.0, 2014.0, 4.0); [2014.0, 2016.0, 4.0); [2016.0, 2018.0, 4.0); [2018.0, 2020.0, 6.0); [2020.0, 2022.0, 8.0); ...
<[2010.0, 2012.0, 3.0); [2012.0, 2014.0, 3.0); [2014.0, 2016.0, 5.0); [2016.0, 2018.0, 5.0); [2018.0, 2020.0, 7.0); [2020.0, 2022.0, 7.0); ...
<[2010.0, 2012.0, 1.0); [2012.0, 2014.0, 2.0); [2014.0, 2016.0, 3.0); [2016.0, 2018.0, 6.0); [2018.0, 2020.0, 6.0); [2020.0, 2022.0, 6.0); ...
<[2010.0, 2012.0, 1.0); [2012.0, 2014.0, 2.0); [2014.0, 2016.0, 5.0); [2016.0, 2018.0, 4.0); [2018.0, 2020.0, 6.0); [2020.0, 2022.0, 7.0); ...

Time intervals across edge weights

Note that the time intervals use both brackets and parentheses for parsing the data. Each interval begins with a bracket, and all end with a closing parenthesis—except for the final interval, which uses a closing bracket to signify the end of the data for a given row.

Now that the data is at least somewhat familiar, it's time to see how this extends to the network graph visualization, using a timeline. This is the key Gephi option for viewing dynamic networks, one which we'll spend more time on in a moment. For now, recognize that the timeline will use our time interval data to build a dynamic network.

Working with timelines

Open the timeline by selecting it in your **Overview** window (it's found at the bottom of the window). You'll see a timeline extending from the start point of 2000 all the way out to about 2037. In its default mode, the entire graph will be displayed. To see how this works, grab the right edge of the timeline and drag it to 2005, and see how the results reflect only those nodes present in the network at that time:

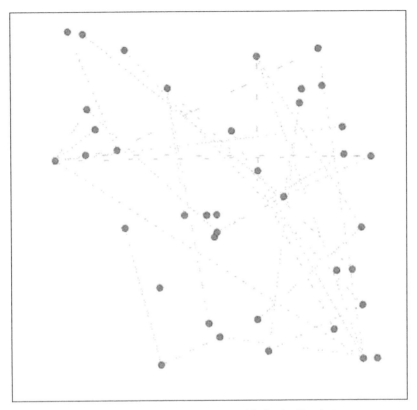

Viewing a network at a point in time with the timeline feature

Now drag the right edge as far to the left as possible, so your entire network is reduced to just those nodes present at the start of the network period. This should leave you with just 6 nodes out of the original 50. Next, click on the large arrow to the left of the timeline to see how the network evolves over the nearly 40-year period. What do we see? Nodes enter the network, connections are formed, nodes leave, connections are broken, and we wind up with just a handful of surviving members in the final years.

If you find the graph changing too rapidly (or too slowly), click on the icon at the bottom-left corner of the timeline, pick the **Set play settings** option, and change the values using the ensuing dialog screen.

While you might find the dynamic graph example to be less than realistic in its depiction of the way most networks behave, it nevertheless provides a useful foundation for our own explorations. To create our own more sophisticated examples, we can follow a series of steps that result in a final graph that can tell a compelling story.

Preparing and importing data for DNA

One essential ingredient for a dynamic network analysis is to have some sort of attribute or attributes that describe one or more units of time. These fields can be in the form of integers, dates, or timestamps, and should correspond with the events in the network at a node level. Here are just a few ideas for what could be represented by one or more of these fields:

- A birth date
- A deceased date
- Date of entry into a network
- Date of removal from a network
- Timestamp of a Twitter tweet

You probably get the idea — virtually any sort of time-related event can be included in a network dataset to help describe specific events, relationships, network entry or exit, network growth, and so on. In cases where networks are fluid, it is very helpful to have attributes representing both start and end points of key behaviors. In the case of dynamic attributes, we will also perhaps want to include some information that reflects changes in stature at a node or edge level.

You needn't worry about merging the data beforehand (although you could use a GEFX format prior to importing to Gephi; more on GEFX later in the chapter), as Gephi makes it very simple to merge individual fields into a time range (start date and end date for example) that can be used to view changes in the network over a span of time. It would be a good idea to populate your network with as many time elements as possible, giving yourself the opportunity to view multiple scenarios in Gephi before deciding which one tells the most compelling story.

Think carefully about what you would like to see in your network graph, as this can save considerable time spent iterating through multiple data pulls. Once you have settled on your general goal for the visualization, there are a few simple guidelines that can make the process as straightforward as possible, especially if the data source is a .csv or other generic file format:

- Make sure your node's file is recognizable when you import it into Gephi. This applies to static as well as dynamic network projects. A critical part of this process is to correctly identify the data type for each attribute. In many instances, Gephi might assume that your data is a string type, even when it actually represents numerical values. Rectifying field types after the import is possible, but it is much more easily done at the outset.

- Your edges table must have source and target values, even when importing an undirected network. Most networks will also benefit with the edge weight values in the data source file.

- If you have multiple node attributes beyond the standard label and ID fields, be sure to import the nodes table before you load an edges table. Otherwise, Gephi will automatically create a nodes table based on the edges data, which will make it very difficult to update your nodes table. Nodes first, edges second.

- Assuming you plan to create time intervals for a DNA (you should be if you are reading this chapter!), be sure to have start and stop points that can be used to build these intervals. Depending on the network you are working with, it is possible to have an open-ended graph, in which case only a start date is required. However, for most networks you will want to have nodes appear and disappear as the graph evolves, so multiple dates are a general requirement.

- Dates can be provided in both a date format that resides in one or more fields in your source data, or they can be manually entered as a calendar date or timestamp when you import timeframes.

We'll see how this all works in a moment as we begin importing files to create our own dynamic networks. Let's begin by taking a look at how to create time intervals using existing attributes, putting into practice some powerful Gephi capabilities.

Implementing and viewing a dynamic network

We're going to use the Red Sox player network familiar to you from *Chapter 7, Segmenting and Partitioning a Graph*, to illustrate some basic yet powerful capabilities within Gephi. The data can be found at `https://app.box.com/s/177yit0fdovz1czgcecp`.

Our first section will work with Gephi timelines to display changes in a network.

> Note that you will always require a starting point to enable a timeline, while the end point is not required, although it can add significant value to a graph when available.

We'll look at two different ways to make our network dynamic:

- First, from an existing project within Gephi. In other words, we don't need to alert Gephi to the fact that our network has dynamic fields when we initially import the data. All it takes is a few simple steps to convert either date or integer values to time intervals that communicate when nodes are added or removed from the network.

- Second, when we are creating a new project, Gephi provides an option to identify time interval values. If we know from the start that certain attributes will be used for dynamic graphs, this option allows a single process to get the job done.

In either case, our dataset has two fields that will serve as both a starting point and an end point in the following examples. The first, **birthYear**, represents the calendar year in which an individual was born. Our second field is titled **deathYear**, and tells us the year a player died, with a null value for those individuals still living.

We'll begin with the existing project approach, followed by a walk through the new project steps.

Creating time intervals in an existing project

Adding time intervals to an existing Gephi project is quite simple, provided your dataset already has some date or integer values (months or years, for example) you wish to utilize. We're going to walk through a simple case where we use the **birthYear** and **deathYear** attributes to create a time interval attribute.

Here are the simple steps to create an interval from the two existing data fields:

1. Navigate to the **Data Laboratory** window.

2. Select the **Merge Columns** icon at the bottom of the window. This will open a dialog box similar to this:

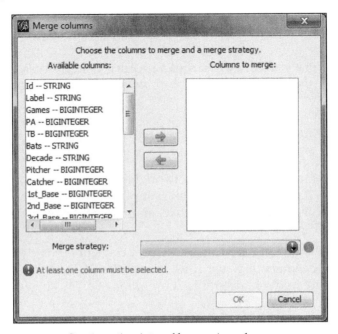

Creating a time interval by merging columns

3. Choose the appropriate fields to merge—in this case **birthYear** and **deathYear** are the two attributes we wish to combine.

4. Next, select the **Create time interval** option from the drop-down menu and click on **OK**.

5. Now you should see a window similar to this one:

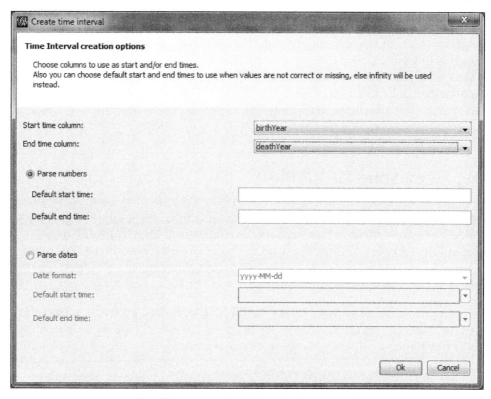

Specifying start and end times for time intervals

6. Specify your start and ending time fields—in this case **birthYear** and then **deathYear**, and allow Gephi to use the **Parse numbers** option. Alternatively, you could specify your start and end times, assuming you are familiar with the dataset. This will allow you to set start and end times that could extend beyond the actual time values, which will act as a bit of a fade-in and fade-out for the timeline; Or the interval could be set to start at a midpoint relative to the time values, enabling you to manipulate the number of nodes shown at the start of the timeline process. That's it—you now have a time interval attribute to perform temporal analysis on your network.

This process has put us in position to begin using timelines that power all dynamic networks in Gephi. So at this stage, you are poised to create and view a dynamic network. We'll resume from this point in a few moments, after we have examined some other approaches to move dynamic network data into Gephi. For our next case, we'll assume that you're working with a new project, and would like to specify some time-based attributes from the start.

Adding time intervals to a new project

There are a couple of ways to incorporate time intervals in a new project. The first approach is to have a GEXF file that already has the presence of time intervals — we'll take a look at how to create simple GEXF files later in the chapter. For now, our approach will be to use an already existing one created in Gephi. The second option is to import a series of static network files that can be identified as timeframes, enabling Gephi to recognize time intervals and act accordingly. We'll look at that process as well.

Using an existing GEXF file

We'll begin with the GEXF option, which involves the import of a single file that is already designed with time intervals. For this example, we'll take the previously used Red Sox player file and save it as a GEXF file, using the **Graph file** menu located at **File | Export**, and then select the .gexf option from the list. We now have a file titled redsox_timeline.gexf that can be loaded into Gephi to illustrate the process.

We're going to start a new project with the GEXF file. Proceed to the **Open** menu under **File**, and filter on GEXF files if needed until the correct file is located. We'll open the file, which loads the following dialog screen:

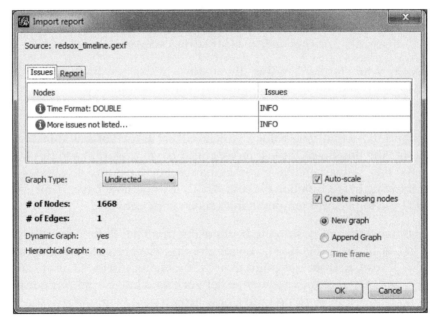

Importing a dynamic network

Notice that Gephi has already identified the presence of a time format while recognizing this is a dynamic network. This will be the case for any GEXF files that include time intervals. We can now begin working with the file using all of the available Gephi tools such as partitioning, clustering, filtering, and so on, and we will also have an immediately available timeline. All we have to do is enable the timeline, just as we did in the dynamic graph example shared earlier in this chapter.

Now that we have seen how easy it is to add time intervals in Gephi, it's time to begin working with them to tell a story. We'll pick up with the existing open project and our already created time interval.

Adding multiple timeframes

The second option is to layer a series of static networks as timeframes for Gephi to create a dynamic network. Suppose in our case that we have various snapshots of the baseball player file we have been using, taken at specific points in time. In this instance, we'll work with a series of three files, titled redsox1.gexf, redsox2.gexf, and redsox3.gexf. We could also follow this process using .csv or other file formats.

Let's start the process by opening the first of these three files. By navigating to the **File | Open** menu, we'll locate the redsox1.gexf file and begin the process. Notice how Gephi handles this static file differently than our prior dynamic file:

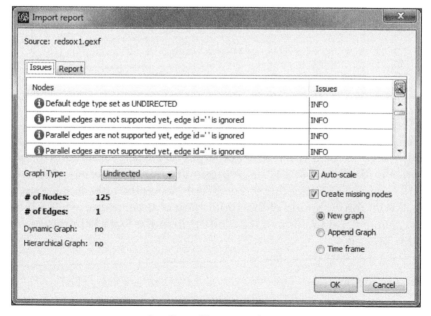

Loading a file as a timeframe

The file is correctly recognized as not dynamic since there is not yet a time interval attribute. Notice also that we have three options at the lower-right of the screen— **New graph, Append Graph,** and **Time frame**. In a nondynamic situation, we would typically proceed with the **New graph** selection, but for dynamic networks we choose the **Time frame** radio button. This selection gives us the ability to convert static files to a file with time intervals that can subsequently be viewed using the timeline feature. After completing this process, a second dialog is presented, which looks like this:

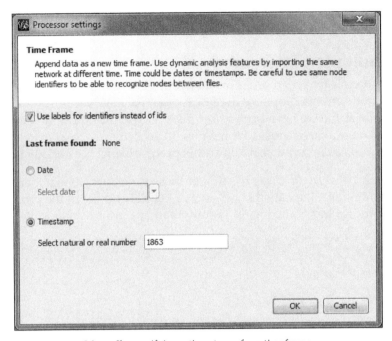

Manually specifying a timestamp for a timeframe

This will help Gephi to orient the timeline based on the underlying time intervals. In this case, I have selected the **Timestamp** option (the screen defaults to the **Date** option) and specified the year 1863 to represent the starting point for this layer of the network. After completing this screen, Gephi loads the data as with any other new project, with the exception of the application of time intervals to each of the data fields. A quick examination of the **Nodes** tab in the **Data Laboratory** window confirms this process.

The process is then repeated for the second and third files, identifying each as a timeframe, and adjusting the timestamp accordingly. Each subsequent timestamp must be higher than the existing values; for this example, I simply entered `1873` and `1883` for the second and third files, although we could certainly be more precise depending on our underlying data. You might have noticed after importing the second timeframe that the timeline became available, as Gephi now recognizes the presence of time intervals across multiple timeframes. After the final layer is loaded, we can enable the timeline and proceed as in our previous examples.

What we've done here is to build a timeline that starts at 1863 and ends at 1883, and displays the network members relative to those time parameters. In this example, the first file had only players who began their Red Sox career from 1900 to 1909, the second has those from 1910 to 1919, and the third file covers 1920 through 1929. So we are layering their birth year with the start of their individual playing careers, which tells Gephi how to visualize each node throughout the timeline. Some nodes will be present at the start of the graph before disappearing, while others enter the network at later intervals. Here is a glimpse of our data in the **Data Laboratory** window:

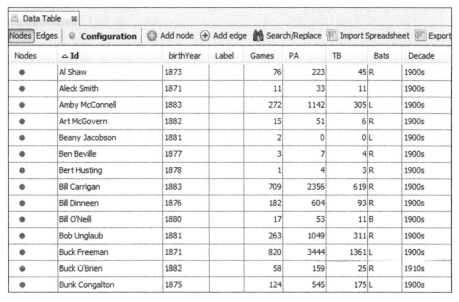

Nodes	△ Id	birthYear	Label	Games	PA	TB	Bats	Decade
✱	Al Shaw	1873		76	223	45	R	1900s
✱	Aleck Smith	1871		11	33	11		1900s
✱	Amby McConnell	1883		272	1142	305	L	1900s
✱	Art McGovern	1882		15	51	6	R	1900s
✱	Beany Jacobson	1881		2	0	0	L	1900s
✱	Ben Beville	1877		3	7	4	R	1900s
✱	Bert Husting	1878		1	4	3	R	1900s
✱	Bill Carrigan	1883		709	2356	619	R	1900s
✱	Bill Dinneen	1876		182	604	93	R	1900s
✱	Bill O'Neill	1880		17	53	11	B	1900s
✱	Bob Unglaub	1881		263	1049	311	R	1900s
✱	Buck Freeman	1871		820	3444	1361	L	1900s
✱	Buck O'Brien	1882		58	159	25	R	1910s
✱	Bunk Congalton	1875		124	545	175	L	1900s

Data Laboratory view with timeline set to 1863 through 1883

Working with timelines

Now that we have seen a couple of examples that incorporated timelines, let's have a more focused discussion for how and why we should use them. Timelines are an ideal way to view changes in the structure of a network, based on the time-based entry or exit of members from a network. There are multiple potential uses of timelines, including the following:

- Timelines help to understand the rate at which nodes enter or exit a network. We can thus address questions about how a network evolved, and whether it continues to grow or is deteriorating. Note that you can also run force-directed layouts while the animated graph is playing.

- A timeline can also help us to identify larger patterns, especially when used in conjunction with a layout algorithm or clustering method applied to the network. This gives us the ability to see if new entrants into the network are linked based on their entry time, or whether they disperse across the graph.

- We can also make judgments about how nodes eventually leave a network, and whether this happens in individual or group fashion—do we see entire clusters defecting from the network at a given point in time?

- Finally, timelines can be used as a filter that allows us to quickly investigate portions of the network using time as a driver of network growth or contraction. As we'll see in a moment, timelines cleverly use Gephi's capable filtering and query windows to restrict the graph display to the selected interval.

Consider some of the types of data that might be abetted by the use of timelines—disease contagion networks, Twitter tweet dispersion, retail shopping patterns, and transportation networks, to name but a few. The list of potential applications is virtually unlimited, as you can undoubtedly come up with many more instances where timelines add to the richness of the network analysis.

Another critical factor for the adoption of timelines lies in their intuitive nature. Just as maps make it much easier to understand geographic patterns, timelines convey a similar sense through the simple left to right time flow. For most cultures, this is consistent with the general concept of time movement and facilitates an easy understanding of the evolution of the network.

Now that we have established some of the potential uses and strengths of timelines, let's create one of our own using the previously created time interval. We'll examine some further uses for the timeline as we proceed through the next section.

Applying the timeline

Working with timelines in Gephi is very straightforward, as we'll demonstrate in this section. To launch the timeline (if it isn't already visible), simply click on the **Timeline** menu offering under **Window**. This will load a timeline bar at the bottom of the screen, viewable in all of the primary work areas. You will see text that states **Enable Timeline**, accompanied by a plus sign. Click on the underlying button, and your previously created timeline will appear, showing the full range of values from 1863 through 2013.

By default, the timeline opens with all values populated, which means you should see a full graph if you are in the **Preview** window. We'll now work through some quick examples for how to use the timeline to scroll through the graph programmatically and then see how it can be used for some quick filtering.

For our first example, grab the right edge of the timeline using your mouse and drag it as far to the left as possible. This will bring your entire timeline back to the earliest starting values and will leave you with a virtually empty graph. This also sets us up to watch how the network evolves, which we'll do by clicking on the arrow button to the left of the timeline. Click on the arrow and watch our graph change through time, growing as players are born across the years, while also losing members as they die. You can see the entire evolution of the network in a few short seconds.

As you might have anticipated, the network was at its peak somewhere in the mid to late ranges between 1863 and 2013, as the growth in the number of new players being born far exceeded the death rate of those leaving the network. As we near the end of the time range, the size of the network diminishes, due to many of the earlier players dying. You can in fact determine the peak period by stopping the timeline at various intervals (click on the arrow key to pause, then again to resume) and viewing the status of the network in the **Context** tab.

Let's look at a few stopping points along the way to see how the timeline can help us assess our network at various intervals, noting that the narrowest interval Gephi allows appears to be in the two-year range for this graph (we'll see how to adjust this manually in the section *Timelines as filters* later in the chapter):

Starting Interval	Nodes	Edges
1875	44	444
1900	412	8,917
1925	735	18,337
1950	909	23,495
1975	1,119	31,210
2000	996	30,763

A quick glance at the table tells us that the network might have peaked in size somewhere near 1975, with more than 1,100 of the total 1,668 nodes present, and over 31,000 of 51,000 edges active. We can become more precise by examining periods on either side of 1975, but this at least provides a general understanding that the network has in fact shrunk and that it likely peaked in or around the 1970s.

Looking at sheer numbers is far from the only pattern we might wish to examine in any network. Viewing the network at specific intervals could also allow us to see critical junctures in either the growth or dissolution of a network. For instance, what happens to the network if a centrally located member (perhaps a hub) leaves the network? Do others follow en masse, or do they reorient themselves to seek out a replacement for the departed member?

In the case of a contagion, viewing the spread of a pathogen might help to inform researchers about the likely path of future diseases, and how changes in a network structure might alter the path, for better or worse. Nodes that are likely to be key transmitters of the disease could potentially be quarantined for a brief period until the threat of contagion passes.

Timelines can also allow us to see the impact of geography or language on the spread of an idea, an invention, a Twitter hashtag, and many more possibilities. For the moment, let's take a look at how timelines double as filters in Gephi, and learn how to take advantage of that functionality.

Timelines as filters

As we noted earlier, timelines invoke the Gephi filtering and querying logic, which then allow us to become more precise with setting filter values. In theory, we could get down to a single date in the evolution of a network, perhaps a single hour if our date format permits. In an instance where the timeline is built on a single Twitter hashtag, the ability to view the growth of a network might need to be viewed in hours or even minutes to be useful.

Using our aforementioned baseball player network, let's examine a few of these cases, and see the potential for creatively using timelines together with additional filtering possibilities. To begin, we're going to view the network for players who were alive between 1925 and 1930 to start understanding other attributes within the dataset. Drag both edges (one at a time) of the timeline to define this period, and notice that the Dynamic Range filter is active in the queries window. Here's a view of those members:

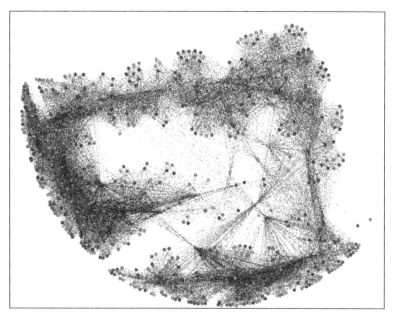

Viewing the player network from 1925-1930

We have 777 members remaining of the 1,668 in our total network. We can now treat our timeline filter just as we would any other filter by adding additional conditions from the filter tab. Now let's assume that we wish to see only those players who started their Red Sox career in the 1950s. To do this, drag an **Equal** filter for the **Decade** attribute down to the **Queries** window (as we learned in *Chapter 5, Working with Filters*) and make it a subfilter of the dynamic range filter already in place. We are now left with just 101 of the 777 nodes.

At this point, we could add further conditions to our filters or even change our timeline settings to view the same conditions for a different time interval, or we could leave things as they are. In either case we should recognize that timelines used as filters provide one more powerful tool for our Gephi toolkit.

Attribute-based DNA

We have explored in detail how to prepare and implement dynamic networks that are topology-based. Now it's time to learn more about implementing attribute-based dynamic networks. We'll begin with a brief review of the fundamental differences between the two, and why we would go to the extra effort of creating dynamic attributes.

As you can recall, in our earlier discussion on topologies we were primarily focused on the changes taking place across and within a network. This included viewing network growth, emerging patterns, changes to the network structure, and perhaps, eventual dissolution of the network. At the risk of oversimplifying, our goal was to understand the collective network, rather than focusing on changes to its individual members.

In contrast, the dynamic attribute approach is heavily oriented toward seeing changes within individual nodes and their relationships to others in the network. To be sure, we can also see some more wholesale changes to the entire network, but the goal is to understand changes at the individual node level. A few of the questions we might ask include:

- When did the node enter the network?
- Did it grow over time, and if so at what rate?
- Was the node a hub through which other nodes connected?
- Did it maintain a relationship with other nodes over a long period, or did it become associated with an entirely different peer group at some point in the network evolution?

With these somewhat different facets to focus on, our approach to create and prepare the network dataset will differ slightly. The general concept is identical, but we need be certain about what we are seeking to understand, with respect to the node behavior.

Preparing the data

We previously walked through how to prepare the data for a dynamic network based on topological changes. Let's follow a similar process for dynamic attribute analysis, making adjustments where needed.

Rather than merely focusing on specific dates where changes occur, we are now highly interested in the level of change; in other words, when Node A changed status at Time B, how significant was the change? To do this, our dataset will require measurable fields such as scores, weights, degrees, or some other quantifiable value that can be shown through color or size changes in Gephi.

These changes will still need to be associated with time intervals in order to create the dynamic network, but our focus has clearly shifted toward viewing individual changes versus network-wide shifts. Consistent with this shift, there are a few considerations to bear in mind when preparing data for an attribute-based dynamic network.

As you might have guessed, if we are to view changes in the structure of network attributes such as nodes and edges, we will need to be certain that our source data has the necessary elements. Now, in addition to the still critical time values, we will want to add other values that are essential to reflect the changing nature of the network. A few possible time-based values to think about include:

- Values that reflect changes in the stature of individual nodes. These could be in the form of weights, sizes, dollar values, populations, or any of hundreds of other measurable values that could be found in a network. These values are most often displayed through changes in the size of nodes, but could also be used to show color changes.

- Values that affect the status (as opposed to stature) of a node can be effectively used in a dynamic network analysis. These might reflect shifts from one category to another, or could also be used to reflect the relative level of some measurable value, perhaps on a 0-100 scale. These types of values will frequently be seen through changes in color.

- Dynamic edge weights can also be used effectively to show structural changes within a network over time. Changes to the relationships between individual nodes or node neighborhoods can be more easily detected if edge weights are calibrated to reflect these shifts.

Exactly what these nodes and edges measure is up to you, but you will likely want to use variables that show enough relative change that can be viewed within the graph.

Implementing and viewing dynamic attribute networks

Given the higher degree of focus on the behavior of individual nodes within a network, we're going to spend some time on a variety of techniques that will highlight changes at the node and edge levels. Much of this will involve using color and size as measures of change, both positive and negative.

So let's begin with nodes, as they will often show changes that are easier to detect when first viewing a dynamic network. We'll walk through a couple of examples— one dealing with changes in size, as dictated by a measurable attribute of the node, followed by another that uses changes in color intensity to display changes in a second attribute.

Let's return to our Red Sox player network and illustrate how to use dynamic sizes in a simple case where an individual player has a single size value that is combined with the time intervals we saw previously. We'll then move to a more complex example where values change for many of the individual nodes.

For our initial instance, we're going to look at the number of seasons played by each individual who ever suited up for the team. Remember that we still have the time intervals that govern when each node appears and disappears (or not), based on each individual's birth and death years. We are now simply adding a size-based variable based on the number of seasons played. So let's begin.

Make sure you have the Red Sox detail timeline file loaded if you wish to follow along. Once the project is loaded, we're going to follow these steps:

1. Move to the **Ranking** window, and select the **Nodes** tab.
2. Find the **SeasonsInteger** field in the drop-down list. We're going to focus on size rather than color, so make sure you're in the size window.
3. You will notice that the data values range from 1 to 23, based on the number of seasons played. Set the **Min** size value to 2 and the **Max** size value to 50.

 Note that this will overstate the differences in the node size, but for now we want to make sure we are seeing those nodes with higher values.

4. Now click on the very small icon to the left of the **Apply** button. This will enable the **Auto Apply** option, which will ensure that time-based values change at the appropriate time interval. For this example, this will be less critical, but for future cases where a single node might have many values, this is a critical step.

5. Click on the **Auto Apply** button.

6. Drag the timeline to the far left of the window, and make it as small as possible by dragging the right edge until it stops. This will give you a small window of about two years duration.

7. Start the timeline animation by clicking on the large arrow. Here's how your settings should look:

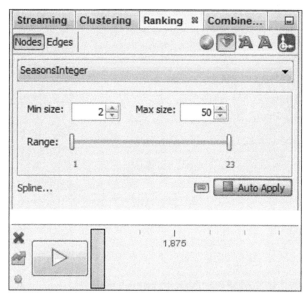

Settings for dynamic network graph example

Now you can watch the dynamic network evolve, seeing both the evolution of the network, as we saw previously, as well as the players who logged many seasons appearing as outsized nodes in the graph. If the network is moving too rapidly for your taste, select the small icon to the left of the timeline arrow and adjust the time settings accordingly.

As we saw earlier, we also have the ability to stop the network animation at any point by clicking a second time on the timeline arrow. We can also take snapshots of the network by manipulating the timeline to include the time interval we desire. Let's have a look at how this works, by dragging the left and right edges to show us the graph from 1920 to 1930. Here's the result:

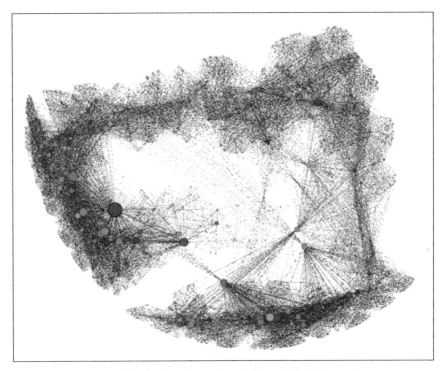

Viewing the player network from 1920-1930

This shows us all the players who were alive in the 1920 to 1930 window, regardless of whether they were retired, active, or future players. We can also see a few prominent nodes who will or already did play many seasons for the team.

If we shift the timeline from 1940 to 1950, the graph grows accordingly, as many of the older players are still alive, and many additional younger players have now been born:

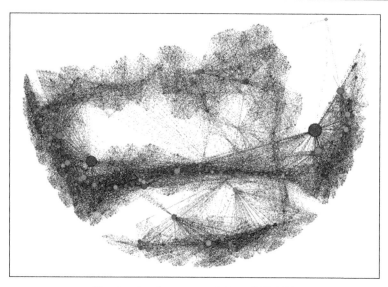

Viewing the player network from 1940-1950

Most of the prior network is still visible, and a sizable section has grown to the right of the earlier graph. In particular, there is a highly visible large hub node present in the new area of the graph. Let's view one more, encompassing from 1970 to 1980, and see the results:

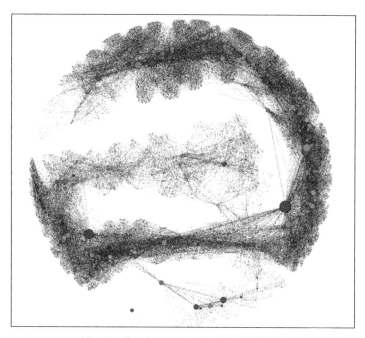

Viewing the player network from 1970-1980

Now the graph has grown to show many more nodes, although a portion of the earlier ones have departed the network. These snapshots show some of the power of using time intervals and the timeline itself, but the real power comes in interacting with the graph in Gephi, exploring, animating, and learning more about your network the entire time.

Once you have this sort of dynamic template set up you can always substitute another variable in place of seasons, as long as it is in the correct numeric format. Then just repeat the above process to see how the new variable changes relative to time.

This was a simple example, in that each node had a static value from the time it entered the network until it is either removed or the timeline simply comes to an end. So we're not completely dynamic yet; for that to happen we need to change the values that correspond with time intervals at the node level. So let's move on to a more complex network, at least from the perspective of changing node values.

Let's look at another example that incorporates changing attribute values across multiple time periods. For this illustration, we're going to use some airline data made available through the US Department of Transportation website at `http://www.rita.dot.gov/bts/sites/rita.dot.gov.bts/files/subject_areas/airline_information/index.html`.

This site plays host to a variety of transportation statistics. What we'll be working with is the data that tabulates travel patterns between US airports by both domestic and international carriers. These files can be very large depending on the data variables you choose to download. For this example, we're going to reduce the data to examine travel patterns originating at a single airport over the course of three calendar months. This will provide us with enough data to make for an interesting graph, but not so much as to lose focus on our goal of showing dynamic attributes. The files are available at `https://app.box.com/s/177yit0fdovz1czgcecp` for you to download if you wish to follow along.

Our goals for the network graph can be summarized as follows:

- We want to be able to understand the general passenger volume patterns flying from our base airport to dozens of destinations
- We would like to see changes by time period in the number of passengers flying to specific destinations
- We would also like to understand how many carriers are flying from the host airport to each destination
- Finally, it would be nice to detect changes in the number of carriers from one time period to the next

The data I've selected for this example is designed to accommodate each of these goals. It is comprised of a single host airport (**Baltimore Washington International (BWI)** in this case) that flies passenger flights to more than 70 domestic locations. This should enable us to fulfill our goal.

The dataset includes three time periods—January, February, and March 2014 calendar months. Thus, we should be able to detect any significant changes in passenger volume by calibrating node sizes to these volumes. This will address our second goal.

If we use the number of carriers to set edge weights (that is, how many airlines fly from BWI to Atlanta) then we should be able to address the third goal as well as the fourth, assuming there are any changes in the number of carriers within this limited timeframe.

The process we will follow is to manipulate the data files to create node and edge files for each of the three time periods, using an identical format in each case. These files can then be processed using Gephi to create three individual timeframes for our eventual dynamic network. So let's begin with the process, starting with the January file. I happened to use Excel for this process, but feel free to use whichever tool you feel comfortable with to create the .csv files.

We'll follow the familiar process for loading these files using the Gephi's capabilities of **Import spreadsheet** found in **Data laboratory**:

1. Import the node file first. This includes fields for `Label`, `ID`, `Passengers`, `Distance`, and `Distance Group`, a categorization used to classify flights by relative distance.

2. Now import the edges table. This will include just three fields—`Source`, `Target`, and `Weight`, which is based on the number of carriers flying a route, as discussed a moment ago.

3. Go to the **Overview** window and select a layout. For this example, the **Layered** layout seems appropriate, using the Distance Category (1-5) to construct an easy-to-understand network structure. Apply this layout.

4. Size your nodes in the **Ranking** tab, using **Passengers** as the attribute value. Adjust the scaling accordingly—I reduced the upper bound so the overall volume associated with the host airport doesn't affect the sizes of the destination airport nodes.

When you've completed each of these steps, your graph should resemble this:

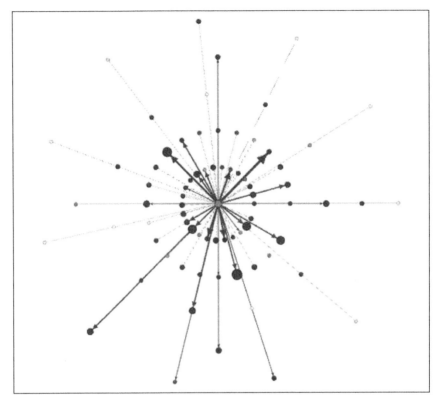

First look at an airline destination network

We can see BWI in the center, surrounded by concentric rings based on the relative distances from the host airport—those with a distance category of 1 are in close proximity, while airports with a 5 are at the far edges of the graph. We can also see by the edge thickness which airports have the most carriers arriving from BWI. The node sizes also tell us where customers are flying. All in all, this is a fairly informative graph. However, our job is not complete—we need to repeat this process for the following two months to answer the remaining questions posed earlier.

Before moving to the February data, be sure to export your current work as a `.gexf` file, so it can be loaded as one of our three timeframes. Then repeat the exact process using the February and March files. After each of these is exported to a `.gexf` format, we'll have the three time-based components for our dynamic network.

Now we move on to the fun part, where we layer the three .gexf files into a single Gephi project. Following these steps will result in a useful dynamic graph that shows month over month changes in the flight patterns emanating from BWI.

1. Open a new project in Gephi.

2. Use **Open** under **File** and locate your respective .gexf files.

3. Import the January file by following the screen prompts. Set **Date** to January 1, 2014 using the built-in calendar.

4. Repeat the process for the February and March files, setting **Date** to February 1, 2014 and March 1, 2014 respectively. This will give the Gephi timeline the parameters for applying time intervals.

When all of the steps have been completed, enable your timeline. Remember to apply **Passengers** as the node size attribute in the **Ranking** tab, and make certain that this will be applied across all time intervals using the **Enable auto transformation** icon to the left of the **Apply** button. As you can recall from earlier in this chapter, this will activate the **Auto Apply** button that enables attribute changes across time intervals.

At this point you can elect to change your layout, apply colors using a partition, and so on. In certain cases, you will even be able to check dynamic graph statistics, although that capability is especially geared to more granular time elements, as opposed to the simple monthly categories used here. Nonetheless, four useful measures can be found in the **Statistics | Dynamic** tab:

- The **# Nodes** statistic will track the growth (or decline) in the number of nodes at various intervals within the timeline

- Similarly, the **# Edges** statistic will do the same for edge counts

- The **Degree** calculation will look at the number of degrees at a given interval and can be set to simply provide the average degree level

- Finally, the **Clustering Coefficient** measure can provide insight into how the network is evolving over time, based on clustering levels

Each of these will provide time series views over the specified time window set using the timeline.

In this instance, I opted to change the layout to a **Dual Circle** layout, using BWI as the only member of the inner circle, resulting in the following graph:

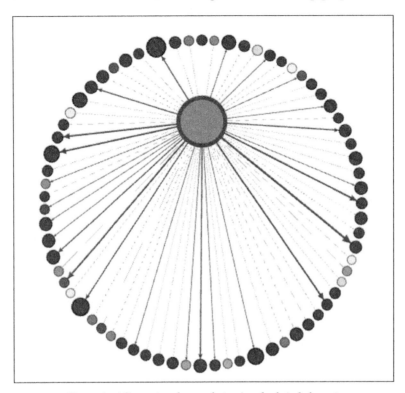

Dynamic airline network snapshot using dual circle layout

One further tweak was to partition the graph using the aforementioned distance group field, resulting in six distinct colors—one for BWI, and a total of five for all the destination airports. The result is similar to the preceding snapshot:

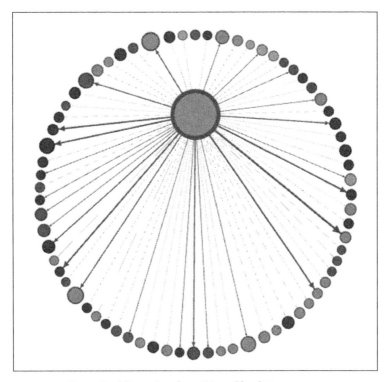

Dynamic airline network partitioned by distance group

You can verify dynamic changes in the graph by running the timeline and observing small changes in node and edge sizes as January changes to February and February to March. While the changes here are slow and somewhat subtle, I hope this provides a bit of insight into what can be done using smaller units of time, such as weeks, days, hours, minutes, and even seconds. The possibilities are almost infinite, depending only on the detail in your data and the processing power of your computer.

We've now seen a few examples of how to visualize networks with dynamic attributes, using files that were previously imported to and enhanced in Gephi. Next, we'll take a brief look at how to create your own GEXF files that will support the creation of dynamic networks.

Creating dynamic GEXF files

While Gephi can be used to create GEXF files, it can be advantageous in many cases to have the file already prepared prior to importing data into Gephi. For any reader acquainted with XML, the formatting and structure will appear very familiar. If you aren't an XML expert, we'll walk through some of the GEXF basics to help you get started.

The code in this section is based on the examples from the `http://gexf.net/format/` site, which provides a general primer for how to structure the data. At a very basic level, the GEXF file is designed to represent a single graph, although that graph might contain many nodes and edges. For a very basic example with two nodes and a single edge between them, the GEXF code would look like this:

```xml
<?xml version="1.0" encoding="UTF-8"?>
<gexf xmlns="http://www.gexf.net/1.2draft" version="1.2">
    <meta lastmodifieddate="2009-03-20">
        <creator>Gexf.net</creator>
        <description>A Web network not changing over time</description>
    </meta>
    <graph mode="static" defaultedgetype="directed">
        <nodes>
            <node id="0" label="Hello" />
            <node id="1" label="Word" />
        </nodes>
        <edges>
            <edge id="0" source="0" target="1" />
        </edges>
    </graph>
</gexf>
```

This file would deliver a simple static graph, which is not what we're after in this chapter. So let's move on to creating a more complex file with time intervals and changing attribute values.

Here's a somewhat more advanced example from the gexf.net site, incorporating time intervals and value changes. We'll break this code into four distinct sections and provide brief descriptions for what is being achieved.

The first section provides basic descriptive information about the file and its format, as well as simple information about who created the file and how it should be described:

```
<?xml version="1.0" encoding="UTF-8"?>
<gexf xmlns="http://www.gexf.net/1.2draft"
  xmlns:xsi="http://www.w3.org/2001/XMLSchema-instance"
  xsi:schemaLocation="http://www.gexf.net/1.2draft
  http://www.gexf.net/1.2draft/gexf.xsd" version="1.2">
    <meta lastmodifieddate="2009-03-20">
        <creator>Gexf.net</creator>
        <description>A Web network changing over
          time</description>
    </meta>
```

Our second section of code pertains to the graph structure, providing the capability for individual nodes to be static or dynamic. Note also that the default edge type (directed) has also been specified:

```
<graph mode="dynamic" defaultedgetype="directed"
  timeformat="date">
    <attributes class="node" mode="static">
        <attribute id="0" title="url" type="string"/>
        <attribute id="1" title="frog" type="boolean">
            <default>true</default>
        </attribute>
    </attributes>
    <attributes class="node" mode="dynamic">
        <attribute id="2" title="indegree" type="float"/>
    </attributes>
```

The third section provides detail about how individual nodes will function, including their respective start and end dates for a dynamic network:

```
<nodes>
    <node id="0" label="Gephi" start-"2009-03 01">
        <attvalues>
            <attvalue for="0" value="http://gephi.org"/>
            <attvalue for="2" value="1"/>
        </attvalues>
    </node>
    <node id="1" label="Network">
        <attvalues>
            <attvalue for="2" value="1" end="2009-03-01"/>
            <attvalue for="2" value="2" start="2009-03-01"
              end="2009-03-10"/>
```

```
                    <attvalue for="2" value="1" start="2009-03-
                        10"/>
                </attvalues>
            </node>
            <node id="2" label="Visualization">
                <attvalues>
                    <attvalue for="2" value="0" end="2009-03-01"/>
                    <attvalue for="2" value="1" start="2009-03-
                        01"/>
                </attvalues>
                <spells>
                    <spell end="2009-03-01"/>
                    <spell start="2009-03-05" end="2009-03-10" />
                </spells>
            </node>
            <node id="3" label="Graph">
                <attvalues>
                    <attvalue for="1" value="false"/>
                    <attvalue for="2" value="0" end="2009-03-01"/>
                    <attvalue for="2" value="1" start="2009-03-
                        01"/>
                </attvalues>
            </node>
        </nodes>
```

Finally, we see the edge parameters, again with start and end values set where appropriate:

```
        <edges>
            <edge id="0" source="0" target="1" start="2009-03-01"/>
            <edge id="1" source="0" target="2" start="2009-03-01"
    end="2009-03-10"/>
            <edge id="2" source="1" target="0" start="2009-03-01"/>
            <edge id="3" source="2" target="1" end="2009-03-10"/>
            <edge id="4" source="0" target="3" start="2009-03-01"/>
        </edges>
    </graph>
</gexf>
```

Note a few changes in the code between the two examples:

- The graph mode value has changed from `static` to `dynamic`
- The second example has now declared node attributes to be either static or dynamic
- Start and/or end dates have been specified for certain nodes and edges
- Values relative to time windows are now specified at the node level

These changes will take us from a simple static graph to a living dynamic graph that shows changes over a time continuum and thus adds a far more insightful view of the network. There are additional structures that can be created using GEXF; for further examples please visit the site at `http://gexf.net/format/`.

The other option for creating your own dynamic GEXF files is to import data into Gephi using `.csv` or other protocols; make your necessary adjustments and customization, and then export the data to a `.gexf` format. This is the process we used in our dynamic attribute example earlier in the chapter. Note that other graph formats can also be created if you are planning to utilize software other than Gephi.

One of the significant advantages of creating a GEXF file is that you will be saving custom analysis performed on a network—colors, sizes, and other attributes can then be easily imported into Gephi at a future date. Similarly, other users could import your network into Gephi and will be able to benefit from your existing work.

It is not essential that you know how to create GEXF files outside of Gephi, as Gephi will do much of the heavy lifting for you within the application. You can certainly continue to load data into Gephi from other formats, enhance it within the application, and eventually output the GEXF format. However, for those who like to do their own coding, or can create processes that download data into an XML framework, there is great potential value in understanding how GEXF functions.

Summary

In this chapter, we covered a lot of ground in understanding how and when to use dynamic networks, and how to implement them in Gephi. Specifically, we discussed the following concepts which have prepared you for effectively creating your own dynamic networks.

We learned how and when to use DNA to view your network data. Next, we addressed how dynamic topology networks differ from dynamic attribute networks, and how to effectively prepare and implement both types in Gephi. We also noted how these two forms can be combined in a single dynamic graph.

Next, we discovered how to use Gephi's timeline functionality to maximize the effectiveness of all types of dynamic networks. Finally, we discussed using GEXF to create dynamic network files outside of Gephi.

Next, we'll look at moving your network analysis beyond the Gephi desktop in *Chapter 9, Taking Your Graph Beyond Gephi*. We'll examine different methods to export your Gephi network graphs to both static- and web-based interactive formats. After providing an overview of many available tools, we'll export some network graphs using the multiple export formats.

9
Taking Your Graph Beyond Gephi

After spending a significant amount of time and effort creating an informative, powerful network graph in Gephi, there is a good chance that you would like to share your work with others. Fortunately, one of the best features of Gephi is its ability to export network graphs for others to view using their favorite web browser.

In this chapter, we will explore the capabilities provided by a handful of Gephi plugins, followed by a walk through the typical steps to make sure your graph is ready. Then we'll spend most of the time on the actual export process. We'll cover the following topics:

- Selecting the best tool for your specific use case
- Customizing available options inside the export plugins
- Exporting and viewing an interactive graph using a web browser

I'll also include links to examples of some existing projects created by me, so you get a better feel of what a deployed network might look like. By the end of the chapter you should be very comfortable with each of these steps, and be able to easily create your own compelling projects.

Overview of the available tools

There are three broad categories of export tools provided for Gephi users. Here are some brief descriptions of your available options, with further details later in the chapter:

- **Graph file**: These exporters simply convert your Gephi project to one of a variety of formats that can be used outside of Gephi, either in other network tools or simply in spreadsheet software. The options here range from simple .csv formats to open formats (.gml), as well as proprietary options for exporting data to Pajek, GUESS, and UCINET protocols.

- **Image exporters**: These exporters enable you to export views of your graph to .png, .svg, or .pdf formats. This is often the fastest way to share a graph, although it doesn't allow interactivity on the user end. The .svg and .pdf options are also useful if your intent is to do further editing in Adobe Illustrator or Inkscape.

- **Web exporters**: These are a family of tools that allow you to push your Gephi network graphs to the Web for others to explore. These tools allow varying degrees of interactivity and represent the most effective means for deploying complex networks. This is where we'll spend most of the time during this chapter, given the many options available within each tool to create and deploy interactive networks to the Web.

Graph file exporters

Gephi provides a wide range of available file exports that enable users to move their network data between tools. This open approach alone makes Gephi a highly valuable tool for all network graph creators, as you will not be limited to a single software platform. To find the available selections in Gephi, navigate to the **File | Export | Graph file** menu. Here's a screenshot of the many options available to you:

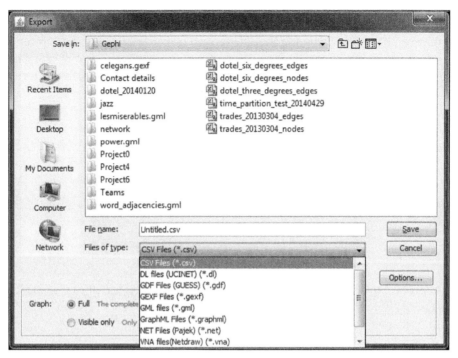

Graph file export options

Let's take a brief walk through each of the available options and their related software tools where applicable.

CSV files

The ubiquitous .csv format is often used for loading data into Gephi, but can also be used on the backend to export data that has been modified inside Gephi. This would enable further exploration using Excel or other spreadsheet tools for statistical analysis.

DL files

This format can be used by the UCINET program (for more information, refer to https://sites.google.com/site/ucinetsoftware/home), a long-standing software used for network analysis. When exporting a file to this format, there are a few simple options that you will get, as shown in this image:

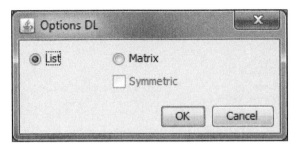

DL file options for UCINET

The data can be exported as a list or matrix, with the symmetric option available for matrix exports. For more information, consult the user guides on the UCINET site.

GDF files

GUESS is another network analysis software (for more information, refer to http://graphexploration.cond.org/). Gephi provides multiple options for this format, as shown in the screenshot:

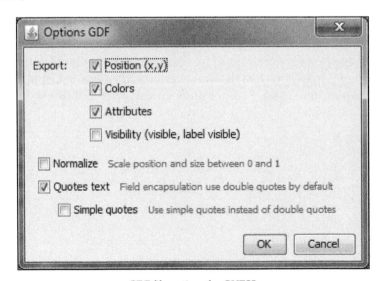

GDF file options for GUESS

We will not go into detail here; to learn more about GUESS and the data options, please visit the GUESS site at `http://graphexploration.cond.org`.

GEXF files

The **Graph Exchange XML Format** (**GEXF**) format is very useful for Gephi users, which is not surprising, since it was created by developers involved with Gephi. In *Chapter 8, Dynamic Networks*, we provided some code examples from `http://gexf.net`. One of the beauties of GEXF is that it is essentially XML repurposed for graph formats. This property will make GEXF's layout and logic very familiar to many programmers.

There are a handful of options available for GEXF exports, as shown here:

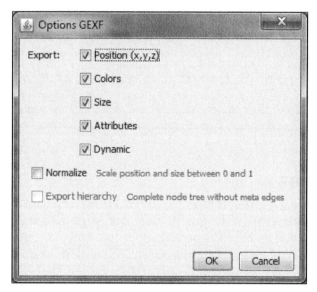

GEXF file options

For additional information, please refer to the GEXF website.

GML files

Graph Modeling Language (GML) is a hierarchical ASCII-based format for describing graphs. The syntax bears a very slight resemblance to JSON. The export options are nearly identical to those of GEXF:

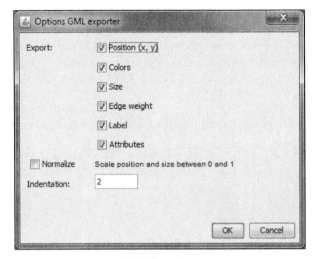

GML file options

GraphML files

GraphML is another XML-based format, so it will look very familiar to some users. There are specific elements (at the graph, node, and edge levels) that make the syntax very easy to interpret. Gephi offers partial support for this format, but once again allows users to export their graph files to GraphML with the following options:

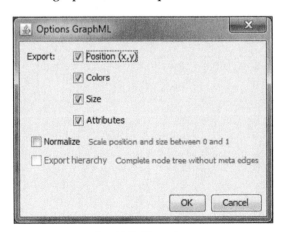

GraphML file options

For the full GraphML specification, visit the GraphML site at `http://graphml.graphdrawing.org/`.

NET files

One of the most prominent network graph solutions is the Pajek program, found at `http://pajek.imfm.si/doku.php?id=pajek`. Pajek uses the .NET format, which Gephi provides two simple export options for:

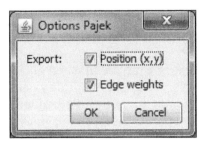

NET file options for Pajek

VNA files

The VNA format is used by a program titled NetDraw and resembles the Pajek .net syntax. Gephi provides a number of export options for this, which are as follows:

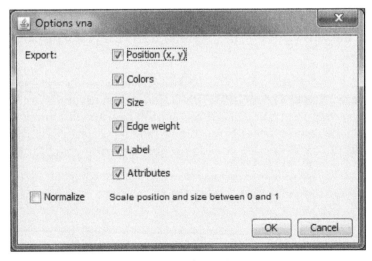

VNA options for NetDraw

To learn more about `.vna` and NetDraw, visit `https://sites.google.com/site/netdrawsoftware/home`.

Before moving to our next section, note that Gephi also provides plugins that enable geo-based data exports for Google Earth (`.kml`/`.kmz` data), as well as shapefile exports that can be used in GIS software as QGIS or MapWindow. For more information, visit the Gephi Marketplace and search for the ExportToEarth, Export to SHP, and Google Maps Exporter plugins. The main requirement to use these is the presence of latitude and longitude (lat/lon) attributes in your network data.

Image exporters

In some cases, your goal will be to produce finished graph output that does not require users to view a network using Gephi or other network graph software. In many of these instances, the graph might be intended for a print publication, or you might simply want to create a specific view of your network for sharing via social media or e-mail. For these cases, the three image export options provided by Gephi offer easy solutions to your needs. Let's look at each of these options, with a focus on the benefits and limitations of each.

PNG export

When your goal is to simply share a static version of an existing graph project, creating a `.png` file is hard to top. This will be the quickest means to share your work with others, with the understanding that the file is not designed for further interaction. On the plus side, .png files scale well and are easily displayed on a blog or website.

Let's have a quick look at the .png export process, which can be initiated by navigating to **File | Export | SVG/PDF/PNG file**. Alternatively, if you are in the **Preview** window, there is a **SVG/PDF/PNG** button near the bottom of the screen that will execute the same process. Suppose we take our example of Miles Davis network and elect to create a `.png` version for quick sharing on a blog or through social media.

We're going to use the **Preview** window and set **Preview Settings** to use the **Default Curved** option, which will display better in this context (versus the black background I used for the Web). Now refresh the window to display with the new format and then export the data to .png using the advice from the previous paragraph. Save the file and then open it in any program where you can view image files. Here's our output image, which should look precisely like the version from the preview window:

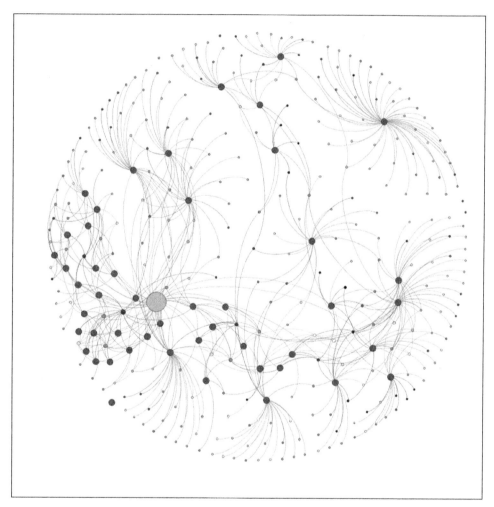

PNG export of Miles Davis network

As you can see, this results in a high-quality image of the network that can be shared through various channels.

SVG export

If you need to move beyond the fixed image provided by a .png export, then you might consider the **Scalable Vector Graphics** (.svg) option. SVG provides an XML-based format that can be edited using either text editors or the more common, image editing software. SVG is also suitable for the Web, as it scales well when zooming or panning a visualization.

In this section, we'll take the same Miles Davis network, save it as a .svg file, and then do some editing using the open source Inkscape program. Following the steps we take might help you determine whether .svg is the best option for post-Gephi editing, or whether you would prefer .pdf, which will be covered in the next section.

Editing an SVG file with Inkscape

So let's begin by repeating the file saving process, but by electing the SVG option in place of PNG. After saving the file, we're going to open it in Inkscape. Feel free to follow along with your own version of Inkscape, or by following a similar process in Adobe Illustrator or any other image editing software.

We already noted that these programs can be used to finish what we already started in Gephi, especially if we are seeking to create a finished graph for print purposes. We could simply leave the graph alone while adding text and titles in the editing software, or we can use the tool to truly edit the graph itself. I'm going to showcase each of these options.

We'll begin with the actual editing of our graph, which can be done by ungrouping the graph elements. This will allow us to edit each and every element in the graph, although it is far more likely that we will want to call out just a few special highlights. So with the .svg file created, we'll open it in Inkscape, which will give us the same sort of view we saw with the .png output.

The key step comes when we click on the **Edit Path by Nodes** icon (or the *F2* key). This allows us to start selecting individual graph nodes and edges for editing. So we will start with a network like this:

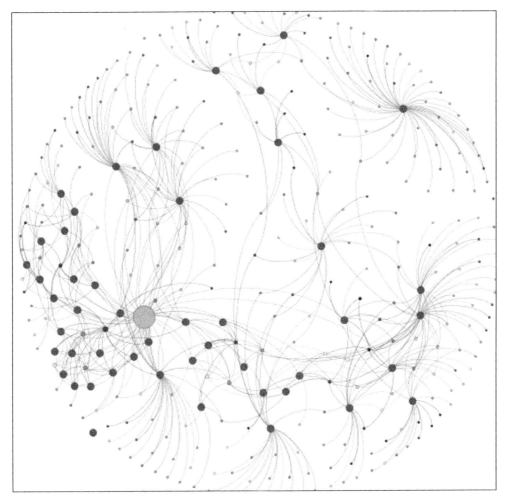

SVG export of Miles Davis network

Suppose that we are not pleased with the yellow shade of the Miles Davis node and would like to change it to blue. All we need to do is select the node using the mouse and then select a new color from the palette at the bottom of the Inkscape window, which will result in the following graph:

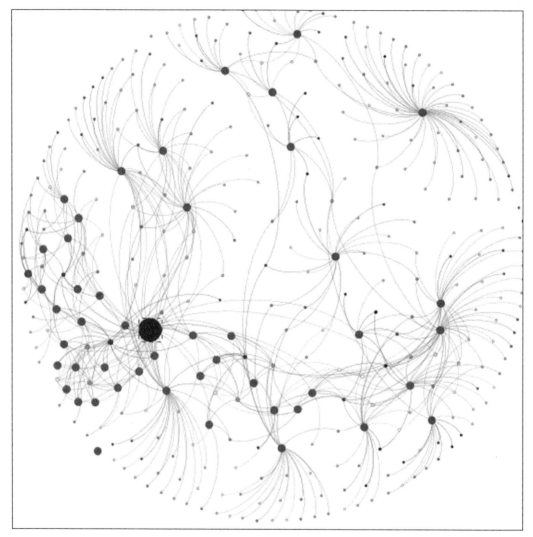

SVG export edited using Inkscape

Let's make a couple more edits to demonstrate how easily text can be added to the graph. Using the **Create and Edit text objects** icon (or the *F8* key) from the Inkscape toolbar, we'll add a small title beneath the network followed by a large label calling out the Miles Davis icon, just in case it isn't obvious enough from the large size and distinct color. We'll also throw in a line as a pointer for the label. Here's our enhanced graph:

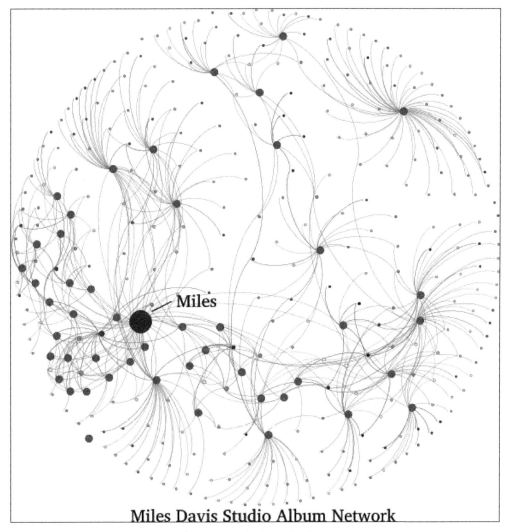

Adding text and titles with Inkscape

This should give you some idea for what can be done to enhance Gephi networks using image editing software. While these were simple edits, there is clearly potential for much more.

PDF export

The Adobe Acrobat PDF format has long been a standard for sharing files on the Web or through e-mail, as it lets all the end users afford the ability to view output without requiring multiple software platforms on their own machine. For the purposes of the Gephi user, it serves as an output option that can produce high quality files for end users to view a network graph. That in itself might be enough to recommend this option, but there is a potentially much more valuable function served by the PDF format, which we'll now discuss.

PDF files can be readily edited using applications such as Adobe Illustrator or its open source alternative, Inkscape. This makes the PDF format highly useful in cases where you wish to tweak your graph beyond Gephi. Much of what you can do within these software platforms is technically possible in Gephi, such as customizing the size and coloring of specific graph elements. However, the ability to add titles and text, strategically position labels, and add images, among a host of other possibilities, makes the PDF export option very useful for Gephi content producers. By the way, there is a Gephi plugin in the early development stages designed for a similar purpose—the **Image Preview** tool, found at `https://marketplace.gephi.org/plugin/image-preview/`.

We'll follow a similar process to what we did with the SVG files in Inkscape. One primary difference is the way in which items are ungrouped; whereas all elements were immediately available using the SVG approach, the PDF might differ somewhat, requiring a few steps to ungroup the file (depending on the export settings). Note that there will often be some transparent layers that need to be removed before all elements can be completely ungrouped.

When you elect to use the PDF export, there are some available options, mostly with respect to formatting of the file, as shown in the following screenshot:

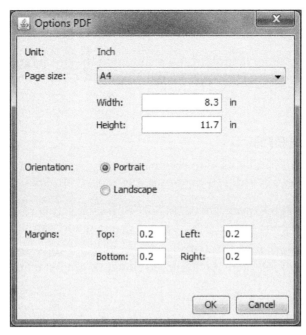

PDF export options

Editing a PDF file in Inkscape

Let's pick it up with the PDF file created and ready for manipulating in Inkscape. When we open the file in Inkscape, another dialog screen pops up, which is as follows:

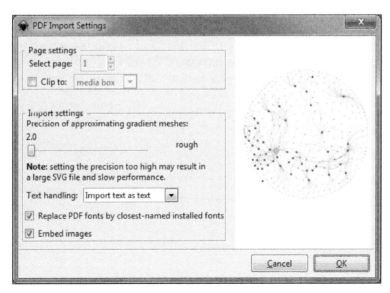

PDF import in Inkscape

Here we can determine how to handle text, whether we should clip the file on import, and how precise we want the file (which will have some cost in the file size).

In this case, I'll go with the default options shown in the preceding screenshot, which will result in a file very similar to what we saw with SVG. We can now begin editing the file in the same fashion we did previously.

Web exporters

Several Gephi plugins can be used to create interactive graphs on the Web. We'll focus on three of these, in order from simplest to most complex:

- **Seadragon Web Export**: This uses the Seadragon software's zoom capabilities to enable traversing large networks using zoom and pan capabilities

- **Sigma.js Exporter**: This is based on the `Sigma.js` software, which facilitates the creation of interactive web-based network graphs using a template-driven approach

- **Loxa Web Site Export**: This also uses `Sigma.js` as the basis for a slightly more sophisticated graph implementation that enables user interaction using filtering and zooming plus the possibility of multiple layered views

Now let's take a tour through each of these options, detailing how they work and what they can deliver for a finished project.

Seadragon Web Export

The Seadragon option is ideal if you want to provide a modest level of interactivity for users. Zoom and pan are the primary features of Seadragon, which makes it suitable for navigating large networks that would prove difficult to decipher as a static graph. What you won't get is any sort of statistical output or additional information about the network.

Let's take a look at the basic options provided by the Seadragon plugin, and then we'll walk through an example later in the chapter. When we select the Seadragon option, this screen pops up:

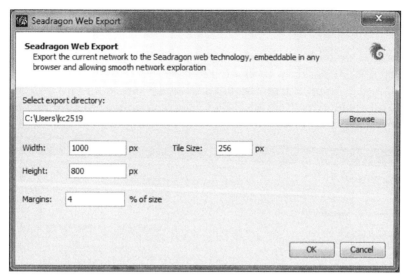

Export dialog box for Seadragon plugin

Here's where the dimensions of the graph can be specified, ideally well suited to the needs of the user. Remember that users can zoom and pan, so there is no need to make the original graph larger than necessary. After selecting the **OK** button, Gephi will export the project to the specified folder location.

We'll see what the output actually looks like, as well as how to interact with it in an upcoming section.

Sigma.js Exporter

If Seadragon doesn't provide the capabilities you're looking for, then it might be time to step up to SigmaExporter, which allows you to create templates that can be used as the base for multiple network instances. We'll spend plenty of time with this option, as it delivers a powerful experience for web users.

Let's assume that we wish to export an existing Gephi network to the Web using SigmaExporter. We'll begin by navigating to the **File | Export | Sigma.js template** menu. The template approach allows us to create specific reference text that can be used again and again, tweaking as needed. Here's what we see after making the menu selection:

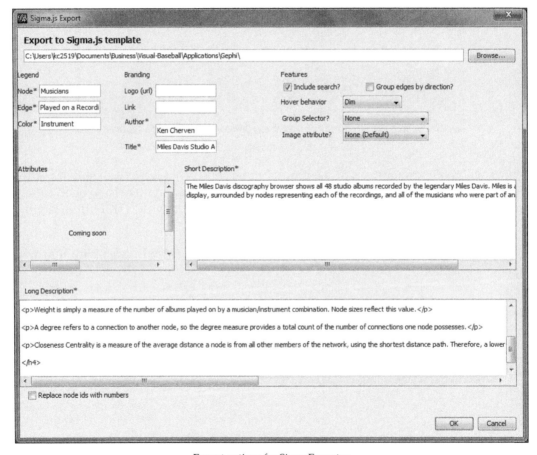

Export options for SigmaExporter

First, we need to specify where the file will be saved. Be careful not to overwrite prior exports, which will be done by default. To avoid this, you can simply add a subfolder for each export within your default directory.

As you can see, there are multiple sections where values can be set, beginning with the **Legend** section. Each of these settings is mandatory for good reason—they deliver critical information to the graph viewer. The options in the **Legend** section can be described as follows:

- In the **Legend** section, there are three options, starting with the **Node** setting, which is essential for the display. This is used to tell viewers what the nodes represent—musicians in our case, but this could just as easily be individuals, places, or dozens of other possibilities.

- The **Edge** setting is also required, and is used to explain what the network connections indicate. In this example, we will specify that edges indicate that musicians *Played on a Recording*.

- We will also use **Color** to encode graph information—in this case it represents the *instrument* a musician played.

Several **Branding** options (for personalizing the graph) are also offered, which are especially useful when you want to link back to your own website or use your own logo. This is also where you specify author and title information; after all, you should get some credit after you've spent time creating a great Gephi visualization.

Several selections can be made in the **Features** portion of the template as well. We'll summarize those here:

- Our first selection, **Include search** allows us to provide users with search capability, which is especially useful when deploying a large network. We'll see just how useful this can be in the next section where we will actually deploy the network graph.

- In the case where we have a directed graph, we have the ability to **Group edges by direction**, making it easier for users to navigate the deployed network

- There is also an option for **Hover behavior**, a simple setting that determines what occurs when users hover over a node. The simple choice is to dim nodes, or to leave them in a normal state. The advantage of using the dim setting is the ability to dim the unneeded sections of the network, which allows a better focus on the relevant areas.

- The **Group Selector** allows you to partition the network using one of the available variables. This could be done using color, centrality measures (if available), or some other categorization.

- Finally, we have an **Image attribute** setting, in the event your network has an image you wish to utilize, based on one of the columns in your dataset. This image will then be used in the **Information Pane** area of the final graph.

Let's move on to a couple more useful options in the template. First up is the **Short Description** text area, where we can provide users with a synopsis of what the network is about. This is where you want to be concise in explaining the network—a couple of sentences should be sufficient.

Our last selection is one where we can really customize the look and feel of the graph, by providing a useful **Long Description**. As you might have noted from the preceding screenshot, HTML styling can be employed here to adjust text sizes, set paragraphs, and so on. This will help give your graph a polished feel by providing essential information for users seeking further information.

In the next section we'll see how to utilize these settings to great effect as we deploy an interactive graph.

Loxa Web Site Export

Another available export choice is the Loxa tool, which uses Sigma.js while providing some alternative options not found in SigmaExporter. We'll walk through the available selections just as we did with the prior tools.

We'll begin again by initiating an export of the existing project, reviewing each of the options as we go. Navigate to the **File | Export | Web site exporter** menu item, which will give you the following screenshot:

Export options for Loxa Web Site Export

You'll notice the relative lack of options compared to SigmaExporter, although there are a handful of options at the bottom of the screen you can choose to export (or not)—**Attributes**, **Colors**, **Dynamic**, **Position**, and **Size**.

In contrast to SigmaExporter, much of the descriptive work for Loxa projects is done behind the scenes by navigating to your project export location. There you will find not only the primary display page (`index.html`), but also two output pages that can be edited in any text editor. The **About** page lets you provide basic information about you or your organization. The **Info** page is where the real meat of the information is supplied, which allows you to specify sources, objectives, metrics, references, and any other information deemed essential to the display.

We'll walk through the process of creating a custom info page when we build our network graph in the next section.

Exporting a web graph

We've just learned about the three primary options for exporting an interactive graph to the Web. We'll walk through the process using each of the three choices. I'll also provide some examples of other graphs created using the **SigmaExporter** option, which I hope will give you an idea of the possibilities.

Let's begin with the Seadragon tool. If you want to follow along, make sure the plugin is installed in your version of Gephi. If not, download and install it using the Gephi plugins option from the **Plugins** menu under **Tools**. For this example, we'll use the familiar project I created that explores all 48 studio albums of jazz legend Miles Davis. The file can be found at `https://app.box.com/s/177yit0fdovz1czgcecp`.

Seadragon

Our first example will be using Seadragon. Follow the process discussed earlier to export the graph by navigating to the **File | Export | Seadragon Web** menu selection. Set your location, size, and margin options in the dialog screen, and create the graph. Remember that if you export the project to a local file, some browsers will not open the graph due to their restrictions on JavaScript files. If you are a Chrome user, you'll want to switch to Firefox for this example, or you can use a local web server powered by Python or Java, as two possibilities.

Let's display the finished graph in the browser:

Gephi Seadragon Export

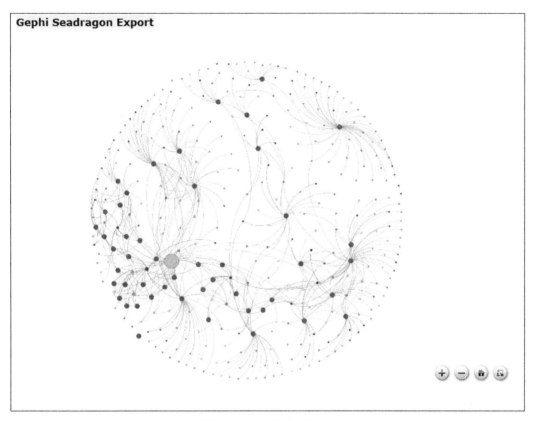

Network output in Seadragon

You can see the controls whenever you hover over the graph. The plus sign enables zooming in, while the minus sign does the reverse. The home icon will return the graph to its original centered position, and the final icon on the right lets you toggle between fullscreen and the original graph size.

Before we move on to the more powerful Sigma and Loxa options, I want to make you aware of the ability to do some style editing behind the scenes for your Seadragon file. All styling information is embedded directly in the .html file created by the Seadragon plugin, although you could create a separate CSS file to refer to if you wish. Here's what the style code snippet looked like when I first exported the above file:

```
<style type="text/css">
        body {
            margin: 0px;
        }
        #seadragon {
            width: 800px;
            height: 600px;
            background-color: Black;
        }
    </style>
```

Here you see some very simple settings that instruct the browser how to display the page — simple width, height, and background color elements. If you have experience with CSS styling, feel free to add more elements using your favorite text editor, but given the relatively limited scope of Seadragon this might not be terribly useful. Perhaps a title element and a textbox or legend would be nice, but these will be easier to implement in the Sigma and Loxa solutions.

Seadragon is a fun tool for manipulating the graph, even if it falls short of the feature sets of the Sigma and Loxa exporters. However, if you want to create a quick, simple network graph for the web browser, Seadragon might be sufficient for your needs.

SigmaExporter

Earlier we saw the many choices available for exporting a network graph using the SigmaExporter tool. Now we'll follow the process right through graph creation. We'll also use the group selection, search functionality, and information pane to learn more about the network. If you wish to follow along, make sure to install the SigmaExporter tool from the available plugins list in Gephi.

So what do we get if we just pursue the initial settings shown earlier in the chapter? Here's the result:

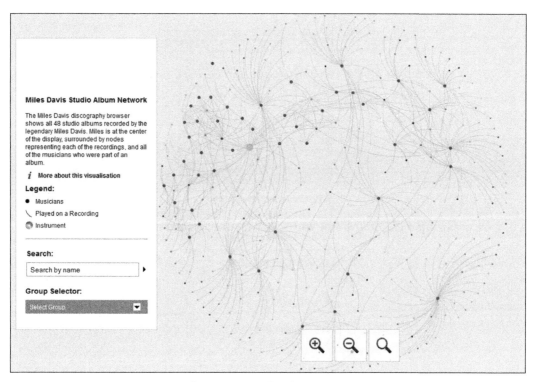

Miles Davis network in SigmaExporter

We have a nice graph that resembles what we just saw in Seadragon, but with additional information courtesy of the template we reviewed in the last section. The graph has an overview, a legend, search box, and group selector based on our partitioning decision (instruments in this case). In addition, if a user clicks on the information icon, the long description text area we saw earlier will be loaded, providing further context on the visualization. So you can begin to see the incremental power these options provide when compared with the Seadragon alternative.

Now let's see how we can tap into some of the Sigma functionality to begin traversing and filtering the network. If we click on the **Group Selector** drop-down menu, we'll see a host of options to choose from—in this case, they refer to specific instruments:

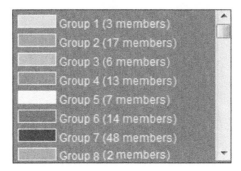

The Group Selector menu

Let's select **Group 4 (13 members)** and see the results in the information pane:

Information pane showing group results

We can now see each of the French horn players employed by Miles Davis on his albums—13 of them, as this was a commonly used instrument in some of Miles' earlier ensembles. We could select any of these musicians using either the information pane or the graph to explore the albums they played on and to which other musicians they are connected. Since this is a bipartite network, each musician is connected directly to albums only, and not other musicians. Selecting any given album will reveal all of the musicians who played on that particular recording, so it's a two-step process to see linkages between musicians.

Now let's use the search tool to learn more about a specific musician. In this example, we'll enter Wayne Shorter into the search box, which results in the following:

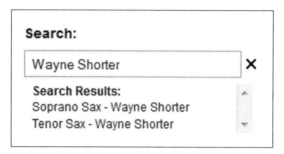

Sigma search option

We have two matches, as **Wayne Shorter** played both soprano and tenor saxophone on various recordings. Selecting the **Soprano Sax - Wayne Shorter** item results in the following information pane:

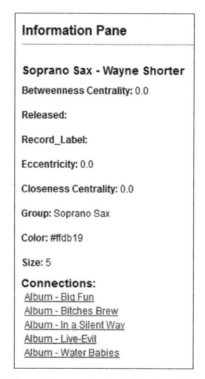

Information pane for individual musicians

Notice that some of the fields here are either empty or meaningless for our analysis. Since Wayne Shorter is a musician, the `Released` and `Record_Label` fields are null; if we select any one of the recordings in the network, those fields will be populated. Notice also that two centrality measures return values of `0`; this is because of the bipartite nature of the network. We could elect to remove these fields from the final result if we so choose, by editing the underlying `data.json` file to remove the unnecessary elements.

We will then see the more interesting information we're after, such as the group classification, the color used for the specific group, and most importantly, each of the recordings where Wayne Shorter played soprano saxophone. Each of these album titles is clickable, which will load new information into the graph display when selected.

A moment ago, I referred to how our results would differ in the event an album (rather than a musician) was selected in the graph. Suppose we selected the album titled **Walkin'** by clicking on the appropriate graph node:

Information Pane

Album - Walkin'

Betweenness Centrality: 0.0

Released: 1954

Record_Label: Prestige

Eccentricity: 0.0

Closeness Centrality: 0.0

Group: Album

Color: #e50000

Size: 25

Connections:
Alto Sax - David Schildkraut
Bass - Percy Heath
Drums - Kenny Clarke
Piano - Horace Silver
Tenor Sax - Lucky Thompson
Trombone - J.J. Johnson
Trumpet - Miles Davis

Information pane for albums

Now we will see the year the recording was released as well as the label that produced the album. We will also see each of the musicians who played on the recording, each in the form of clickable links. Selecting the **Bass - Percy Heath** link will then display every recording he played on, providing further insight into the network content. This ability to navigate the network from either the graph window or the information pane makes for a very powerful, easy to use visualization.

Another powerful capability within the Sigma plugin is the ability to create advanced styling. While there are a few ways to customize the output via the basic template, there are many more options behind the scenes. To access these files, go to the directory where your visualization is parked (it will be an index.html file), and locate the css folder.

Inside the css folder you will find two files—a primary file titled style.css and a second one called tablet.css. Most of your tweaking will be performed in the style.css file, where you have dozens of elements that can be adjusted. If you aren't familiar with CSS, it's worth learning the basics, as it will allow you to truly customize your output in so many ways. Let's have a look at a small snippet of CSS code from the file:

```
#maintitle h1 {
  display: none;
}

#mainpanel {
  margin-top: 50px;
  margin-left: 25px;
  background:#fff;
  background-color:rgba(255,255,255,0.8);
  border:1px solid #ccc;
  z-index:20;
  position:fixed;
  top:0;
}

#mainpanel .b1 {
  padding: 0px 0 0 0;
}

#mainpanel .col {
  width: 240px;
  padding: 18px 18px 18px 18px;
```

```
      margin: 0;

  }

  #title {
      font-weight: bold;
  }

  #titletext {
      padding: 6px 0 10px 0;
  }
```

Just in these few selections you begin to get a sense of the possibilities, such as being able to customize the width, margin, and padding for your main information panel. You could also change the positioning of the panel, adjust its coloring, and decide whether to create a border surrounding the panel. This is just a very small glimpse into the style file—there are literally hundreds of adjustments you could make to create a unique look and feel for your published visualization. Even more edits can be made within the `config.json` and `sigma.js` files, for instance. It is important to remember that any edits you make will be overwritten if you need to recreate the network, unless you create a new folder location for each version.

Loxa Web Site Export

We just used SigmaExporter to create multiple versions of a single network graph; now we'll follow a similar process using the Loxa plugin. If you wish to create your own graphs, make sure to install the Loxa Web Site Export tool from the available plugins list in Gephi. Our primary difference for this example will be the need to edit some of the Loxa files using a text editor, so get your favorite tool ready if you wish to do a little tweaking.

If you wish to follow along, you'll need to have the Loxa plugin installed—you should find it in your available plugins directory. The export process for the tool was detailed earlier, and is just as simple as for the other web exporters. Remember that there weren't a lot of settings to modify in the dialog screen (as there were for SigmaExporter), so we're going to proceed with the default options checked. Depending on the speed of your computer and the complexity of the network, the export could range from a few seconds to upwards of a minute. Locate the exported file and open it up in a non-Chrome local browser session. The results will be along these lines:

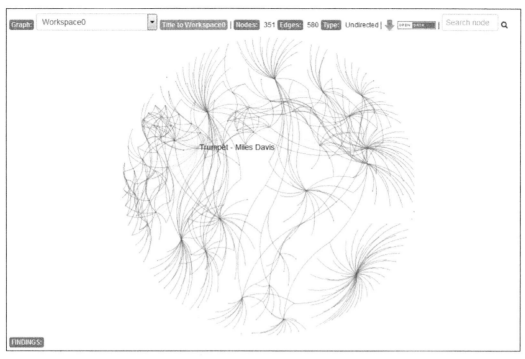

Default Loxa display window

Your version might have a darker background; I have adjusted the background color by editing some of the inline styling within the `index.html` file produced by Loxa. While more than 90 percent of the styles are set using a standalone CSS file, a few of the rudimentary elements are stationed within the main page, like so:

```
<style type="text/css">
    label {
       display: inline-block;
       width: 5em;
    }
 /* sigma.js context : */
 .sigma-parent {
    position: relative;
    border-radius: 4px;
    -moz-border-radius: 4px;
    -webkit-border-radius: 4px;
    background: #666;
    height: 530px;
 }
 .sigma-expand {
    position: absolute;
```

```
    width: 100%;
    height: 100%;
    top: 0;
    left: 0;
}
.buttons-container{
    padding-bottom: 8px;
    padding-top: 12px;
}
</style>
```

The initial `sigma-parent` element had a background setting of `#222` (almost black) which I have changed to `#fff` (white) for the benefit of the print settings in the book. I have also tweaked the label styling by editing the `loxawebsite-0.9.1.js` file (your version might differ). Node and edge styling can also be manipulated by adjusting settings within this file. Use your own discretion when making changes to the styling.

Taking a look at the Loxa display window, there are a few important items to note:

- Notice that at the top of the graph there are three tabs—the **SNA** page, **About analysis** tab, and **About us** page that can be customized to provide additional information about the network. The **SNA** page refers to the actual graph, while the **About analysis** tab is intended for descriptive information about the project, much as the SigmaExporter template that provided descriptive fields. Finally, the **About us** page serves as a placeholder for information about the authors of the visualization. We'll come back to these in our next example.

- Next, there is a graph dropdown that shows all workspaces belonging to the current project. In this case, we have but a single workspace, but Loxa can accommodate multiple instances within a single project. We will discuss more on this shortly.

- Basic network information is displayed at the top of the graph, such as the numbers of nodes and edges, and whether the network is directed or undirected.

- The download image arrow will convert the network to a PDF file for offline viewing.

- Finally, there is a search box function that assumes that the search functionality is enabled

One of the outstanding features of the Loxa tool is the ability to zoom in using the scroll wheel on your mouse. Seadragon also features this option, but Loxa adds more functionality, including the ability to see node labels at different levels. So where we saw only the Miles Davis label on the initial load, watch what happens when we begin to zoom in:

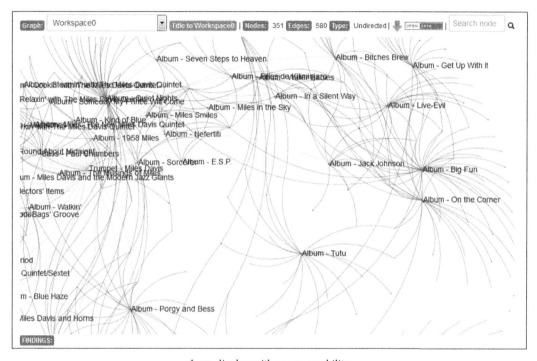

Loxa display with zoom capability

Now we are able to see each of the album titles displayed automatically, but no musicians yet as the visualization would become very crowded. Zooming in another level does just that, however, the individual musicians from each recording are now labeled along with the recordings, as shown in the following screenshot:

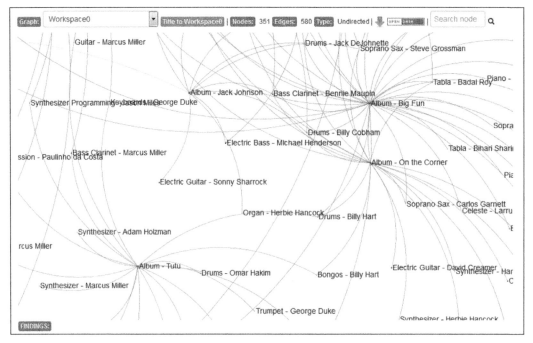

Loxa display with additional level of zoom

This capability, along with the ability to drag-and-drop the graph, makes for a very powerful, highly interactive environment that will provide a great experience for your users.

Before we conclude this chapter, I wanted to go back to a couple of the previously discussed tabs in the Loxa output and show you how these can be customized to make for a more polished visualization. In our initial example, you saw the plugin defaults, which serve as placeholders for additional information. We're now going to provide some of that information by editing the `about.html` and `info.html` files found in the project folder. These will be minor edits done in a matter of a few minutes. The capability to provide much more information is at your disposal.

Here is a look at a few of the newly customized pages, with placeholder text updated to match the project:

The customized About the Project page

The **Objectives** tab can also be customized with the goal of stating why the visualization exists, as well as any secondary aims behind the network graph:

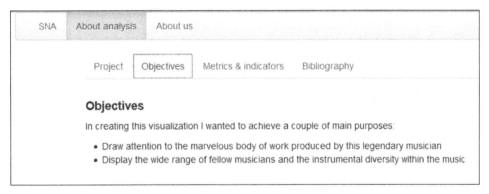

The customized Objectives page

More customization can be done on the **About us** tab. While I just placed a website link here, much more could be done to tell the world who you are,

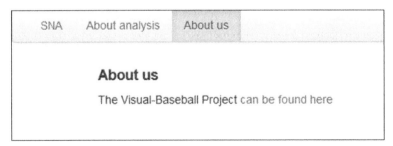

The customized About us page

The sky is the limit for customizing your Loxa project—all you need is some very basic HTML and CSS skills to create a unique, informative and interactive project.

Summary

In this chapter you learned how to take advantage of the many available tools that will take your network graphs beyond the Gephi application and into the hands of external users. We learned about three main categories of exporters in Gephi.

We discussed graph file exporters, which export your network data into formats that are readily accessible by other network graph software, as well as by Gephi. We went onto discussing image exporters, which facilitate turning your graph into static files via PNG, SVG, or PDF exports. We also elaborated on web exporters, which turn your Gephi network graphs into interactive displays for the Web

We also covered how SVG and PDF exports could be further edited using a tool such as Adobe Illustrator or Inkscape and shared some examples using Inkscape.

Our final sections covered the process of creating and exporting network graphs for the Web, including sections on editing the underlying templates and source files to achieve a finished, professional look for our graphs.

In *Chapter 10, Putting It All Together*, we'll take a look at using the best practices from this book to begin building your own networks, and we'll also have a brief discussion about the future of network analysis.

10
Putting It All Together

Until this point in the book, we have focused on many aspects of Gephi that can be used to create effective and interactive network visualizations. In many cases, these topics were discussed in isolation within their respective chapters. We have managed to merge multiple functionalities on some occasions, but never the entirety of what Gephi can help us create. In this final chapter, the goal is to pull all of these elements together at a more holistic level and build some Gephi projects from start to finish.

We'll focus on three primary goals in this final chapter as we seek to further develop your own network analysis skills. The first two will make an effort to fully leverage Gephi's considerable capabilities, while the third section will focus on what the future of network graph analysis might encompass. Here's what we'll cover in this chapter:

- In the first section, we'll look at how we can use Gephi to interpret and enhance existing networks

- We'll spend the majority of the chapter creating a couple Gephi projects from start to finish, eventually deploying each to the Web

- Our final section will look at where network analysis stands today and where it is likely to go in the future

Let's begin by using Gephi to interpret an existing network visualization.

Using Gephi to understand existing networks

In previous chapters, we've examined a variety of techniques and functionalities present within Gephi that act on the existing network data. These included topics such as filtering, partitioning, running statistics, styling, and ultimately exporting our projects. As I mentioned in the introduction, much of this has necessarily been done in isolation, with periodic instances where multiple approaches were merged. In this section, we are going to utilize a considerable portion of the Gephi application to understand and potentially improve on some of the existing network graphs.

The hope is that performing many of these operations on existing graphs will prepare us to create better projects when we begin with our own raw data. Think of this as a bit of a warm-up exercise before we tackle the more challenging goal of building our own projects.

So let's begin by exploring a single challenging graph, and begin flexing our creative muscles using a variety of Gephi techniques. It's time to locate an existing project to modify—either `.gexf` or `.net` formats should work, or even existing the `.gephi` files. The Gephi wiki is a good place to start, although you could search for any of these file types on the Web and find some additional resources. Let's get started.

The example we'll walk through, the **Marvel Social network**, is available in the `.gephi` format on the Gephi wiki at `https://wiki.gephi.org/index.php/Datasets#Social_networks`. The network represents thousands of Marvel comic book characters and how they have interacted with one another throughout decades of comic book editions. This is a rather dense network of roughly 10,000 nodes and nearly 180,000 edges, which gives us a graph that is nearly impenetrable at first glance. At a minimum, we would like to take this network and give the user some tools to help them navigate the graph effectively. Beyond that, the ability to make the graph more visually appealing would also be a good idea, as long as it is not simply for aesthetic purposes alone. In other words, let's make it look nicer within the context of increased efficiency for the user.

Here's our starting point of the network graph:

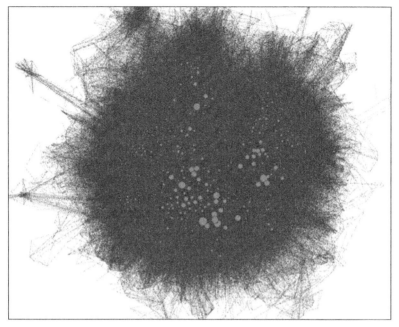

The Marvel hero network graph

A bit overwhelming at first, isn't it? We do have a few visual cues to begin working with—there are clearly some high degree nodes sized accordingly. There also appear to be some outlying clusters at the extreme edges of the graph, and we do have the ability to understand the structure a bit by hovering over selected nodes. Nonetheless, the graph suffers from the infamous hairball effect that we generally seek to avoid in network visualization. So where to begin?

Some of the more obvious opportunities to improve the graph are not available in the data. For instance, there are no categorical variables informing us when or where a character originated. Nor are there any fields indicating in which of the many Marvel comic books the characters appeared. Our best (and only?) option would seem to be to improve the graph by creating our own variables and filters using either statistical measures or created variables. We can do this—it isn't as hopeless as we might have originally feared. Gephi provides some powerful tools to enhance even the most challenging networks.

I'm going to start with a tool that we haven't previously explored in the book, but one that's especially useful when confronted by a dataset with few variables to work from. At the bottom of your **Data Laboratory** window are a series of icons, including the **Merge columns** function we previously used and will encounter again later in this chapter. However, for this example, we'll slide to the right of the window and employ one of the useful regex commands to create some new variables for our graph. You might recall the **regex** (short for **Regular Expression**) functionality from *Chapter 5, Working with Filters*, where we used it to create wildcard filters. This time we're going to use it to create some new field values to make network navigation far easier for the end user.

We'll use the second of the two regex functions (Create a boolean column from regex match, Create column with a list of regex matching groups) — the one with the lengthy title of **Create column with list of regex matching groups**. Click on the **Create column** button to open the dialog box, where we'll create a new field titled **Man**. Why Man, you ask? Because our quick perusal of the dataset and slight familiarity with Marvel characters (and comics in general) suggests that there will be many characters with man in their title. For starters, we have Iron Man, Spiderman, and likely dozens of others. We'll have to be careful with the filter so that we don't identify all the characters with Woman in their title as well, since man is also represented within those five letters. For that matter, we don't want portions of a character named Norman (for example). So this can get a little complex, but we'll get there using regex.

For our example, we can use the \b modifier to find only those instances where the term MAN is found in the dataset (this data is in uppercase). This allows us to create a new column using the dialog screen:

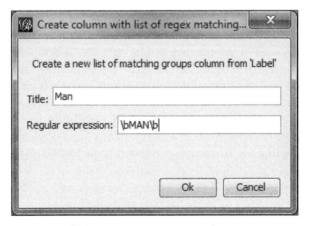

Using regex to create a new column

Now that we've created the column, let's use it to filter the graph by working with the **Equal** filter and dragging the Man field down to the **Queries** window. We then need to enter the matching value for the filter to work properly, as follows:

Setting the query pattern with equal filter

Clicking on the **Select** and **Filter** buttons results in a network graph that displays only the records that match our criteria, as shown in the following diagram:

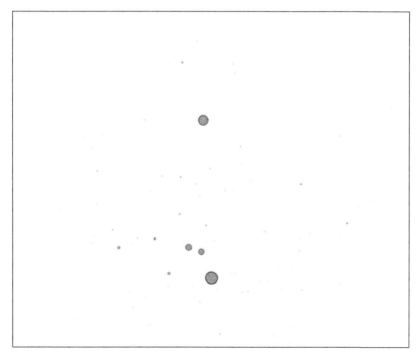

The graph results from applying the MAN filter

We can verify the efficacy of the filter by perusing our results in the data laboratory:

Label	Man
IRON MAN/TONY STARK	MAN
IRON MAN IV/JAMES R.	MAN
MAN-THING/THEODORE T	MAN
SEAWEED MAN	MAN
SPIDER-MAN/PETER PAR	MAN
WONDER MAN/SIMON WIL	MAN
,"WONDER MAN/SIMON WIL	MAN
,"IRON MAN/TONY STARK	MAN
,"IRON MAN IV/JAMES R.	MAN
COBALT MAN	MAN
,"COBALT MAN	MAN

The partial results from application of MAN filter

So we've accomplished something that's potentially very useful as we attempt to create a more easily navigated network. There's clearly more that can be done, including coloring the graph nodes based on our filter. All we have to do here is right-click on the **Reset colors** icon and select a color that will be applied only to our filtered members (make sure the filter is applied—otherwise the entire graph will be re-colored). We'll choose a dark blue shade to identify the *Man* characters, and then remove the filter to see the following result:

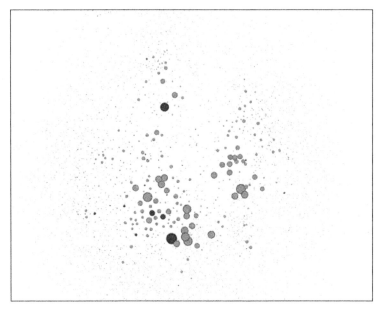

The updated graph with new color for all MAN characters

We can then repeat this series of steps to create other new fields. For example, I created a field titled `Woman` and another titled `Black` in recognition of the many cartoon characters (often villains) with black as part of their name. By the way, you might need to hit the **Reset** button to see your new values in the **Filter** window. Performing the filtering and coloring on each in sequence results in the following graph where we now have three distinct colors beyond the gray for the remaining members of the network:

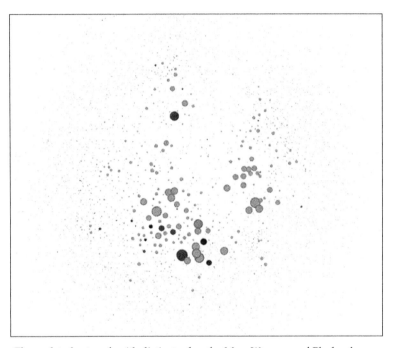

The updated network with distinct colors for Man, Woman, and Black columns

We can also use graph statistics to filter the graph more effectively. Bear in mind that this might take a while given the size and complexity of this graph (it might even fail, depending on your available memory). Memory settings can be adjusted by editing the `gephi.conf` file found in the `Gephi-0.8.2\etc` folder, or refer to `http://gephi.github.io/users/install/`; however, you might be able to calculate some centrality measures, or at the very least we can work with degrees to segment the graph. We could even elect to use an **Erdos Number** (for more details on the Erdos Number Project, refer to `http://www.oakland.edu/enp/`) to see how close each graph member is to a specific character (say Iron Man). In fact, let's try the Erdos Number approach to partition the graph.

After calculating the Erdos Number for the Tony Stark Iron Man character (as opposed to the various other Iron Man incarnations) we can begin to segment the graph based on how each character relates to Iron Man. The average number turns out to be 2.103, indicating that a typical character is slightly more than two edges away — direct connections would have an Erdos Number of one. We would like to see the distribution of these visually to better understand the role of Iron Man in the Marvel pantheon, and who is most closely identified with him.

To do this, we will simply select **Erdos Number** as our partition criteria, which will show us the numbers ranging from **0** (for the central character) through **6**, as follows:

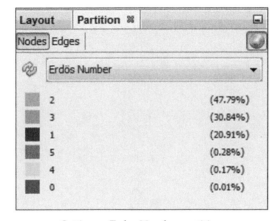

Setting an Erdos Number partition

We can then apply the colors (modify these first if you wish to create a personalized color scheme) to see the final result:

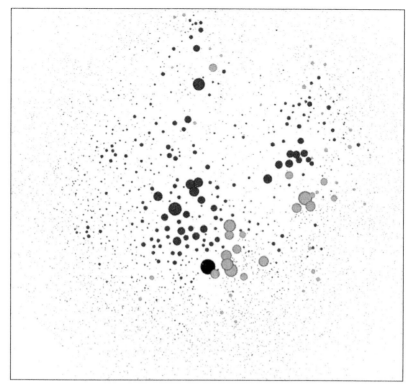

Marvel hero graph partitioned by Iron Man Erdos Number

Looks a lot better than where we started, doesn't it? There are obviously many other ways we could have modified the graph—different field creation, alternative partitioning strategies, new color schemes, or filtering approaches. The point is that Gephi provides a powerful array of tools to help you move in almost any direction when working with an existing network graph.

We'll now move on to create our own projects from start to finish.

Creating new Gephi projects

Now that we've dissected and improved upon some existing network graphs, the time has come to develop our own projects from scratch. This will involve a number of steps, and will allow us to fold in much of what has been covered thus far in this book. Here's a summary level synopsis for everything we'll do to create our projects—it's a long list, but you should be well prepared to handle each of these steps based on what we've covered to this point.

Here are the steps, arranged in a typical order, although some of these steps could be swapped (such as the steps involving statistics and filtering):

1. First, we'll locate a dataset that is suitable for network analysis. The data might or might not be in a suitable format when we find it, which will dictate whether the next step is necessary.

2. We might need to format the data so that Gephi can read it without issues. Remember that Gephi is able to handle a variety of input sources created in various graph file formats. If we are sourcing data that isn't already in one of these formats, then we'll have to create either a pair of .csv files (one each for nodes and edges) or have the data available via some MySQL (or other database) tables.

3. When the data has been imported by Gephi, the first thing we see is a random layout. After a cursory inspection of the data in the data laboratory, we'll want to apply one of the many layout options made available in Gephi. This is typically an iterative process, as your initial selection might not deliver the results you are seeking. Stay with this process until you get something that makes you comfortable.

4. After finding a suitable layout, it's time to do a visual inspection of the graph. Are there obvious patterns such as **homophily**, or does the network take on a more random appearance? Do we have a single **giant component**, or are there multiple disconnected subnetworks? Do we see obvious **hubs**, or are there many alternative ways to traverse the graph? Does the graph have a large or small **diameter**? These are just a few of the questions we should ask ourselves as we inspect the graph.

5. Now we can further understand the network by employing any of the many filters provided within Gephi. These can be especially helpful when faced with a dense network, but are certainly not limited to just that condition. We can also gain insight by filtering the data based on degree levels, by classifications or partitions, or based on a combination of criteria using an intersect query.

6. It's time to apply some statistical measures to the graph to help confirm our initial impressions. The centrality measures are especially important, as they will apply real numbers that can help identify the network influencers, regardless of their placement within the network. Other statistics will help confirm initial impressions about diameter, clustering, and homophily, among other measures.

7. From here, we can begin segmenting and partitioning the network using a variety of tools in Gephi. This step will often highlight graph patterns through visual means such as sizing and coloring, making it easier for the graph viewer to understand the message.

8. In cases where the network has some sort of time element, we can create dynamic graphs that call out temporal changes in the network. This might come in the form of a node entry and exit as time passes, or it could reflect time-driven changes in status for individual nodes. In either case, dynamic networks can convey a very powerful story to viewers.

9. Our final step in most cases will be to make the graph available for external users, often through deployment to the Web. This then makes the network interactive for all users without requiring any knowledge of Gephi. In other cases, we might elect to simply share an image of the network via a `.png` file, or we could choose to tell a story using the `.svg` or `.pdf` output formats.

Sounds like a lot, but as you become more comfortable with Gephi, much of this will become second nature. We're going to put this into practice by creating a pair of projects, the first a dynamic network that remains within Gephi, and the second a project that we will push to the Web for user interaction.

Project 1 – Newman NetScience dataset

Our first example will use the NetScience dataset created by noted network scientist Mark Newman. Newman's data examines the working relationships between hundreds of academic network science practitioners through a co-authorship network. Nodes represent authors, and edges the connections between co-authors. This data can be found in multiple places on the Web, including Newman's own site. We'll begin with a `.gml` version of the data, which you can find at `https://app.box.com/s/177yit0fdovz1czgcecp`.

All that exists at the start of the project are the respective nodes and edges tables, which will give us full control over the ensuing steps. From this raw data, we will create a project that incorporates a wide range of Gephi techniques and methods, resulting in a finished network graph that tells a compelling story. We'll follow the steps outlined a moment ago, although we might make a slight detour here and there.

Exploring the network in Gephi

Once the data has been loaded in Gephi, we'll see the following network in a random layout, as provided in detail in our chapter on selecting a layout algorithm. This won't look like much, but it does provide us with enough to get underway:

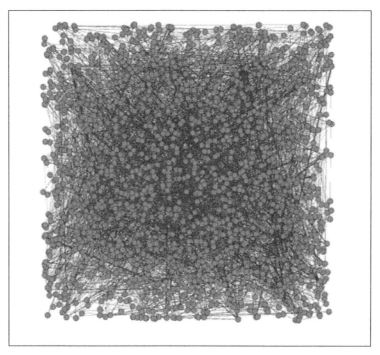

The Newman network science collaboration network

We need to get the data into some sort of layout that will help us to understand the network structure. The context window tells us that the network has 1,589 nodes and 2,742 edges; fewer than two edges per node on average. Thus, our network is not very dense, which might help point us to a specific sort of layout. We also know that the network has enough nodes to perhaps eliminate some other algorithms from consideration—a circular layout might not work effectively for displaying this network.

Given this information, I am going to begin with the **ARF** algorithm, which I find to be useful for small- to medium-sized networks of this sort. We'll see whether ARF effectively displays the network; if not, then another option will be considered. For instance, if our network turns out to be highly clustered, the ARF might not distinguish the clusters as well as something like Force Atlas (remember that ARF creates largely circular layouts). We'll need to make that determination after seeing the results.

After running the ARF algorithm for nearly 10 minutes (your time might vary) using the default settings, we will be able to see the following output:

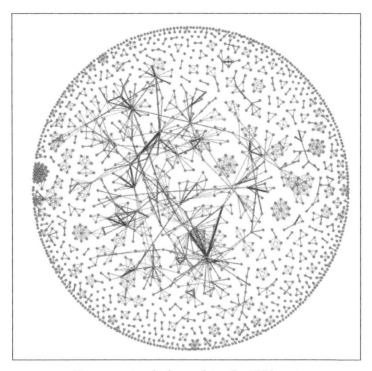

Newman network after applying the ARF layout

Based on these results, I believe we can move forward. The graph quite clearly displays a number of clusters, an indication of network scientists collaborating on projects. We also see some instances where nodes are linked to more distant members of the graph, an indication of some cross-cluster collaborations.

Something else is very clear— this is not a single connected network. Instead, there are multiple cases where smaller subnetworks exist. This is going to influence some of our statistical measures, as we'll see momentarily. For instance, there is no way to calculate a single diameter measure, as it is impossible to traverse the entire graph.

Next, let's begin using some filters to better understand the network. Here are a few questions we can attempt to answer:

- Which nodes are the most influential, as measured by degrees?
- Where are the heaviest edges an indication of frequent collaborations?
- How large is our largest connected component, and who belongs to it?

We will quickly discover an issue—there is no explicit degree measurement in our nodes table, as we had in some prior datasets. Fortunately, we have several easy ways to measure degrees. We could take the data outside of Gephi and calculate a degree value for each node, we can use the Gephi ranking function to size all nodes based on their individual degrees, or we could simply use the filters within the **Topology** folder to look at **Degree Range**. So even though we don't have an explicit field for degrees, Gephi recognizes the network structure and lets us filter using the degree attributes. We can note that the degree range runs between 0 and 34, so let's examine all the values of 15 or greater. The graph now shows just 34 nodes, roughly 2 percent of the network, clearly concentrated in three distinct areas of the network.

Now let's look at edge weights to see where the most frequent collaborations occur. In this case, the source file does provide the edge weights, making it very easy for us to filter on. We have multiple ways we can go about this, but using a range would be a sensible approach. Let's set the range to 2.0 or greater, which leaves us just 14 edges from our initial total of close to 3,000. We can easily note who the collaborators are by navigating to the edges table in **Data Laboratory**.

Finally, let's apply the **Giant Component** filter to the network to understand what proportion of the network is connected in the largest area of the graph and we will get the following result:

Giant component of Newman network

As you can see, there is a large connected component, but it represents just 24 percent of the entire network, suggesting a very fragmented graph with multiple pockets of isolated activity. So, fully three of every four researchers are not a part of the largest network. This could change significantly if just a few of the external nodes were to collaborate with something in the giant component, and would make for an interesting temporal study to check whether the network evolves significantly over time.

Let's apply some statistical measures to the graph to understand patterns even better. Remember our earlier mention about the difficulty of calculating diameter across the network, due to the many component groups. However, we still have the ability to run many statistical functions, but must recognize their limited meaning in certain contexts (such as a component with just five members). So our primary goal should be to examine the giant component and its member nodes, as this is where the most significant interactions are taking place.

After running a battery of statistical measures, we have the official validation for what we already suspected. Here are a few examples of the official validations:

- Graph density is 0.002, an exceptionally low figure, which confirms what we knew about the low number of connections relative to the node count

- The average clustering coefficient is 0.878, which confirms that the graph is highly clustered, something that is visually apparent

- There are 396 components in the network, which gives further evidence of the fragmented nature of the network

- The average degree is 3.45, which means that a typical member of the network has between three and four collaborations

Everything we note confirms our expectations, with no hidden surprises. Now that we've done our due diligence on the filtering and statistical fronts, it's time to make the graph more accessible and informative for users. We'll do this through the use of partitioning and segmentation, which will bring to our attention the most critical elements and patterns within the network.

For starters, we'll rank the nodes based on their degree level, which will quickly highlight some of the more evident patterns in the network. While we're at it, let's apply color using the same criteria. Set the size range between 2 and 25 and use one of the built-in color themes, and then open the **Preview** window for improved aesthetics. Let's increase the edge thickness to 2.0 and we see the following result:

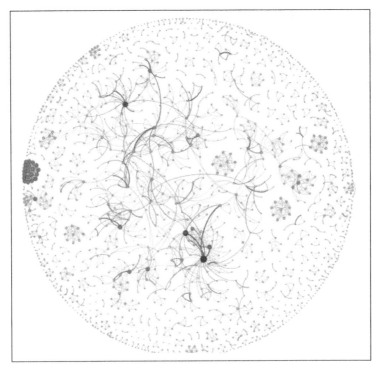

Newman network with node size and color customization

These edits call out the high degree nodes in the graph, and also help to highlight unusual patterns like the tight cluster at the left of the graph. So performing the simple ranking exercise has helped make the graph more understandable at first glance. We could have employed some other approaches to segment the graph, such as using one of the available clustering algorithms, or perhaps through the use of a partition. The latter is a bit problematic with this dataset, as we don't have any information about institutional affiliations, professional credentials, or some other unifying characteristic.

Deploying the project to the Web

Our next step at this point is to take the graph beyond Gephi, perhaps as an image or a PDF file, or even an interactive web project. Let's make this one interactive, as it will give end users an opportunity to explore the graph and find answers to many potential questions. For this example, we'll proceed using the Sigma.js Exporter to create a straightforward interactive network for the Web.

If you are unfamiliar with the SigmaExporter process, refer to *Chapter 9, Taking Your Graph Beyond Gephi*, where we employed it to build our Miles Davis example for the Web. As you can recall, we used the template process to fashion an informative network about the 48 studio albums created by the pioneering musician. For our new instance, we'll need to edit the text to tell a relevant story about the network science collaboration network assembled by Newman.

I've gone ahead and edited the template settings to reflect the data in this particular network and published the graph to the Web. You can find it at:

`http://visual-baseball.com/gephi/NetScience/network/`

Here's a screenshot that shows the familiar layout using ARF and `Sigma.js`, hovering over the Mark Newman node:

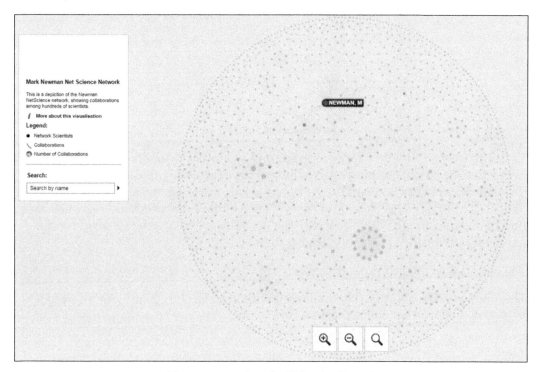

Newman network on the Web using Sigma.js

If we select the same node, we'll see all of Newman's collaborators and then have the ability to view their respective connections through a simple click. This is the same approach we shared with the Miles Davis network in *Chapter 9, Taking Your Graph Beyond Gephi*. Here's what we get after selecting the Newman node:

List of collaborators for M. Newman

To recap, we started with a raw graph file and wound up with an engaging, interactive graph out on the Web. Now users have the ability to easily navigate through this network, to learn more about the various collaborations as they go. Had the dataset provided the dates and titles of each of the collaborations, we could have turned this into an incredibly rich experience, but we'll have to be satisfied for the moment with this still powerful visualization.

The output files can be found at `https://app.box.com/s/177yit0fdovz1czgcecp`.

This gives you the ability to begin playing with the CSS styling and other settings that allow you to personalize the network.

Project 2 – high school network with dynamic edges

For our second project, we're going to have some fun working with a dataset that shows interactions between students at a high school in France over the course of seven school days. The original dataset can be found and downloaded from `http://www.sociopatterns.org/datasets/high-school-dynamic-contact-networks/`.

The data provides a history of active contacts between individual students within a single high school, measured in 20 second intervals. As you can imagine, mapping the edges in this fashion could lead to a lot of connections appearing, disappearing, and then reappearing, making for some light entertainment without adding a lot of insight into behavioral patterns. Feel free to create your own time intervals in this fashion if you want to explore this; our finished project will take a slightly different approach.

Rather than mapping the slightly spurious 20 second connections, I wanted to view the patterns that build over the duration of the study. To do this, we will add new connections as time elapses while still retaining previously existing ones. This will give us a better idea of how patterns evolve over the course of a day or a week, while simultaneously drawing attention to frequent connections that might highlight a variety of relationships in the network.

We're going to step through the project using a number of Gephi methods to set up our working project. Once everything is in place, we're going to capture images of the network at the end of each school day to note what changes have taken place. We'll also capture some fundamental graph statistics at a macro level (feel free to explore individual students on your own) to confirm our visual impressions. Finally, we'll pull everything together in an Adobe PDF file that tells a useful story for viewers.

If you wish to start from scratch, the source node and edge files can be found at `thiers_nodes.csv` and `thiers_edges.csv` at `https://app.box.com/s/177yit0fdovz1czgcecp`.

Using Gephi to explore the network

Let's begin by opening the node and then the edge file using the Gephi data laboratory import spreadsheet functionality. Once the files have been imported, we need to create a time interval so Gephi can display a dynamic graph. Remember that we covered this process in *Chapter 8, Dynamic Networks*. In **Data Laboratory**, select the **Merge columns** icon, and then select the **Start Time** and **End Time** columns, followed by the **Create time interval** option from the drop-down menu. Click on **OK** to load this dialog screen:

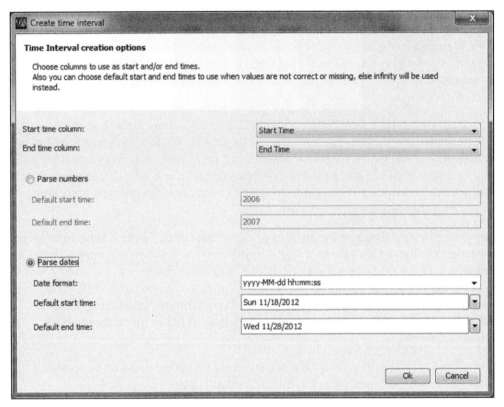

Setting time intervals by merging columns

Select the **Parse dates** option, and make sure that the format is entered in the same form as in the image. After clicking on the **OK** button, you should see an **Enable Timeline** icon at the bottom of the Gephi window. Selecting this will load a timeline that looks like this:

Timeline after creating time intervals

As you can see, Gephi has identified the day of the month element in the data, giving us the range of days from the 19th through the 27th of the month. You'll also see the typical random layout in the **Preview** window, waiting anxiously for you to provide a proper layout option. To make the project a bit more fun, hide the edges using the **Show edges** icon (it toggles the edges on and off) in the preview window. This way, we won't spoil the fun for the dynamic edges we'll see in a moment.

Now move to the **Layout** tab and select the **Yifan Hu** option if you wish to follow this example to the letter. Feel free to play with other algorithms if you want to create something a little different from this example — the underlying statistics and network structure will remain the same regardless of your selection. I tinkered slightly with the default settings to spread the network out just a bit:

Yifan Hu settings for a dynamic high school network

Here's what the Yifan Hu yields (edges still hidden) using the settings in the prior screenshot:

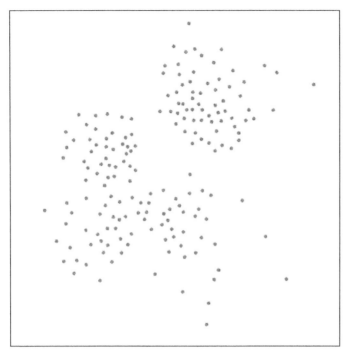

Network graph after applying the Yifan Hu layout

Our next step will be to size the nodes by degree and then to color them according to the **Class** element in the data. These steps will serve two purposes:

- Sizing will give us an indication for which nodes have the highest contact levels in the network.

- Partitioning by class will provide the formal structure of the network as defined by the school authorities. In this case, we have five classes, so the number of colors in the graph will be quite manageable.

For this example, the nodes have been given a size range of 2 to 20, as shown in the following screenshot, (actual values range from 2 to 56 degrees), which should allow us to see the higher influence members without distorting the graph or obscuring the smaller nodes:

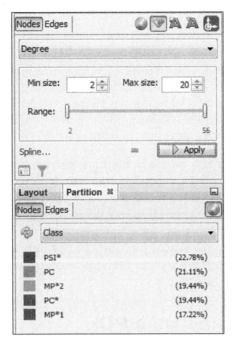

Sizing and partitioning nodes in the high school network

After running each of these steps, we now have a graph that effectively illustrates the formal class structures while also showing the range of influence across all nodes:

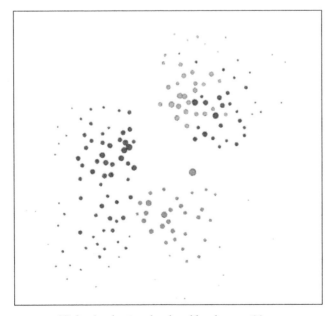

High school network colored by class partitions

It's now time to show the edges between nodes — toggle the **Show edges** icon to make the connections visible again. Once that's complete, move to the timeline and drag the bar to the very start of the timeline. Shrink it as far as possible, by grabbing the right edge of the bar with your mouse. This puts us at the start of the first day (the 19th). Notice that there are just a few connections showing in the overview window, that reflect the handful of students already connected early in the school day. Now let the timeline run by clicking on the arrow to the left. Watch how connections build as we move through the school week.

If you find the graph moving a little quicker than you prefer, adjust the timeline settings (covered in *Chapter 8*, *Dynamic Networks*) to the left of the arrow. Watching the network build over the course of the study period reveals patterns of how members connect within their own class as well as with nodes in other classes. In some cases, there is little interaction between members of two classes, perhaps due to the physical structure of the school building, or perhaps related to the curriculum constraints. In any case, we have a potentially interesting story we can turn into a sort of time-lapse static presentation.

Creating the project as a PDF

In order to tell a compelling story about a dynamic network in a static format, we're going to have to provide a little more background information than in our interactive web example earlier in the chapter. We cannot afford the luxury of networks where users can zoom and pan for more information. So our approach must be slightly different, in that we have to provide users with enough information to tell the story. Everything is in our hands in this case — the user cannot craft their own story via interaction.

So what will we need to craft a compelling story? Here are a few ideas:

1. Our first step will be to create snapshots of the network at the end of each school day to show how the network evolves over the study period.

2. We'll also want some essential network statistics to help support the graphs, preferably in a visual format that shows the network trends.

3. We might also need to provide more of a narrative than we would in an interactive network situation. As I noted a moment ago, we need to tell the story of this dynamic network.

I'm going to provide a glimpse into what the final visualization will look like. The entire PDF is available at `https://app.box.com/s/177yit0fdovz1czgcecp`.

Here's one of our visuals that shows the network at the end of day 1 (November 19, 2012):

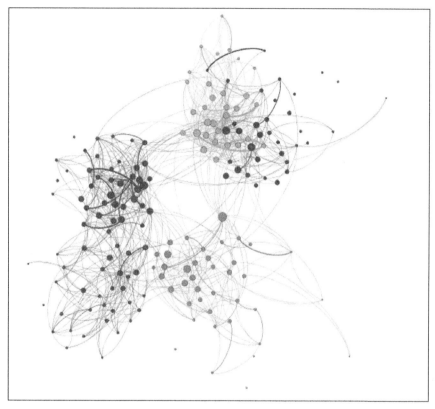

Dynamic high school network at the end of day 1, November 19, 2012

There will be a series of these visuals (one each for the 19th, 21st, 23rd, and 27th), showing the evolution of the network over the course of the study period. Viewers will be able to detect some of the changes, especially when comparing the first and last day. Yet the story would be incomplete without sharing some of the critical graph statistics that fill in the gaps. So with each end of the day snapshot, I also captured several critical network structure measures and pulled them together in a single page. This allows users to see how the network evolved, and when major changes (if any) took place:

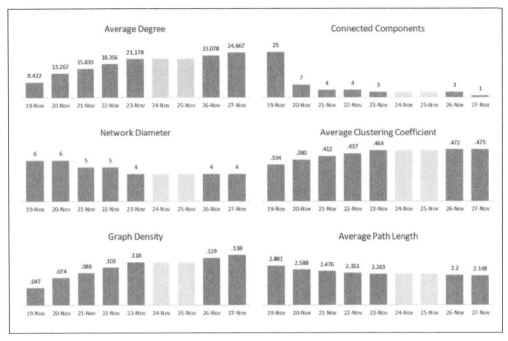

Statistical measures tracking network evolution

Notice that the two weekend days have been grayed out so as not to lead the user to the wrong conclusions. Placing all of these graphs on a single page lets the viewer see the evolution of the network in statistical terms, perhaps confirming their initial visual impression. Key changes in the network are also called out in the final visualization, completing the entire story.

Anticipating the future of network analysis

So we've seen in the course of this book the many wondrous things that can be done using Gephi, and we've still really just scratched the surface. There are now so many opportunities to process, analyze, and visualize network datasets that it can be overwhelming at times. Countless examples of Twitter, Facebook, and other social networks proliferate across the Web, some of them thoughtful and powerful, some others far less so. Likewise, we have all seen many instances of collaboration networks, protein networks, cell structure networks, citation networks, and so on. Where does it all go from here? Will the future look like the present, simply with more examples?

One outcome that seems a near certainty will be the increasing involvement of end users in interacting and perhaps even participating in the creation of the eventual network display. Imagine a case where users can adjust and adapt to the graph on a real-time basis, affecting the outcome of the network. Look no further than many of the massive multiplayer online games for proof of what can be done at the user level. Perhaps game theory examples will involve multiple end users acting according to their own preferences of the moment, with the network adapting and evolving to reflect the instantaneous input of hundreds or even thousands of users. These real-time examples could change much of today's analysis from a dependence on static historical datasets to an environment that is plugged into the ongoing changes in an evolving network.

Imagine also the possibilities of delivering additional insight by providing relevant information behind every node and edge in a network. In today's world, we have the ability to craft templates and provide generally static information to accompany our network graphs. In some cases, this is abetted by external links that provide additional information. This approach, while useful, puts the burden on the user and provides something less than a seamless process. How can we improve this process?

In the near term, are there untapped opportunities where network analysis can work more closely with **ontological** resources to deliver richer information and interactivity to the end user? In the slightly more distant future could all relevant information be accessed within the bounds of a single network page, enabling users to travel through the network as if they were in a gaming environment? Consider the possibilities of adding relevant information that activates multiple senses, and how users could leverage the power of sight, sound, and touch to examine and understand the network. Users could perhaps access a sort of virtual world, but one that is based totally on the reality of moment to moment interactions, not on some fictional construct created by game designers.

Beyond the evolution of network graph analysis through technological advances there is the question of additional use cases. We have seen the many instances of social media, citation, collaboration, biological, and infrastructure networks, but are there other opportunities to leverage network analysis to understand systems? Could network graph analysis be a powerful tool for exploring topics such as chaos theory, tracking the impact of specific stimuli on a surrounding network? Might we also be able to explore connections within the body that could help combat disease or infection? Are there greater opportunities to use these tools to better predict long-term effects of specific short-term decisions, in a modeling sort of environment?

These are merely a few examples for where network graph analysis could be heading. You no doubt have additional thoughts about the future and where the opportunities will emerge. Regardless of our individual ideas, I believe we can all agree that the future will be filled with exciting opportunities to employ these methods to better understand our world and all of its interactions. The future of network graph analysis and all its manifestations promises to be both challenging and rewarding, and will evolve and grow through the efforts of readers like yourself.

I also invite you to view my personal explorations and discussions at `http://visual-baseball.com/wordpress/?gallery=network-graphs` as well as the great work of users in the Gephi communities on Facebook and LinkedIn. Some truly exceptional work is being shared in these forums.

Summary

In this final chapter, we covered a few key areas that focused on Gephi and network graph analysis at a more holistic level.

We learned how to understand and ultimately enhance existing network graphs through the use of many of Gephi's capabilities. We learned how to use regex to provide additional insight into an existing network, particularly when the network data provides no obvious starting points for analysis. From there, we employed our more familiar skills of filtering, sizing, and coloring graph elements to create a more accessible user experience.

We then created two projects from scratch using publicly available datasets. In the first example, we took a static network, enhanced its appearance, and made it interactive on the Web. In our second case, we created a dynamic network by building time intervals that documented member patterns, and ultimately created a time lapse project as a PDF output.

In our final section, we took a look at the future of network graph analysis and where it might be heading. We looked at the possibilities enabled by advanced technology as well as opportunities for horizontal expansion through the application of network analysis methods to additional disciplines.

I hope this book has helped provide you with opportunities to leverage Gephi more effectively to address your own network analysis needs. In addition, my hope is that I have triggered some additional ideas that you might pursue as you continue to investigate this fascinating yet largely untapped field.

Data Sources and Other Web Resources

This appendix lists various data sources, web resources, and references which you can use as supplementary material for the best use of this book.

Data sources

Here are a number of data sources that provide network data as well as links to other data sources:

- **Stanford Network Analysis Project (SNAP)** has a website `http://snap.stanford.edu/data/links.html` with links to many network datasets (large and small).

- Mark Newman is one of the most recognized network scientists who maintains a number of network datasets at his site `http://www-personal.umich.edu/~mejn/netdata/`.

- Albert-László Barabási is one of the foremost network scientists and runs the Barabasi Lab at Northeastern University. More information about him can be found at `http://barabasilab.com/rs-netdb.php`.

- The Gephi wiki has many network datasets as well as a number of files that are already in various proprietary formats. These can be found at `https://wiki.gephi.org/index.php/Datasets`.

- **KONECT** is the **Koblenz Network Collection** available at the University of Koblenz-Landau. The University's site houses one of the best collections of network data, and provides easily accessible symbols that identify specific network attributes, which can be found at `http://konect.uni-koblenz.de/`.

Web resources

Here are just a few websites that provide practical or theoretical insights into network analysis. There are, of course, dozens more that can be discovered by a simple web search:

- The **Center for Network Science (CNS)** at Central European University hosts a variety of resources of interest for network scientists and practitioners at `https://cns.ceu.hu/`.

- The Carnegie-Mellon University houses the **Center for Computational Analysis of Social and Organizational Systems (CASOS)**. A variety of informational and educational resources are provided that will be of interest to network analysts. More information can be found at `http://www.casos.cs.cmu.edu/index.php`.

- NetLogo is a site where you can run model simulations online or using the downloaded NetLogo software. Many interesting examples are available at `http://ccl.northwestern.edu/netlogo/index.shtml` to help you understand network growth and evolution patterns.

Import processes

For additional details on how to import datasets, refer to *Chapter 4, Network Patterns*, from *Network Graph Analysis and Visualization with Gephi*, available at `https://www.packtpub.com/big-data-and-business-intelligence/network-graph-analysis-and-visualization-gephi`.

Bibliography

There are hundreds of papers available on the Web dealing with various aspects of network graph analysis, as well as multiple books available in PDF versions. This list provides some of the resources I have found most useful while preparing for and writing this book:

- Barabási, A. *Linked: The New Science of Networks*. 2014.

- Bearman, P., Moody, J., Stovel, K. *Chains Of Affection: The Structure of Adolescent Romantic and Sexual Networks*. American Journal of Sociology. 2004. 44-91. Retrieved April 19, 2014.

- Easley, D., Kleinberg, J. *Networks, Crowds, and Markets: Reasoning About a Highly Connected World*. Cambridge University Press. 2010.

- Kourtellis, N., Alahakoon, T., Simha, R., Iamnitchi, A., Tripathi, R. *Identifying high betweenness centrality nodes in large social networks: Social Network Analysis and Mining*. 899-914. Retrieved November 2, 2014.

- Lattanzi, S., Sivakumar, D. *Affiliation networks*. 2009.

- Newman, M. *The Structure and Function of Complex Networks, SIAM Review*. 2003. 167-167. Retrieved March 27, 2014.

- Steen, M. *Graph Theory and Complex Networks: An Introduction*. 2010.

- Tang, J., Musolesi, M., Mascolo, C., Latora, V. *Temporal distance metrics for social network analysis*. 2009. Retrieved March 21, 2014.

- Wimmer, A., Lewis, K. *Beyond and below racial homophily: ERG models of a friendship network documented on Facebook*. American Journal of Sociology. 2010. 583-642. Retrieved June 22, 2014.

Index

graph
  analyzing 48, 62-64
  applications 8
  collaboration 8
  exporting 68
  information linkages 9
  modifying 49, 65-67
  natural-world networks 9
  technological networks 9
  Who-Talks-to-Whom graphs 9
graph aesthetics
  about 107
  example 108-111
graph density, network measures 183
graph density, network statistics 200
**Graph Exchange XML Format
     (GEXF) files**
  about 283
  URL 283
graph file exporters
  about 280, 281
  CSV files 281
  DL files 282
  GDF files 282, 283
  Graph Exchange XML Format (GEXF)
     files 283
  GraphML files 284, 285
  Graph Modeling Language (GML) files 284
  NET files 285
  VNA files 285, 286
**graphing needs, Miles Davis network
     example**
  about 87-89
  analysis goal 89
  dataset parameters 89, 90
  interactivity 92, 93
  network behaviors 91
  network density 91
  network display 91
  temporal elements 92
GraphML files
  about 284
  URL 285
Graph Modeling Language (GML) 284
graph statistics
  about 182

  centrality measures 185, 186
  centrality statistics, interpreting 193
  clustering and neighborhood measures 188
  clustering statistics, interpreting 196
  interpreting 190
  network measures 182
  network measures, interpreting 190-193
  used, for filtering 207-215
graph window 25
GUESS
  URL 282, 283

H

hairball effect 34
Hiveplot layout 34, 82, 95
homophily
  about **19**, 123, 124
  identifying 144-147
**Hyperlink-Induced Topic Search (HITS)
     function, network measures 184**

I

image exporters
  about 280, 286
  PNG export 286, 287
  SVG export 288
Image Preview tool
  URL 292
import processes 346
in-degree centrality 194
in-degree centrality (directed graphs) 187
In Degree Range filter 155
inflation 221
initial graph layout
  viewing 45, 46
Inkscape
  PDF file, editing 293, 294
Inter Edges 152
INTERSECTION filter 175, 177
INTERSECTION operator 154
intervals, topology-based DNA
  creating, in existing project 251-253
Intra Edges 152
Isometric layout 84, 95

web sources 346
Who-talks-to-Whom graphs 9

Y

Yifan Hu algorithm 76, 96
Yifan Hu layout 60
Yifan Hu multilevel approach 77, 96
Yifan Hu Proportional layout 76, 96

Thank you for buying
Mastering Gephi Network Visualization

About Packt Publishing

Packt, pronounced 'packed', published its first book, *Mastering phpMyAdmin for Effective MySQL Management*, in April 2004, and subsequently continued to specialize in publishing highly focused books on specific technologies and solutions.

Our books and publications share the experiences of your fellow IT professionals in adapting and customizing today's systems, applications, and frameworks. Our solution-based books give you the knowledge and power to customize the software and technologies you're using to get the job done. Packt books are more specific and less general than the IT books you have seen in the past. Our unique business model allows us to bring you more focused information, giving you more of what you need to know, and less of what you don't.

Packt is a modern yet unique publishing company that focuses on producing quality, cutting-edge books for communities of developers, administrators, and newbies alike. For more information, please visit our website at www.packtpub.com.

About Packt Open Source

In 2010, Packt launched two new brands, Packt Open Source and Packt Enterprise, in order to continue its focus on specialization. This book is part of the Packt Open Source brand, home to books published on software built around open source licenses, and offering information to anybody from advanced developers to budding web designers. The Open Source brand also runs Packt's Open Source Royalty Scheme, by which Packt gives a royalty to each open source project about whose software a book is sold.

Writing for Packt

We welcome all inquiries from people who are interested in authoring. Book proposals should be sent to author@packtpub.com. If your book idea is still at an early stage and you would like to discuss it first before writing a formal book proposal, then please contact us; one of our commissioning editors will get in touch with you.

We're not just looking for published authors; if you have strong technical skills but no writing experience, our experienced editors can help you develop a writing career, or simply get some additional reward for your expertise.

Network Graph Analysis and Visualization with Gephi

ISBN: 978-1-78328-013-1   Paperback: 116 pages

Visualize and analyze your data swiftly using dynamic network graphs built with Gephi

1. Use your own data to create network graphs displaying complex relationships between several types of data elements.

2. Learn about nodes and edges, and customize your graphs using size, color, and weight attributes.

3. Filter your graphs to focus on the key information you need to see and publish your network graphs to the Web.

Google Visualization API Essentials

ISBN: 978-1-84969-436-0   Paperback: 252 pages

Make sense of your data: make it visual with the Google Visualization API

1. Wrangle all sorts of data into a visual format, without being an expert programmer.

2. Visualize new or existing spreadsheet data through charts, graphs, and maps.

3. Full of diagrams, core concept explanations, best practice tips, and links to working book examples.

Please check **www.PacktPub.com** for information on our titles

Network Analysis using Wireshark Cookbook

ISBN: 978-1-84951-764-5   Paperback: 452 pages

Over 80 recipes to analyze and troubleshoot network problems using Wireshark

1. Place Wireshark in the network and configure it for effective network analysis.

2. Use Wireshark's powerful statistical tools and expert system for pinpointing network problems.

3. Use Wireshark for troubleshooting network performance, applications, and security problems in the network.

Untangle Network Security

ISBN: 978-1-84951-772-0   Paperback: 368 pages

Secure your network against threats and vulnerabilities using the unparalleled Untangle NGFW

1. Learn how to install, deploy, and configure Untangle NG Firewall.

2. Understand network security fundamentals and how to protect your network using Untangle NG Firewall.

3. Step-by-step tutorial supported by many examples and screenshots.

Please check **www.PacktPub.com** for information on our titles

Printed in Great
Britain
by Amazon